Making Knowledge Count
Advocacy and Social Science

At the height of anti-Vietnam war protest, social advocacy was inseparable from youth militancy. It is now a common means of intervention – a component part of the way society searches for reform, examines cultural attainment, or adjudicates quality of life. *Making Knowledge Count* explores transformation in the advocacy process and its implications for social activism.

The essays in this collection use case studies to address four vital issues of modern social advocacy. The first, a positive result of world-wide human rights legislation, is a new social framework which legitimizes advocacy. The second concerns the development of advocacy strategies for social empowerment, including favourable precedents in court, government funding, and an array of media opportunities. A third issue is the link between social conflicts and social movements. In the past, collective conflict centred on the confrontation between capital and labour, but in recent years social movements have focused on an array of middle-class issues concerning quality of life. Fourth, the essays examine the role of researchers in the process of advocacy. At the very minimum, advocacy tends to involve active participant-observers, which runs against the myth of objectivity in social sciences.

Case studies of advocacy in this collection include those concerning human rights in Chile, race relations, refugees, community and labour advocacy, alternative work training, and advocacy in the women's movement. The final part of the book shows how social advocacy also reforms research methods by uncovering hidden issues in social science, such as reflexiveness, social commitment, and interested knowledge.

PETER HARRIES-JONES is an Associate Professor in the Department of Anthropology, York University.

Making Knowledge Count
Advocacy and Social Science

EDITED BY
PETER HARRIES-JONES

McGill-Queen's University Press
Montreal & Kingston • London • Buffalo

© McGill-Queen's University Press 1991
ISBN 0-7735-0819-8

Legal deposit second quarter 1991
Bibliothèque nationale du Québec

Printed in Canada on acid-free paper

This book has been published with the help
of a grant from the Social Science Federation
of Canada, using funds provided by the
Social Sciences and Humanities Research
Council of Canada.

Canadian Cataloguing in Publication Data

Main entry under title:
Making knowledge count
Includes bibliographical references
and index.
ISBN 0-7735-0819-8
1. Social sciences – Philosophy. 2. Social
action. 3. Political participation.
4. Social scientists – Political activity.
I. Harris-Jones, Peter, 1937–   .
H53.C3M34 1991   300'.1   C91-090070-1

This book was typeset by
Typo Litho composition inc.
in 10/12 Baskerville

To Elspeth Heyworth, social advocate, in memoriam

Contents

Don Dippo

PART THREE: FROM ADVOCACY TO
SOCIAL MOVEMENTS

Ronnie Leah

John Cleveland

PART FOUR: THE OBSERVERS AND THE OBSERVED —
ADVOCACY AND METHOD

Metta Spencer

Gareth Morgan

Stewart Crysdale

Acknowledgments

This book began as a series of papers presented at the annual conference of the Ontario Association of Sociology and Anthropology, 18–20 October 1984. The annual conference, organized by the editor when he was vice-president of the association, was entitled "Advocacy and Practice." I would like to acknowledge all those who gave papers at the conference, for it was they who provided first evidence of a coherent and focused topic. The project could not have continued without the continuing support of OASA towards defraying costs of pre-publication preparation.

Robert Paine of the Institute of Social and Economic Research, Memorial University, Newfoundland, was instrumental in promoting the idea of this book, and gave freely of his time in the early stages of editing. It was a conference organized by him in August, 1983, and later published by Memorial University as *Advocacy and Anthropology: First Encounters*, which laid the groundwork for the OASA venture. Both Gareth Morgan and Stewart Crysdale made valuable suggestions as to the book's format. All of the contributors have been most helpful during the drafting process and have made editorial tasks enviably easy.

I would like to give special thanks to Philip Cercone, executive director of McGill-Queen's University Press, who has gone out of his way to encourage this project. Pat Cates, Grace Baxter, and other members of Secretarial Services, York University have also given time, care, and energy in preparation of the manuscript.

Lastly, the book is published with a grant in aid from the Social Science Federation of Canada and I would like to acknowledge those SSFC readers who gave helpful comments at all stages of preparation.

Making Knowledge Count

PETER HARRIES–JONES

Introduction: Making Knowledge Count

Events in Eastern Europe in 1989 demonstrated in a most extraordinary manner the ways in which spontaneous social action can transform the political order of a nation-state. It is still too early to judge whether the street demonstrations constituted a political revolution in some definitive sense of the term, but clearly the lives of millions of people in Eastern Europe became transformed with improbable speed and decisiveness.

All the circumstances contributing to such dramatic change are not yet known, but some of the key factors are obvious. The courage and foresight of individual dissenters who were willing to risk their lives to challenge the authoritarianism of the state is one key factor. Another is the networks of dissent that underpinned the street demonstrations and gave a semblance of coherence to "spontaneous" protests. For a brief time they aided in the transfer of power from communist to non-communist government.

Networks of dissent in these countries were not clandestine cells seeking the overthrow of the state, nor did they have a well-developed alternative political ideology. Their focus was on specific issues, the ecology, peace, human rights, or a combination of these. The reason that "eco-glasnost" networks were permitted to exist was that Eastern European governments had themselves been signatories to international accords on these issues and found it useful to give lip service to these aims.

Issues of peace, ecology, and human rights and women's rights brought out demonstrators in Western Europe and North America as well. In fact, the rise of new social movements during the 1970s and 1980s was a global phenomenon. Third World social movements formed around the lack of urban housing and services (Slater 1985) and cultural genocide – the deteriorating state of the world's indigenous peoples (Burger 1987).

The origins of each movement appear to be separate from the others. Each also seems to have different historical aims. As single-issue organizations, the new social movements do not have an overall ideology, nor do the issues which they espouse fall easily into the ideological formats of socialism and capitalism. Only the environmentalist movement in industrial countries seems to be creating an ideology of its own (Paehlke 1989, 273–83). Yet, as a collective phenomenon, the rise of social movements becomes an increasingly important phenomenon in its own right.

The new social movements are extra-parliamentary but not revolutionary. They formulate cultural objectives and contest these outside the scope of political parties and parliamentary process. Their very existence narrows the political possibilities for existing parties, conservative, liberal, or socialist, to continue as umbrella organizations channelling political dissent. Traditional social movements were class-based and mainly tied to the interests of industrial workers. By contrast, membership of the new social movements is mixed. They are predominantly middle-class in highly industrialized countries with some support from other social classes, and predominantly under-class in Third World countries, with linkage support from the middle class in industrial countries. The organization of "old" social movements was based on a representative federalism. For example, international labour organizations were based on an institutional hierarchy at international, national, occupational, and local levels, even though the international federations gave wide scope for autonomous action at each one of these levels. By contrast, the "organization" of new social movements lacks any top-down hierarchy. The new social movements are *both* local *and* global. Their globalism is structured more by grass-roots participation than by institutional practices. Local activity tends to overflow the geographical boundaries in which it is conducted and converges with other local activities to give a perception of globalism. This pattern of global-yet-local is related to the development of modern communication systems, particularly television broadcasts via satellite. On occasion there has been formal satellite linkage for entertainment extravaganzas in support of human rights or peace or the environment.[1] Another important difference about the new social movements is that they embody *positive* forms of protest and proactive organization. For this reason the membership of new social movements cannot be simply categorized as political "contras," "masses on the streets," or "anarchists."

The divergence between the events of May 1968 and the activities of the new social movements is striking. In May 1968, student radicals in France proclaimed a new political alliance between workers and intellectuals and marched to their barricades in the Latin Quarter of Paris chanting the slogan "L'imagination au pouvoir! (All power to the imagination!)" (Birnbaum 1969, 164). This utopian sentiment is very different from that which motivates the new social movements. They perceive that political transformation cannot succeed without a concomitant change in cultural values, neither more nor less than a "change of heart." In Western Europe and North America the "change of heart" in the new social movements is closely identified with a change in prevailing notions of "peace," "progress," and "civilization."

ADVOCACY AND EMPOWERMENT: A WORKING DEFINITION

The positive form of protest in which the new social movements engage is a type of consciousness raising for alternative values. Consciousness raising of this sort is not to be confused with "public education," the attempts of governments to channel public opinion in a preferred direction through leaflets and advertising. Nor is it to be confused with lobbying, the process through which special-interest groups put pressure on government decision making in order to bring about legislation favourable to corporate entrepreneurs. While social movements may employ both, the broader process in which they are engaged challenges the "objective facts" by which current policy is rationalized. In effect they engage in a form of advocacy which challenges the "reality" of dominant values. It is a process of making an alternate form of social knowledge count.

The advocacy of social movements is bound up with a lengthy process of political empowerment. This type of advocacy, while it might involve lawyers and the justice system, is distinct from the usual forms of "pleading" in the courts. A dictionary definition of advocacy places emphasis on an advocate "pleading in support of" – that is arguing for, defending, maintaining, or recommending a cause or a proposal within the existing rules of law.

The most striking feature of advocacy through empowerment is "advocacy with" the group challenging dominant values, rather than "advocacy for" a client or class of clients (see Heyworth below). In Canada, the closest legal practitioners come to "advocacy with" is when lawyers make an "appearance" before a duly constituted commission. An "appearance" is not a hearing, nor is it an application. It is a hybrid form of legal action which has arisen in recent years directly linking social issues to the practice of law. The advocacy process in an "appearance" is usually directed towards social policy or proposed legislation on social issues. Advocacy of this sort makes some lawyers nervous precisely because the process of "pleading" lies outside well-defined rules of legal representation.[2]

Advocacy through a process of political empowerment tries to raise social issues to the level of a clearly defined collective or "class" interest in which that "class" is given a capacity to act. Using "class" in quotes here indicates that "class action" in this sense is distinct from the Marxist formulation of social class. Advocacy of this sort is usually concerned with *equity* and equitable distribution of social rights rather than with more abstract principles of *social equality*. Nevertheless, "class" and social class may overlap. Any issue in which the new social movements are involved may have, in addition to claims for equity, an underlying conflict of social class. Current legislation which social movements attack often coincides with the cultural values of the political élite.

A significant feature of advocacy is that the overlap between "equity" and "equality" may not be evident at the time of the formation of a social movement, or at the beginning of an advocacy process. Visibility of the opposition emerges from the very conflicts which the process of empowerment generates. Empowerment is a circularity in which social class and social inequalities are revealed as the process goes on.

At first objectives are fuzzy. Often they can only be grasped retrospectively. What is dimly understood at the outset is that those holding power distort or control expression of interests though manipulation of ideas and means of communication. Subordinate groups find themselves socialized into compliance, accepting definitions of reality offered by dominant groups or government institutions – even though the groups are partly aware that their own position does not accord with these definitions. Advocacy begins on a general claim of equity, but then the process generates conflict around the ideology of social equality. An example of this is Leah's discussion below of the overlap between social class issues of working women and the equity claims made by the women's movement for provision of day care facilities.

The history of social service work in North America is an example of the linkage between advocacy and empowerment. Prior to the 1960s the social service field was full of examples of advocates who acted "on behalf of a client" with a view to achieving specific objectives laid down by a client according to the client's instructions. Social workers were trained in a clinical model of social welfare and had little concept of how the practice of social work linked to political reform (Anderson 1985, 54). At the beginning of the 1960s the success of grass-roots organization of Black communities in the Chicago ghettoes began to change the whole approach to social service work.

A new premise emerged that the poor can be organized into groups and that through this process of self-empowerment many of the barriers to equity and equal opportunity can be broken down. The equation of grass-roots advocacy with political self-empowerment and community organization began to become embedded in a much wider conception of social action. The original premises which linked advocacy to community organization for self-empowerment became transformed as the War Against Poverty, a social movement demanding equality and reform of the politics of social class in America. An overall strategy emerged by which the poor would compel the United States Congress to redistribute resources through some national guaranteed income plan.

The strategy involved a coalition of civil rights groups and militant anti-poverty groups but required a formidable level of political skill both to mobilize massive grass-roots demonstration and to form alliances with organized labour, civil rights organizations, and other groups supporting welfare reform. A guaranteed annual income program also required the consent of us Congress. As the arena of conflict shifted, Congress, which had started as neutral, itself became the major political opponent of the strategy and aims of the War Against Poverty.

In the early 1970s the us Congress began to preempt the demand for a major redistribution of wealth and power by sacrificing the interests of the poor to the interests of those who determine welfare policy. It imposed institutional sanctions against those who would strengthen the organizational power of the deprived. Advocacy for the poor became transformed into a mandated process, carried out through the various levels of government bureaucracy (Kutchins and Kutchins 1978, 29–37).

ADVOCACY AND HUMAN RIGHTS

A major shift in the 1970s and 1980s has been the emergence of human rights as a focus for advocacy. Human rights are moral fictions, but they are fictions with highly specific properties, the most important of which is that they are incommensurable with concepts of utility. When claims invoking rights are matched against claims appealing to utility, or when either or both are matched against traditional concepts of justice or morality, there is no rational means of deciding which claim is to be given priority or how one can be weighed against the other (MacIntyre 1984, 70). Nevertheless, the concept of rights can undermine the legitimacy of any claim to "util-ity." Thus human rights can be used in an advocacy process to counter claims based on economic utilities or the bureaucratic criteria of "efficiency."

In states where no specific individual rights have been acknowl-edged before, the admissibility of human rights changes the form of social advocacy. The overall effect of a constitutional shift towards recognition of individual rights is one of reducing the power of the legislature of the nation-state. The executive arm of government is curtailed in some of its abstract powers to control its citizens the way it thinks fit, as legal action in court becomes a predominant coun-terbalance to arbitrary legislation.

The Universal Declaration of Human Rights was proclaimed by the United Nations on 10 December 1948. The Universal Declara-tion did not create positive law directly binding on member states. Instead, it left the way open for member states to adopt Conventions consistent with the principles of the Universal Declaration later, dur-ing the 1970s.

As part of domestic law, the Conventions mark off specific atten-tion to areas in which human rights ought to have effect, and give explicit enumeration of rights in each of these areas. For example, article 2 of the Universal Declaration of Human Rights encourages respect for human rights and fundamental freedoms without regard for race, colour, sex, language, religion, political or other opinion, national or social origin, property, birth, or other status. The titles of Conventions giving effect to these principles are the Convention for the Prevention and Punishment of the Crime of Genocide; the International Convention on the Elimination of All Forms of Racial Discrimination; and the Covenant on Civil and Political Rights. Other Conventions prohibit slavery and protect indigenous and tribal populations (Kallen 1982).

Ratification occurred while domestic politics were shifting from the left of centre to the right in several key industrial countries, and this shift affected the context in which human rights legislation was introduced. In the United States, Great Britain, and elsewhere, con-servatives used human rights issues to deflect criticism of capitalist economic policies and inequalities in world trade. Their view is that economic inequality is quite unlike any other and, no matter how gross, does not in itself constitute economic discrimination. The Marxist-socialist claim that economic inequality is discriminatory is fundamentally wrong, they argue.[3]

Conservatives have had to accept political costs in making their stand. The most obvious cost is that if their version of human rights is to succeed, they must be seen to respond to evidence of violations of human rights, even if the violations occur among right-wing political allies. As the Pinochet regime in Chile revealed, the governments of "Marxist terrorists" are not the only governments to repress and torture citizens. Human rights became a means of subjecting sovereignty of right-wing nation-states to some form of external monitoring and control (see Landstreet et al. below).

The other political costs are more subtle. First, conservatives have been unable to install right-wing versions of morality. Often a conservative vision of government's based on a conceptualization of efficiencies and functional rationality and tries to make the decision-making process appear autonomous – disconnected from the social interests of any one social class, as if rational administration and technical rules precluded class interest. Science and technology help in legitimizing this form of government by supporting the view that rational decision making is the only possible formulation for government. Yet neither science nor technology can provide the necessary moral criteria for ethical standards of conduct, even as para-ideology. Where rationality of science fails to provide a satisfactory code for moral values, the settlement of moral issues has had to be left to the courts (Mueller 1973, 101–10).

Second, in the conservative vision, political loyalty can be obtained through material compensations, primarily through fulfilling consumer demands and maintaining a high standard of living. Provision of social service such as education, medical care, and welfare is a secondary issue. No significant problems of legitimacy arise so long as the lower classes alone suffer the consequences of an underdeveloped social sector.

Yet when the system of economic growth begins to buckle under the strains of its own success, the middle classes also become vulnerable to the deterioration of the social infrastructure. Noise, pollution, urban crowding, increased crime, spread of chemical poisons, and a deterioration of the quality of life become middle-class issues. The middle classes perceive this increasing deterioration in quality of life as a systemic defect. When they realize that these conditions are not a temporary aberration, a gap begins to open up between privately experienced deprivation and publicly exercised power. The middle class begins to demand that if those in power will not or cannot act, then the situation must be remedied outside the boundaries of party politics (Mueller 1973, 159–61).

For these reasons, the spread of human rights has had the effect of promoting progressivist rather than conservative ideas of moral and cultural values. This is particularly the case in Canada, where a Charter of Rights and Freedoms was proclaimed in 1982. The outcome on a range of moral issues has been profound. By invoking the Charter, the pro-choice segment of the women's movement has been able to strike down the abortion law. The peace movement has challenged the legality of testing U.S. Cruise missiles in Canada, and the environmental movement has won significant approval for extension of anti-pollution legislation. The Supreme Court has also extended the grounds of discrimination listed in the Charter of Rights and Freedoms. In another human rights case the Supreme Court also ruled that judges can scrutinize the merits of government legislation to decide whether it is legal. This particular curtailment of arbitrary action on the part of government may become extremely important for all social movements in Canada during the coming decades.

The Charter of Rights and similar legislation fall short of being a panacea for ensuring progressive social change primarily because the United Nations Declaration skirts the issue of collective interest. When it comes to the rights of peoples protecting their own culture against the rights of nation-states, the Declaration prefers to assume that peoples who are not part of mainstream culture ought to assimilate to it. The assumption plays straight into the hands of those who wish to deny the very existence of ethnic minorities and imposes a heavy burden on those who advocate for indigenous rights in multicultural polities (Maybury-Lewis 1985, 134).

Adequate definition of aboriginal rights was deliberately left out of the Canadian Charter of Rights and Freedoms, and since then there have been considerable difficulties in reversing this omission. The clash between collective rights and Charter of Rights has also led to inconsistent decision making with respect to language rights in Quebec and was at the heart of the failure of recent constitutional negotiations, the Meech Lake Accord. The United Nations' solicitous regard for rights of nation-states has also led to peculiar biases in conventions governing the entrance of refugees into Canada (see Adelman below).

FROM ADVOCACY TO SOCIAL MOVEMENTS

Governments, together with dominant political élites, like to convince the public that "objective knowledge" is on their side and that evidence to the contrary is worthless. The fiction of certainty is always attached to "objective knowledge" as if it were authoritative and as if it could not be controverted. It is the task of the advocate to ensure that such knowledge is put to the test of alternative interpretation.

The advocate has to show that the supposed "commonly shared assumptions" or the "irrefutable evidence of science" (Gusfield 1981, 22) has in fact been constructed by social processes of selection and interpretation. In that process, political and bureaucratic interests intervene at every point.

An essential part of advocacy is to make the public understand the worth of an alternative framework of argument. Yet devising strategy for successful counter-argument is far from easy. It requires much more than rhetoric during the advocacy process. Over the years governments have come to realize that increased public awareness on any issue is a two-edged political weapon. Judicious use of advocacy organizations can aid implementation of government policy as much as create serious opposition to it. Tactics of opposition become mired in the possibilities of reciprocity where each is out to assure the other that they should be supporting each other in the construction of policy (see Adelman below). Rees and Tator also show how their advocacy group, the Urban Alliance on Race Relations, began in opposition to government but later became co-opted in policy making.

Many governments spend public money to aid advocates, and on these occasions the construction of consensus is an exercise more in the circularities of feedback than in adversarial conflict. Typically, governments will finance advocacy group presentations before organized hearings. When prodded hard enough, governments have even sponsored advocacy research. How much finance advocacy interests obtain depends on the extent to which the issue captures the public eye.

For the advocacy groups, the pathway to success weaves in and out of multiple forums of opinion. Controversial issues have extensive treatment in the mass media. Conferences both national and international precede publication of a scholarly journal. Subsequently, funding of special opinion polls and social surveys will bring mass media and scholarly attention together in the forum of daily political discourse. On the other hand, governments can and do play the imperial game of divide and rule among these multiple forums when they wish to delay taking action. The history of environmental advocacy during the 1970s in the United States is one long process of governmental divide and rule among multiple forums of opinion.

THE SPECIAL CASE OF ENVIRONMENTALISM

More than any other issue, environmentalism has been responsible for advancing the strategy of advocacy and forging the link between advocacy, human rights, and social movements. Modern environmentalism began in the 1960s as an inclusive part of general protest and dissent. Environmentalism was interpreted in many different ways – as a social movement, as a set of ideas based upon ecology, or as a back-to-nature movement. It housed two contrasting categories of people – those who espoused a planned ecology, and those who doubted whether science and technology were compatible with humanistic principles. The first category saw their priority as sustaining a viable physical and biological environment, and was essentially conservative in character, while the second was anti-establishment, calling for alternative uses of technology, solar power, wind power, new designs for housing, and so forth. Their solution was for the option of technology that did not alienate humanity from either society.

The solutions proposed were clearly incompatible, but the strategy which emerged is somewhat different from that which might have been imagined. Instead of reducing environmentalism to a set of core demands, environmentalism has built and sustained a broad front of public sympathy over a number of interrelated issues. For example, the nuclear power issue during the 1970s brought environmentalism into contact with anti-nuclear movements, while the early 1980s extended the issue yet again by bringing it into contact with anti-war movements as well. In the late 1980s the environmental movement became caught up in demands for global sustainable development (Keating 1989).

The formation of these coalitions is reminiscent of the War Against Poverty but has proceeded at a slower pace. Environmentalism combines a whole array of issues, including pollution, safety, conservation, civil liberties, and all-round personal or community-based welfare. The greatest impetus for keeping these in a unified perspective came from the near-accidents and catastrophic failures of nuclear technology itself. Three Mile Island in Pennsylvania and Chernobyl in the USSR cast permanent doubt on the validity of scientific assurances about the safety and viability of nuclear power.

In the 1980s there was a dramatic turnaround of perspective within science. Where atmospheric scientists gave dire warnings of the consequences of global warming, they established a "rational" basis to fears of pollution, waste management, overuse of material resources, and other aspects of environmental degradation, including the continued use of nuclear power.

A current Canadian perspective is that of Paehlke (1989, 273ff), who argues that environmentalism is becoming an ideology, the first ideology to be deeply rooted in the natural sciences. The movement grew up in an aura of non-partisan politics but is at the point of losing its political neutrality. As environmentalists become more ideological, so neo-conservatives become the major opponents of the movement's proposals for reform. Paehlke argues that in future the movement is likely to become the home for a new type of progressive politics, linking economic equity, peace, and environmental protection.

This book does not include a case study of ecological advocacy. This is a weakness.[4] Nevertheless, the links between advocacy and social movements, so prominent in the case of environmentalism, are well supported in the other case studies in this book.

ADVOCACY AND SOCIAL THEORY

A number of well-known sociologists, including Falk (1987), Frank (Frank and Fuentes 1988), Habermas (1984), and Touraine (1981), have taken up the issue of how the formation of new social movements affects social theory. Touraine and Habermas fashion arguments similar to those of Mueller given above. The propensity of the state to promote technology and technical solutions for their own sake, especially in the military sector, gives rise to demands for compensations in the name of "forms of life" or quality of life. These protests are often carried on outside nation-state legislatures. Governments of mixed economies provide quantities of goods and services as a substitute of quality of life and qualitative dimensions of "the good life" have not been important aspects of governmental activity.[5]

Touraine points out that the existence of new social movements does not obviate class conflict, for new social movements are to some extent built upon older movements. The situation for sociological theory is one of *both* conflict over the older forms of social equality *and* distribution of equity in society arising from conflicts over "the programmed society," as Touraine puts it.

The major benefit of Touraine's argument is that he is able to combine analysis of local social conflict with the more abstract notion of mode of production, showing the connection between the narrow and the wider setting. Through his analysis it becomes quite clear how the practical actions of social movements "ceaselessly attack the reproduction of the established order, smash open the social order, disclose social relations to the view behind principles, values, and techniques" (Touraine 1977, 447).

Both Marshall and Dippo show (below) how conflicts of social class require continuing attention from advocates. Marshall argues that advocates in the labour movement should recognize quite clearly the adversarial nature of past struggles with capitalism. Though researchers acting as advocates in the labour movement have neither the credentials for leading labour nor the mandate to do so, research can be crucial in union officials' policy making. For Dippo, the focus of advocacy is the gap between "work" as an abstract category under the control of the "owners of work," and young workers' awareness – or lack thereof – of the social unity of work.

Frank and Fuentes state that, while new social movements display much variety, the strength and importance of social movements is related to long-term politico-economic and ideological cycles. The majority seek autonomy rather than power and are more defensive than offensive, yet social movements often support in one way or another "delinking from capitalism" (Frank and Fuentes 1988, 27–45). The success or failure of social movements has to do with relative advantages they gain over their opposition. They also succeed as a result of how well they write their own scripts. As Frank points out, there is an element of "street theatre" in the progress of social movements (see also Adelman below). The movements will constantly challenge current definitions of social roles, controls on social order, and the actual functioning of politics.

There are advocacy groups in all facets of the political spectrum. Liberal advocates find themselves confronting the radical right, while centre-right counter-movements oppose the left. Each constructs a strategy to secure relative advantage. Movement and counter-movement form opposing visions of future society but political directions are subject to splits and fragmentation. The best current example is the women's movement. Cleveland (below) shows how the women's movement in Toronto has been unable to turn personal experience of male dominance into the realm of public issues because the women's movement is split between alternative conceptions of feminist empowerment. This is the major reason why the women's movement in Toronto remains politically marginal.

ADVOCACY AND METHOD

The construction of social knowledge through advocacy ought to revamp outworn criteria of method in social science. The stumbling blocks to a rapid development of a sociology of advocacy are the requirements of "advocacy with," as Heyworth puts it (below). These raise considerable problems. Students of advocacy find it difficult, if not impossible, to adopt a stance "neutral" or "above" that which the advocate takes, even if the language of social science enters into the process of mediation.

According to mainstream sociology, building up a sound body of knowledge depends upon an objective understanding of a social phenomenon. This knowledge will not come about if the results of the study were distorted by the intrusion of investigator's values. Such a study challenges canons of "objectivity" on which social sciences have flourished. Yet, as Crysdale argues (below), most professional bodies of social researchers make clear statements about justice and injustice, good and evil, right and wrong, efficiencies and inefficiencies, without fear of betraying objectivity. Today "interested knowledge" is a valuable part of human discourse. A social science which recognizes the nature of its own interventionist activity is better placed to engage in the making of social policy – which is inherently interventionist – than a science which pretends to be neutral.

The canons of method in social science have a chilling effect on social intervention. Wherever knowledge continues to be defined as a product of the rational application of scientific method, the social sciences are administratively enjoined to retain a "scientific approach" in their research. Many social scientists are aware that application of science and technology threatens the survival of civilization, but individual social scientists feel great unease arguing against the effects of unbridled rationality.

Recently feminist writers reflecting on the experience of the women's movement have argued that requirements for "objectivity" are a consequence of the Adversary Paradigm in science and philosophy. The Adversary Paradigm has assumed that the best way of evaluating academic work is to subject it to the strongest or most extreme opposition. Any thesis which survives this method of evaluation is likely to be more correct than one that does not.

Yet the adversarial use of counter-example is not a good way to reach conclusions about complex and holistic issues. Abortion is a case in point. The adversary method requires that example and counter-example be limited to explicit premises. In the case of abortion the premises of the argument have been narrowed to the "personhood" of the fetus. The explicit premises of "personhood" are then taken to be the grounds which will determine the outcome of the abortion issue and the rules made in society with regard to terminating a pregnancy. Yet, when a decision has to be made, individuals invoke a much wider system of ideas about abortion than the "personhood" of the fetus. This wider system of reasoning, moral in origin, is largely ignored in adversarial confrontation. The method of adversarial argument and counter-argument may logically defeat an opponent but, to be morally convincing, reasoning must be related to a much larger system of ideas: "What are the most plausible premises that would make this argument a good one?" "Why is this argument important?" (Moulton 1989, 5–20). Methods of objective reasoning reduce the relationship of part to whole to a very narrow causal determination and the narrow causality then becomes the primary determinant of "reason" and "method."

Advocates, by contrast, insist that part-to-whole relations are fundamental to their methodology, and are determined to devise methods which will embed this form of reasoning. Spencer, in her article below, argues that "objectivity" in research should not oblige researchers to estrange themselves from their own interests. It is the task of all social science to undertake active intervention, for only by intervention will any program of social research "uncover" its own interests in a wider dimension.

Advocates have to convince. In his contribution to this volume, Morgan argues that, since knowledge is a socially constructed process, the method of advocacy should be built upon an epistemology of practice. Contrary to its claims, conventional method does not necessarily derive insightful knowledge from research. Instead, the validity of research depends on the stance taken by the researcher. Morgan suggests that the appropriate facility, or method, emerging from advocacy is that of critical reframing of issues. A practitioner able to reframe issues provides more insightful knowledge than any generalization from empirical data. He suggests advocates adopt an epistemology of practice which requires researchers to undertake "reflection-in-action."

SUMMARY

Case studies in this book include participants' views of advocacy in process (see Rees and Tator below). In conventional social science, discussion "about advocacy" would be regarded as theoretically superior to that of the advocate reporting his or her own case. To separate the two discussions would go against the object of this volume.

The case studies bring into a single framework three dimensions of inquiry. First, they demonstrate order in the tangle of issues surrounding advocacy. Making knowledge count includes political empowerment, consciousness-raising, and collective self-analysis. They also demonstrate the continuing importance of social class in underpinning conflict.

Second, they show how advocacy is amplified by the presence of television. The construction of social knowledge is often a construction of "reality" via the media. The communicative framework of the social construction of knowledge is crucial to its theoretical understanding.

The third dimension evaluates the methodological issues of "making knowledge count." Whether these involve local activities or global social movements, the inherent circularities between observer and observed bring a totally new dimension to traditional methods of social science. Recognition of the new relationship between the social observer and patterns of dissent permanently alters the academic study of society. Conventional social science has not yet come to terms with the type of research in which observer and observed are in circular, reflexive contact with each other (Science Council of Canada, 1985, 259). Advocacy, on the other hand, thrives on reflexive circularities. Advocacy helps to develop the consciousness of social groups, and, as a result of raised consciousness, empowers them to act on their own behalf. This is a key to achieving critical reframing of issues and constructing knowledge congruent with new contexts of action.

This book is in four parts. The first part establishes the relation between advocacy and the implementation of human rights; the second relates advocacy to empowerment; the third relates to social movements; and the fourth relates advocacy to its own methodology – advocacy as a form of social science.

NOTES

1 While technology creates a medium facilitating development of social movements, the argument that technical facilities automatically bring about a change in the ratios of perception, a "global village," to use Marshall McLuhan's term, are far fetched. Any technological system operates within a complex political context. Satellite broadcasting is intimately tied to national governmental control. News about dissent is dependent on national government policies permitting interviews, taping, and rebroadcast, so that the reporting of social movements is always uneven and discontinuous.

2 This point arose from a discussion in a seminar on Pension Benefits at the Canadian Bar Association meeting in Toronto on 22 September 1989.

3 A quite opposite position is taken by politicians in many of the newly independent states of the Third World (the Group of 77). They maintain that economic discrimination is fundamental to worldwide erosion of fundamental human rights and freedoms, and that the u.s. along with other Western industrial nations must share the responsibility for this state of affairs. The conservative reply is that those accusing the United States and other capitalist nations of perpetrating global inequalities are themselves guilty of a double standard. Most nations making accusations have a far worse human rights record, and such selective morality threatens the whole question of human rights (Glaser and Possony 1979, 390).

4 The original draft for this book contained an article on the pollution of Canadian Indian land. Unfortunately, the author faced a lawsuit arising out of the issues presented and had to withdraw. Lawsuits are one of the practical hurdles which advocates may have to face.

5 Habermas' primary thesis is very close to that of Touraine. Touraine speaks of "conflicts of the programmed society." Modern sources of conflict lie in modern governments' social engineering outside the sphere of work. To this end they have thoroughly immersed themselves in human management policies and harnessed science and economics in support of their schemes. Habermas argues that social conflict in the last two decades has turned away from issues surrounding social welfare and the pattern of state redistribution towards a new set of conflicts which relate to "the grammar of forms of life." By this he means that modern social conflicts are to be found in ecology and anti-nuclear movements; in women's movements; in conflicts over regional and cultural autonomy; and in the proliferation of religious sects – especially those propounding a return to conservatism. These conflicts involve systemic opposition to the way in which modern states seek to organize and control social life. Thus modern social conflicts are matters of incompatible epistemologies rather than contestations over political authority.

REFERENCES

Anderson, David. 1985. "The Rubicon of Involvement – Social Work and Anthropology." In Robert Paine, (ed.), *Advocacy and Anthropology: First Encounters*, 45–58. St John's: Institute of Social and Economic Research, Memorial University of Newfoundland.

Birnbaum, Norman. 1969. *The Crisis of Industrial Society*. London: Oxford University Press.

Burger, Julian. 1987. *Report from the Frontier: The State of the World's Indigenous Peoples*. London: Zed Books.

Falk, Richard, ed. 1987. *Towards a Just World Peace: Perspectives from Social Movements*. London: Butterworths.

Frank, André Gunder, and Marta Fuentes. 1988. "Nine Theses on Social Movements." *International Foundation for Development Alternatives (IFDA) Dossier* 63: 27–44.

Glaser, Kurt, and Stefan Possony. 1979. *Victims of Politics: The State of Human Rights*. New York: Columbia University Press.

Gusfield, J.R.. 1981. *The Culture of Public Problems: Drinking-Driving and the Symbolic Order*. Chicago: University of Chicago Press.

Habermas, Jurgen. 1981. *The Theory of Communicative Action: Reason and the Rationalization of Society*. Volume 1. Boston: Beacon Press.

Kallen, Evelyn. 1982. *Ethnicity and Human Rights in Canada*. Toronto: Gage Publications.

Keating, Michael. 1989. *Toward a Common Future: A Report on Sustainable Development and Its Implications for Canada*. Ottawa: Minister of Supply and Public Services Canada.

Kutchins, H., and S. Kutchins. 1978. "Advocacy and Social Work." In George H. Weber and George J. McCall, eds., *Social Scientists as Advocates*, 13–47. Beverly Hills: Sage Publications.

MacIntyre, Alasdair. 1984. *After Virtue*. 2nd ed. Notre Dame: Indiana University Press.

Maybury-Lewis, David. 1985. "A Special Sort of Pleading – Anthropology at the Service of Ethnic Groups." In Robert Paine, ed., *Advocacy and Anthropology: First Encounters*, 130–48. St John's: Institute of Social and Economic Research, Memorial University of Newfoundland.

Moulton, Janice. 1989. "A Paradigm of Philosophy: The Adversary Method." In Ann Garry and Marilyn Pearsall, eds., *Women, Knowledge and Reality: Explorations in Feminist Philosophy*, 5–20. Boston: Unwin Hyman.

Mueller, Claus. 1973. *The Politics of Communication: A Study in the Political Sociology of Language, Socialization and Legitimation*. New York: Oxford University Press.

Paehlke, Robert C. 1989. *Environmentalism and the Future of Progressive Politics*. New Haven: Yale University Press.

Science Council of Canada. 1985. *Social Science Research in Canada: Stagnation or Regeneration?* Ottawa: Ministry of Supply and Public Services.

Slater, David, ed. 1985. *New Social Movements and the State in Latin America*. Dordrecht, Holland: Floris Publications for the Centre for Latin American Research.

Touraine, Alain. 1977. *The Self-Production of Society*. Chicago and London: University of Chicago Press.

– 1981. *The Voice and the Eye: An Analysis of Social Movements*. Cambridge: Cambridge University Press, and Paris: Editions de la Maison des Sciences de L'Homme.

PART ONE: ADVOCACY AND HUMAN RIGHTS

Advocacy and Human Rights

The case studies in this section relate in some manner to the issue of human rights. In the liberal democracies, human rights issues tend to elicit a grass-roots response in a way that political criticism rarely manages to do. The visibility and ease with which human rights violations can be demonstrated, through television broadcast and videotape replay, and the ease with which the images can be absorbed, are clearly factors promoting the salience of human rights issues.

Consider United States–Soviet Union relations during the presidency of Ronald Reagan. Instances of Soviet violations of human rights were well documented. They were relatively simple to present and could be visually interpreted. They could therefore be "explained" within the limited format of the six o'clock TV news program, and reach a mass audience instantly. The same was true of racist suppression in South Africa, or, in an earlier period, of the horrendous suppression of human rights in Chile.

The flow of media images leads to immediate consciousness raising, but whether or how this can be turned into collective discourse is much more difficult to assess. Writers in the field of mass communications studies are agreed only in that the incidence and kinds of effects which mass media have on political behaviour are very uncertain wherever there is a variety of issues entering into the political spectrum. In the contested area of morals and opinion, which attracts much media attention – and human rights are essentially a moral issue – it is difficult to name a case where the media can be identified as sole cause of any given social effect.[1]

Military-authoritarian regimes, on the other hand, are almost always anxious to cut the interpretative loop between media images and the development of political discourse. The potential for the combination of media presence and human rights to galvanize political opposition in this loop of communicative activity is far more obvious and direct.

In their article on Chile, Landstreet et al. provide an outstanding example of the communicative loop between social research activity, human rights, and national political resistance. They divide the repression of the Pinochet regime into three phases. The first phase was a long, dark period from the coup in 1973 until 1977. It was a period of indiscriminate brutality and repression in which major institutions such as the universities were totally subdued. In the second period, lasting one or two years, the military junta tried more subtle mechanisms of control. As they did so, there was a gathering of information on the effects of repression by dissenting research groups, now staffed by academics dismissed from the university. By 1980–82 a third phase had come into being. Groups like the Agrarian Research Centre (GIA) began to put into effect socially oriented programs supporting the peasantry or the urban poor, and in some way helping fulfil basic needs and restore human rights. These dissenting research groups – advocacy groups – were becoming a basis for formal political opposition.

The contrast between the slow and painful response to human rights violations in Chile and the response to alleged violations of human rights in liberal democracies is quite remarkable. Responsibility in Canada for human rights lies both in provincial and federal jurisdiction. In 1960 the federal government of Canada passed a Canadian Bill of Rights as a Canadian counterpart of the Universal Declaration of Human Rights, but its application did not apply provincially. In 1962, in response to federal initiative, Ontario passed the Ontario Human Rights code, which had the Ontario Human Rights Commission as its executive arm. By 1975 all Canadian provinces had established Human Rights Commissions to administer anti-discriminatory legislation.

At the federal level, a formal Charter of Rights and Freedoms was incorporated in the Canadian Constitution Act of 1981. But Quebec interpreted the Constitution Act as a denial of its status as a "founding people" within Canada, equal with anglophones as the other founding nationality.[2] The premiers of Quebec, René Lévesque and Robert Bourassa, demanded that before Quebec agreed to become a signatory there should be full recognition of Quebec as a society distinct by its language, culture, and institutions, possessing all the attributes of a distinct national community.

This means that the areas of human rights and freedoms covered by Canadian law have been selectively tailored. Many ambiguities and weaknesses remain with regard to the status of aboriginal peoples, Status Indians, Metis, and Inuit. The Canadian Charter of Rights and Freedoms almost foundered on the aboriginal question. Subsequently, the Meech Lake Accord foundered on the intractable combination of the status of aboriginal peoples and the "distinct society" i.e. collective rights in Quebec.

Wherever there is a multicultural society, or wherever distinctive ethnic or cultural groups exist, there also exists a potential political conflict between majority and minority ethnic groups. This question could have been addressed in human rights legislation in Canada, but has not. Ethnic, religious, and linguistic minorities, wherever they exist, could be accorded the positive right in law to express and enjoy their own distinctive culture, language, and religion. As the issue currently stands, majority/minority ethnic relations have become "a powerful political tool wielded by the dominant ethnic collectivity to disadvantage, disprivilege and deny the fundamental human rights of ethnic minorities" (Kallen 1982, 43, 107, 230).

This is the context for Rees and Tator's discussion on race relations advocacy. Rees and Tator's organization, the Urban Alliance on Race Relations, began its advocacy by challenging the dominant assumption that no racial discrimination existed in Canada. In the mid-1970s racial incidents of one sort or another were commonly reported in the press and on television. But the official administrative view remained that in Canada a climate of racial harmony existed. For administrators, racial harmony was equated with the absence of racial conflict, and the official view proposed that any advocacy or any public confrontation on racial questions would only fuel a storm of racial tension.

The advocacy group had to get their own alternative vision of racial intolerance firmly established and did so by both undertaking social research and using media events to transform the media's own assumptions about racial harmony and intolerance. The Urban Alliance on Race Relations is, therefore, an excellent example of how advocacy groups can undertake the task of constructing social knowledge.

Modern media studies recognize that "the media" are an enormously diverse set of messages, images, and ideas which originate in society and which are fed back to the originators in modulated form. The "effects" of the media on any one issue are difficult to discern because the communicative loop is circular, with the "media" being its physical channel of circulation. Far more is known about situations where media focus on institutionalized behaviour *within* established norms and values. A typical example would be a national political campaign, in which the campaign is concerned with directing and reinforcing socially approved objectives.

Advocates trying to transform social situations can hardly emulate the media tactics of the political campaign, and yet advocacy is, by its very nature, a sort of campaign, and access to media an important part of advocacy. "Campaign requirements" are fourfold – information, interpretation, expression, mobilization (McQuail 1984, 190–211):

- informing about aims and activities of given organizations,
- interpreting information and events and image-building,
- giving voice to beliefs, values, ideologies and principles,
- helping to develop a consciousness of belonging to a party, class, group, or social movement,
- mobilizing and guiding the activities of followers,
- fund-raising.

In effect, advocates are required to double up as researchers and political lobbyists. Researchers fit more easily into the "expressive activity" of advocacy, where they can give voice to beliefs, values, ideologies, and principles. They are less well fitted for the other range of communicative functions. As Adelman points out in his discussion of refugee advocacy, the two roles of "objective expert" and "media theatre director" are difficult to keep in balance.

As each of the following essays indicates, advocacy is a series of activities, separated in time, place, and personnel, which aims to change, in some manner, the conventions of existing practice or the existing institutional order. The study of advocacy supports the notion that *all* values are artifacts of the social. There is no meta-communicative order that prescribes social values; communication is the activity which gives rise to standards and norms and creates a diversity of viewpoints at the same time.

In liberal democracies the ongoing construction of a diversity of values cannot be confused with anomie or lack of coherent social norms. Instead, advocacy is a key process in the way that particular forms of knowledgeable activity are made to count.

NOTES

1 Modern mass communication theory is split between two forms of argument about "media effects," with one group believing the exercise to be worthwhile, and another group believing that all arguments about

"effects" begin from false premises. The group wishing to renew research on the effects of mass communication recognizes that prior research on the effects of media on individual behaviour was in error. Research on media effects should concentrate on the study of cognition, not the study of behaviour. Mass media effects should be considered together with collective phenomena such as belief, ideology, and cultural patterns. The group of researchers who discount attention paid to media effects is well represented in Great Britain. There some institutes have refrained from calling themselves "media research" or "mass communications" institutes because they think of themselves as "institutes for cultural studies." Stuart Hall and Raymond Williams, both of whom support this position, argue that all communication is a cultural, or social, production.

2 The original document creating the Dominion of Canada, the British North America Act, makes no explicit reference to human rights. It does provide for protection of the English and French languages, and the rights of both Protestants and Catholics to denominational schools. From the time of the British North America Act language provision become the focus for perennial conflict of rights of different cultural groups.

REFERENCES

Kallen, Evelyn. 1982. *Ethnicity and Human Rights in Canada*. Toronto: Gage Publishing.

McQuail, Denis. 1983. *Mass Communication Theory: An Introduction*. Beverly Hills: Sage Publications.

PETER LANDSTREET, JINNY ARANCIBIA,
MARCELO CHARLIN,
HARRY DÍAZ, AND JACQUES DOYER

Human Rights Advocacy in a Repressive Context: Chile, 1973–89

INTRODUCTION

This article examines advocacy in an authoritarian context – the Chilean military dictatorship ushered in with the 1973 coup d'état.[1] More specifically, it focuses on how social scientists responded to a repressive state, and the way in which much of their work came to take on the character of *human rights advocacy*.

The main institutional means through which this transformation of social science practice in Chile occurred was a forced and massive transfer of academics out of the formal university system, and the creation of a large number of independent (private) social science research centres.[2] These constituted what became known as the "dissident" research centres, the main loci of humann rights–related social science activity in Chile.

We will address the concept of "human rights" later in this article; here we wish to clarify that by "advocacy" we understand the espousing or supporting, by argument, of a cause or social actor(s). It is understood that interests other than one's own are being supported, though one's own may also be served in the process. The word derives from the Latin *advocatus*, meaning "legal counsellor." Advocacy thus involves empathy. A fine line, however, may separate it from presumptuousness: for example, quite an array of parties regard themselves as the vanguard and lucid consciousness of the working class, and it is not clear that many Nicaraguans regard the U.S. government as an advocate of their freedom. When advocacy oversteps itself, and advocacy and its object are largely nonsynchronous, it enters the realms of error, vested interest, projection, or wishful thinking. Many Chilean academics now believe that this was a source of problems in social science advocacy in Chile in the decade prior to the military coup, in the intensely ideologized national political environment of that time. (See Garretón 1983, 7–10, and Brunner and Barrios 1987, 75–82 for discussions of this issue.) We will see later how the following years saw a loosening of tight linkages between ideology and social science practice.

THE AUTHORITARIAN STATE

The 1973 military coup took place in what had been one of Latin America's oldest and most stable democracies. Chile was experiencing a process of economic and social reform initiated by the 1964–70 Christian Democratic government of Eduardo Frei. This period of reform was widened and deepened by the socialist Unidad Popular (UP, or Popular Unity) government led by Salvador Allende, elected to power in 1970. The UP was a coalition of two major, mass-based leftist parties (the Socialist and Communist Parties), plus several smaller ones. The reforms, and the ideological debate[3] surrounding them, led to an intense political polarization of the population, and the whole process was stopped by a military coup led by General Augusto Pinochet in September 1973.[4]

The coup and the junta's subsequent policies caused enormous dislocations throughout Chilean society. From 1973 onwards, policies – some public and some secret – were aimed at destroying, dismantling, reorganizing, or controlling all organizations and institutions considered to be an expression or support of the previous order.[5] Political parties were declared illegal (the leftist parties) or "in recess" (all other parties); labour organizations were brought under tight control; many media outlets (TV and radio stations, magazines and newspapers) were closed down; and all universities were put under military control. An unprecedented number of Chileans left the country.

The ruling junta was composed of four persons: the heads of the army, navy, air force, and the national uniformed police (Carabineros). At first the junta governed as a team, but then General Pinochet, commander-in-chief of the army, became increasingly central within it, formally becoming president in June 1974, and the authoritarian government took on a markedly personalistic character. In this process, Pinochet was assisted by the creation of a secret police service, known by its acronym, DINA. Emerging in June 1974, the DINA represented a new centralization and professionalization of repressive activities. It took many of these activities out of the hands of the three branches of the armed forces and the two national police systems. The head of the DINA reported directly to Pinochet, a procedure that promoted and reinforced his personal power within the junta. Following a series of international scandals, including foreign assassinations, the DINA was cosmetically reorganized in 1977 into the CNI, which continued as an indispensable prop to the regime (Branch and Propper 1982; Dinges and Landau, 1980).

Beginning with the coup, the Chilean population experienced human rights violations transcending, both qualitatively and quantitatively, anything experienced in the country in this century. We present below a list of types of such violations, grouped under the right that they violate; following each type of violation a brief explanation or example is provided. The examples are chosen to cover a range of both time and social actors. The list is a heuristic device, adapted from an organizing scheme in Charlin 1984, 61–2. It takes into account the United Nations' Universal Declaration of Human Rights, though our list is much shorter than the range of rights specified in that document's thirty articles. In essence, we have selected those rights whose violation clearly constitutes political *repression*. Only in the case of one type of violation, "maintenance of massive unemployment" (8.b. below), have we gone beyond the set of overtly repressive measures. We include this one precisely to signal the incomplete nature of our list of rights. There is a whole set of what may loosely be called "social and economic rights," the violation of which does not necessarily constitute repression, at least not in the restricted sense of the term. The UN document, for example, refers to rights having to do with working conditions, marriage, rest and leisure, standards of living, health and education. We recognize the importance of these rights, and thus include massive unemployment as an example of the range of rights violations which, for reasons of space, we cannot examine in this article.

One other qualification is indispensable. The main purpose of repressive measures is to control behaviour of an oppositional, or potentially oppositional, sort. But the measures achieve their full force in society not only through what we call their "primary effects" on the persons directly repressed, but also – via fear – through their secondary effects on the family and friends of the directly repressed, and then through tertiary effects that occur when the population in general "knows that such things happen" in the country, even though any given person "knowing" this may not have been affected personally, either directly or in his/her immediate social network. These tertiary effects, then, represent politically induced fear having become a component of the nation's culture.

Further, we would argue that the prime incapacitators are thoughts of torture and death. Thus, fear checks behaviour by means of a set of associations that could be exemplified by: "If I go to the demonstration tomorrow, I may be arrested. If I'm arrested, they might torture me. They could kill me."

The point is that under authoritarian rule, the behaviour-controlling consequences of human rights violations are wider than the set of directly repressed individuals, owing to this ripple effect. People are taught to control themselves, so that political repression, once internalized, becomes self-repression. In short, repression's effects are both wider and deeper than they might seem at first. There is always more repression than there appears to be.

HUMAN RIGHTS VIOLATIONS

1 The right to life

Killings. Serious estimates of the number of politically motivated killings within the first year of the dictatorship range from five thousand to thirty-thousand (Amnesty International, cited in Brown 1983, 47). Subsequent levels were much lower, as killings became more selective.

2 The right to physical and moral integrity

a. Torture (both physical and psychological). Statistics on this practice are seriously incomplete, but it was a consistent policy under the junta, used mainly by the secret police. For documentation see Amnesty International (1983), and Brown (1983, 67–79).

b. Intimidation. This involved a range of relatively low-profile techniques designed to warn people that they were under observation; the implicit message was that they should moderate their behaviour. Examples include following people in an obvious fashion, searches of residences and offices while occupants were away, threats against family members, surveillance from cars parked in front of buildings, obvious opening of mail, and anonymous phone calls. Documentation is sparse, but all members of the opposition knew these techniques.

3 The right to freedom of person

a. Disappearances. In this practice, the authorities denied knowledge of the fate of missing persons. Estimates of the total number of disappeared between 1973 and 1978 range from 1,600 to 2,500 (Brown 1983, 80–6). The practice attracted very negative international publicity, and from 1979 onward disappearances were rare. Human rights specialists assume that all or almost all of the disappeared were killed either in the moment of apprehension or (more commonly) while under detention, often after torture.

b. Arbitrary arrests. These are politically motivated arrests, and three patterns were discernible: individual arrests, "mass arrests" (associated with demonstrations), and "raid arrests" (associated with raids on entire neighbourhoods). A standard practice over the years, the incidence of arbitrary arrests increased greatly from 1983 onward, when demonstrations began occurring more often. In 1983, for example, conservative counts (based only on verified instances) showed 641 individual arrests, 14,436 mass arrests, and 17,699 raid arrests, for a total of 32,776 (CCHDH 1984, 16–24).

c. Banishment. This is the practice of internal exile, in which persons were banished to remote parts of the country – the cold and rainy south or the desert north. It occurred in waves over the years, with sentences lasting from three months (summary banishment by simple order of the Ministry of the Interior) to several years (judicial banishment). From March 1981 to June 1983, 311 persons were banished (Brown 1983, 97–102).

4 The right to live in country of nationality

Involuntary exile. We see this as having had four sources: 1 those who fled due to perceived threats to their life or liberty, but whose reentry to Chile was not legally barred; 2 those administratively or judicially expelled from the country; 3 those political prisoners who were allowed to convert prison terms into exile; 4 those who, while outside of the country, had their reentry to Chile prohibited. Precise figures are not available, but with regard to the last three categories it may be noted that towards the end of the 1970s the government publicly referred to some ten thousand citizens who were prohibited from reentering the country; Chilean human rights organizations, however, had documentation indicating that the number was at least thirty thousand, and probably higher. (This figure, of course, does not count the family members living in exile with those whose reentry was officially barred.) The first category above undoubtedly contains by far the largest number of exiles, but insuperable measurement difficulties would confront any attempt to distinguish between those who left having "genuine" reasons for fear from those who emigrated primarily for other reasons (such as economic).

5 The right to justice

a. Denial of legal defence. The day of the coup, the junta decreed a state of siege, which lasted until March 1978 and allowed the creation of "wartime" military courts. These courts tried political prisoners, and in many instances gave death sentences. All trials were brief, and whole groups of prisoners were tried in less than twenty-four hours. In some cases defendants were allowed no access to a lawyer at all; in others a lawyer was present but not allowed to interview defendants before or during the trial (Frühling 1983, 517–18; Arancibia, Charlin, and Landstreet 1987, 54–6).

b. Ineffectiveness of habeas corpus. From 1973 to 1979, of more than five thousand writs presented to the courts, only four were accepted (vs 1982, 80).

6 The right to freedom of peaceful assembly and association

a. Controls on public assembly. From the coup until August 1988, Chile was continually under "states of exception": states of "siege," of "emergency," and of "risk of disturbance of internal order." Public gatherings, whether meetings or demonstrations, needed authorization from the military authorities. Permission for assembly of a non-supportive political character was usually denied, and when assemblies "became" political, they often were violently repressed (Brown 1983, 8, 28–33).

b. Banning of organizations. Immediately after the coup, Chile's national labour union confederation (the Central Unica de Trabajadores, CUT) was dissolved, and, as mentioned, political parties were banned or placed "in recess." Though many plant-level unions survived, and labour leaders gradually built new federations, and though the parties never disappeared entirely (in fact they showed a marked resurgence from 1983 onward), government controls fragmented the opposition sufficiently to prevent it from reaching the critical mass necessary to bring an end to the military regime.

7 The right to freedom of expression and access to information

Banning of communications outlets and censorship. Media outlets belonging to the left were closed down after the coup. In addition, the states of siege and emergency allowed military commanders to establish censorship. Nevertheless, several Christian Democratic–

associated outlets were allowed to continue (a weekly news magazine and a chain of radio stations), and the Catholic church gave protection to a variety of other oppositional outlets (another chain of radio stations and several magazines). In the 1980s a number of low-circulation magazines associated with the moderate left emerged; their existence was generally tolerated, though their right to publish was periodically suspended. Television is generally considered the most influential mass medium in Chile, and at no point was any sort of oppositional TV station allowed.

8 Economic rights

a. Firing of employees for political reasons. In the one and a half years between the coup and March 1974, some three hundred thousand public and private employees were dismissed for political reasons (Anonymous 1975, 13).

b. Maintenance of massive unemployment. Unemployment reached unprecedented levels, averaging 20 per cent of the labour force from 1974 to 1987, as compared with a pre-coup average of 5 per cent from 1965 to 1973 (Cortázar 1988, 10–11).

THE EDGE OF SURVIVAL

The junta's economic policy was a "neoconservative," market-oriented one, epitomized by the Chicago school of economics led by Milton Friedman (Foxley 1983, Vergara 1986). Social service expenditures were reduced, state enterprises privatized, tariffs cut, and the Chilean economy was laid open to the discipline of international market forces. The impact on the majority of Chileans was severe. Beyond the unemployment mentioned above, real earnings (wage and salary income relative to the cost of living) deteriorated; by 1988 earnings were still 12 per cent lower than in 1970 (Jadresic 1989, 21). Personal income was redistributed regressively, becoming concentrated in the top 10 to 20 per cent of the population (Cortázar 1980, Délano and Traslaviña 1989, 168). In terms of food, calorie consumption per capita dropped by some 12 per cent, and proteins by 20 per cent, from 1974 to 1987 (Martner 1989, 24).

Post-coup Chile thus experienced widespread damage from the junta's repression and its economic policy. Both were central to human rights violations and social science responses to them. We now illustrate some of the types of problems advocates faced by a brief glance at three groups living on the edge of survival: Natives, the urban poor, and low-income women.

Chile has close to half a million Native people, among whom the Mapuche, in the south-central part of the country, are the most numerous (Foerster 1989, Leiva 1985, Doyer 1985, Bengoa and Valenzuela 1984). Following the coup some Mapuches, like other peasants, were searched out by landowners, the military and police, and killed, often following torture, and often in groups. After this period of relatively indiscriminate repression, another followed during which Mapuche leaders "disappeared" or were jailed under harsh conditions. The aims seem to have been to eliminate leaders antagonistic towards the military government, and to instil enough fear that new individuals would be reluctant to take on vacant leadership roles. After an interval, the regime came under international criticism and the balance of these types of actions shifted towards other methods, including internal exile, death threats, and deprivation of the right to be in certain parts of the country.

A threat of a different sort was posed by the 1979 Decree-Law entitled "For the Division of Reserves and the Liquidation of Indian Communities." The central point of this law was to promote the privatization of Mapuche land ownership, and transfer what had previously been community-owned land into private parcels. This created conditions under which non-Mapuches would be able to purchase what had been reserve lands, thus undermining the residential ethnic homogeneity which helped support Mapuche collective identity.

Any observer in the region could see that both the Mapuches' situation and prospects were dismal. Mapuche unemployment was well above the national average. Many had little more than a hut and the land on which it was built, and church organizations often had to provide direct food aid. Most men were either working a small plot of land inadequate for their needs or staying home for lack of employment. The employment shortage, with its depressing effect on Mapuche morale, coupled with the prevailing ethnic prejudice and the government's lavish attitude towards the alcohol trade, accounted for a high level of alcoholism among the adult Mapuche population. While alcoholism and malnutrition were threatening Mapuche health, shortage of clinics annd hospitals worsened the situation. The first victims were the children, and Mapuche infant mortality was some 30 per cent higher than the national average.

The Mapuches' educational situation was also bleak. The government, as part of a national policy, transferred responsibility for public primary education to the municipalities, some of which encouraged the private sector to expand into this area. The result among the Mapuche was lowered access to education. Although the only language studied was that of the conqueror, not Mapudungu, at least the Mapuche had basic schooling. This now became harder for the young Mapuche to achieve.

Like the peasantry and indigenous people, who were pushed to the verge of emaciation by state policies, the urban poor also endured setbacks.[6] The advantages of cities, such as a greater and wider range of employment choices, access to public services, and entertainment, were substantially eroded during the process of economic privatization. In addition to paying relatively high prices for services that had been inexpensive or free, the urban poor faced serious unemployment. To this must be added the problem of urban underemployment, mainly taking the form of poorly paid, low-productivity jobs, which multiplied. There was an increase in the "informal sector" of the labour force, which includes marginal self-employed persons (such as street vendors), the sporadically employed, and non-wage workers (such as household members working in family stores).

One of the most serious problems faced by the urban poor was in access to housing. The privatization of state housing services entailed rising prices, and the cost of urban land also increased appreciably. The result was a large increase in the number of homeless urban dwellers, who typically had to move in with relatives or friends.

State repression brought additional ordeals. Given its view of poor neighbourhoods as refuges for political agitators and criminals, the cities' shantytowns were frequently subjected to massive occupations and searches by police and military. The searches disrupted families' daily activities: people awakened at night, homes searched and sometimes ransacked, and men taken to police stations or other holding areas where they were checked for possible criminal or political activities.

Chilean women shared general problems with other collectivities with which they were associated (urban poor, peasantry, native people, etc.), and also confronted problems specific to their gender.[7] In a society where the role of breadwinner traditionally has been assigned to men, men's difficulty in finding work and providing for the family produced feelings of failure and demoralization. With channels for social participation blocked, these men tended to vent their frustrations in the most accessible place: within the family. In this adverse atmosphere, where shouts and arguments were frequent, relationships between husband and wife, and between parent and child, deteriorated.

The traditional division of labour was reinforced constantly by the military regime. The Chilean military has an exceedingly conservative conception of women's roles in society, viewing them solely as wives, mothers, and housekeepers, a view also commonly found in the mass media. But with urgent need to obtain money for their families' survival, many women were compelled to leave the home and accept menial jobs, usually as maids or street vendors, or in poorly paid government job-creation programs. In all these occupations, women worked without social service benefits or day care centres for their children, while earning less than the minimum wage. Unemployed husbands generally assumed little responsibility for child care or domestic tasks, activities heavily sex-typed as female. Accordingly, women in this situation had the double burden of domestic work and menial employment.

The role changes within the family, the harsh household economic situation, the mother's absence, and the father's diminished figure led to considerable disruption in the lives of children in low-income families. Increased numbers dropped out of school and sought work to supplement family income. It became common to go through the day with only tea and bread. Malnutrition levels among shantytown children rose alarmingly.

Women experienced major setbacks in labour legislation originally designed to facilitate their employment. Where the military reimposed the free market, employers found it expedient to fire women because the protections for women built into the Labour Code made their labour's cost proportionately higher than that of men. Another solution to the same problem was found: government began eliminating protective legislation. Working women lost their previous rights to day care for their babies in factories, time off to nurse them during working hours, job protection during pregnancy, and maternity leave. Age of retirement and receipt of pension was also raised for women. Thus women became "free" to compete with men for jobs.

No small number of women experienced political repression as well, especially women involved in leftist political parties. During torture sessions, women frequently were told, in effect, that since politics was not a field for women, they were traitors to their gender.

In short, the lower echelons of the social pyramid were besieged from political, economic, and ideological directions. Hunger, unemployment, lower wages, discrimination, withdrawal of state services, and repression became endemic in the daily lives of the poor. A range of advocates, including clergy, lawyers, social workers, and journalists, attempted to deal in various ways with their problems. Among the advocates were social scientists, especially those expelled from, or denied entry to, positions in Chile's formal university system. We now deal with the universities and the rise of private research centres.

THE UNIVERSITIES

At the time of the coup, university campuses were invaded by the armed forces and police. Persons were killed, prisoners taken, buildings occupied and ransacked, and books burnt. Existing rectors were removed, and military "delegate rectors" were put in their places – generals, admirals, colonels, and captains, retired or in active service. Captured, the universities were held under direct control by the armed forces. The new uniformed rectors were given wide discretionary powers, backed up by the continuing presence of secret police on campuses.

The first purges were targeted mainly at the left. It has been estimated that in the initial months after the coup some 30 to 35 per cent of the teaching personnel, 10 to 15 per cent of the non-academic staff, and 15 to 18 per cent of the students were expelled, for a total of about eighteen thousand persons (Elgueta et al. 1978, 416). The military's own terms for this process were "purification" and "cleaning up." Starting in 1976, large-scale dismissals of Christian Democratic faculty members also occurred. Although the expulsion of the left was performed in a relatively public manner, the subsequent firing of Christian Democratic professors was often carried out using budget cuts as the pretext (Garretón 1980, 102).

The personnel purge was accompanied by an institutional purge. All units (faculties, schools, departments, and institutes) in which the left had a significant presence were at least restructured, and many were eliminated entirely. In some cases, units simply ceased functioning because so many of their faculty members had been ejected or had fled. In those socially oriented academic units which remained, ideological control was imposed and curricula were reorganized to eliminate materials offending against "state interests" or "national unity."

HUMAN RIGHTS ADVOCACY: LEGAL, RELIGIOUS, AND ACADEMIC

During the first years after the coup, academics were faced with the simple problem of survival. During this period, the most visible human rights advocates in Chile were lawyers and clergy. In fact, those among both groups who rose to the challenge can be thought of – occupationally – as functionally specialized human rights advocates. Each profession involves the normative and/or practical obligation of assisting others. Each appeals to frameworks of values – the law and religious ethics – having a certain autonomy from the political values so heavily under attack by the military regime. From these early legal and religious efforts, much else evolved. Without the ground traversed by lawyers and clergy, the academic response would have been slower in coming and smaller in scale.

As Frühling states:

The organized presence of lawyers defending victims of political repression in the courts is not unique to Chile. But in Chile it is especially significant because of the institutional and human resources invested in it and the impact it had on the internationalization of the Chilean human rights situation ... The continuous recourse to the courts met with some success and even managed to limit the freedom of action of the government's repressive apparatus. Legal defense activities from 1973 to 1978 enjoyed public notoriety through press coverage of major cases. For each act of repression, a response was prepared to bring a suit or an appeal before the courts. In the case of disappearances and the permanent use of constitutional "states of emergency" to inhibit the exercise of individual rights, judicial action was part of a political strategy designed to keep similar incidents from recurring (Frühling 1983, 510–11).

But during these years, human rights–oriented legal action was carried out almost exclusively within organizations having some degree of religious protection. Two were central. In October 1973, the Committee of Cooperation for Peace (COPACHI) was formed by Catholic, Protestant, and Jewish representatives. It grew to over one hundred employees in less than a year, and its main activity was legal aid to victims of political repression. The government forced its closure by December 1975, but Raúl Cardinal Silva Henríquez, archbishop of Santiago, created a new organization in January 1976: the Vicariate of Solidarity. The Vicariate included almost all the personnel formerly working in COPACHI, but was established as a formal part of the Archdiocese of Santiago, thus invoking the Church's legal autonomy vis-à-vis the Chilean state.[8]

While legal aid was always central to the Vicariate's activity, it also developed a wide range of other human rights functions. As Smith (1982, 289) has pointed out, the Catholic church was able to exercise its human rights role because "while all other major social organizations in the country had been outlawed or placed under heavy surveillance or in recess, the Church was the one remaining institution allowed to function openly."

While this was happening in church circles, what occurred among academics who were openly or tacitly opposed to the military regime? At the outset, it is important to realize that the "purification" of the universities, though massive, was not total. Some opposition academics – more Christian Democrats than leftists – escaped the purges and learned how to cope by keeping a low profile and exercising great caution in their teaching, research, writing, and public statements. For some it also involved learning how to chip away at previous constraints and take advantage of whatever political openings presented themselves. By the beginning of the 1980s it was possible to identify several departments or units in the Santiago-based universities as being composed mostly of opposition academics. Subsequent years saw a certain crumbling of ideological control within the universities, as the military government found itself mired in a perpetual legitimacy crisis.

Generally speaking, most opposition academics were expelled from their universities during the 1970s, and among them, three trends stand out. First, many hundreds of professors left Chile, establishing new lives abroad. Second, many others who were expelled managed to stay within Chile, shifting to non-academic spheres of work.

The third trend was the one encompassing human rights–related academic work in Chile; it involved the creation of alternative, oppositional spaces of social science activity. A few of what were to become the set of "dissident" private research centres existed before the coup and survived it, but their most important origin lay in the founding, in November 1975, of an institution named the Academy of Christian Humanism. Like the Vicariate of Solidarity, it was the creation of Cardinal Silva Henríquez, and was also lodged legally within the Archdiocese of Santiago. An umbrella organization (not an actual research centre), the Academy grew from very small beginnings to shelter nine opposition research centres. And by setting an example, it also helped stimulate the emergence and growth of other such centres, not protected by the Catholic church but having other means of legal incorporation.

These research centres were almost completely dependent on foreign funding from Western European and North American sources: government ministries and agencies, non-governmental organizations committed to international development and cooperation, foundations, political parties, churches, and the like. Politically, most centres were associated – however informally – with either the left (mainly the non-Marxist-Leninist sectors of it) or the Christian Democratic Party. Some were composite, but as the division between Christian Democracy and the left is a deep one in Chilean political culture, these were in the minority.

By 1984, at least thirty-one dissident centres existed in Chile, employing several hundred opposition academics working in the social sciences (see Díaz, Landstreet, and Lladser 1984). By 1986 their numbers had grown to forty (Lladser 1986). The centres specialized in many different fields of inquiry: education, economic policy, labour economics, sociology, communications, culture, agrarian matters, religion, women's studies, human rights issues, native peoples, regional problems, and others. Most combined research with action programs and a range of services to organizations forming part of what was loosely known as "the opposition." The relative balance of these kinds of activities varied from centre to centre (Brunner and Barrios 1987, 111–113).

In what sense were these private centres involved in human rights activity? The answer has three parts. First, the primary orientation of these centres' research – the thread connecting the majority of their research products – was the analysis of the ways in which the military regime, and its economic and social policies, were adversely affecting different sectors of Chilean society. Research focused on collectivities of persons in their varying subordinate social statuses: peasants, workers, the unemployed, the marginally employed, women, youth, the homeless, the elderly, students, native people, the banished. It also focused on organizations and institutions that were subordinate either in terms of their relationship to the class structure, or in relation to powerful corporations or the all-powerful state: small businesses, labour unions, cooperatives, schools, the media, political parties. This was research done "from below," showing how people's political, civil, economic, social, and cultural rights were being violated, even when not specifically cast in human rights vocabulary.

Research was also done "from above," on the junta, the armed forces, different government agencies, and the large corporations, banks, and holding companies that benefited from state policies. But here an informal rule expressed to us by one academic was *"No hay que tocarle la cola al mono"* ("Don't touch the monkey's tail"). The reference was to Pinochet, but by inference it included the radius immediately around him. Research became more dangerous the closer it came to the centre of state power. It required exceptional personal courage for an opposition researcher in Chile to take as his/her topic the junta, the armed forces, or, especially, the secret police.

The second part of the answer is that these research centres actively generated "outreach" activities to organizations composed of persons whose rights had been violated. Activities included advisory services, program development and evaluation, technical assistance, and provision of information about social, economic, and political issues. This was drawn from the centres' own research, but written in a form understandable to persons who were not highly educated. Among the recipients of these services were labour unions, cooperatives, neighbourhood soup kitchens, church units providing direct aid to the poor, small businesses, women's groups, peasants, artistic and cultural groups, and self-help housing projects.

The third part of the answer is that during the 1980s the centres became heavily involved in generating detailed proposals for alternative state policy measures, not with the hope that the military regime might adopt them, but rather that a future democratic one might do so. These policy proposals were developed as a means of attempting to ensure that the basic rights in each centre's social sector(s) of interest would be protected under a future government. That is, a research centre specializing in agrarian issues would be especially attentive to the needs and rights of peasants, a women's studies centre to those of women, etc. Some also hoped that an ensemble of such policy proposals, integrated into a coherent whole, would provide a sufficiently compelling vision of a possible alternative that the country might actually reorient itself in that direction.

The human rights advocacy of these social scientists occurred first through their research on the *problems* of subordinate sectors; second through direct *assistance* activities for organizations attempting to ameliorate the problems of these sectors; and third through the elaboration and advocacy of *policy alternatives* designed to enhance development prospects while working towards the satisfaction of basic human rights.

Having given this sketch of academic advocacy, we now trace in a little more detail some of its main lines of development over sixteen years of dictatorship.

THE EVOLUTION OF SOCIAL SCIENCE ADVOCACY

Overall, academic advocacy grew dramatically in terms of the number of persons and institutions involved and the scope of their activities. It also evolved in markedly more open and political directions.

The initial years of advocacy were quiet ones. The few opposition research centres existing or created during the first years after the coup kept a low profile, taking care to be seen as engaged in inoffensive (technical, historical, or abstract) projects. Church institutions provided outlets for research results that would have been difficult to publicize elsewhere.

By 1978–79 repression was operating at lower levels, was more selective, and used less obtrusive techniques of control (psychological harassment rather than disappearances, for example). The military regime felt more stable and secure, allowing some limited space for oppositional activities. This climate facilitated the emergence of new private research centres; by the end of 1979 some twenty existed, covering a wide range of fields from cultural studies to labour economics.

During this period, the research centres' main form of advocacy was to criticize, through their publications, the negative effects of the regime's policies. Until 1978, almost all of the information available in Chile about the country's social, economic, and political situation had been coming either from official sources or from ones supporting the regime. The private academic organizations' studies now generated *alternative knowledge* about important trends in society. The studies began to reveal the magnitude of the deterioration of the population's standards of living.

Research results were published by the centres themselves in mimeographed form. Several monthly magazines controlled by the "accepted opposition" – Church institutions and the Christian Democratic Party – also published their research.

When researchers wished to venture into dissemination beyond the bounds of safety, anonymous documents were written and circulated. The most ambitious work of this sort was *Cinco Años de Gobierno Militar en Chile: 1973–1978* (Five Years of Military Government in Chile: 1973–1978, by Elgueta et al. (1978). Researchers from various centres contributed to this 656-page mimeographed document containing chapters on the junta's self-created political and legal foundations, state repression, international relations, economic policy, labour, the agrarian sector, education, mass media, and the churches. The authors used pseudonyms to avoid retribution. The report had limited circulation within Chile, and untranslated, its influence abroad was slight.

Academic advocacy by the end of the 1970s still suffered from the overall political constraints – the regime's strength and the opposition's weakness – and more specifically from legally restricted channels of public communication. Nevertheless, in retrospect two accomplishments are clear. First, the beginnings of an alternative information base about the regime's policies were established, a base on which further information would accumulate and from which new questions could be posed. Second, an important threshold was breached as *some* dissident academic voices broke through the prevailing silence, moving outward the boundaries of the possible. These boundaries would be stretched further in the future.

During 1980–81 repression remained relatively relaxed and more political space opened for the opposition. Economic development seemed stronger, largely due to the inflow of foreign credits and imported consumer goods. In mid-1981 Milton Friedman spoke of a Chilean "economic miracle" comparable to post-war Germany's (Délano and Traslaviña 1989, 66). However, the situation for most Chileans remained dismal; there were high rates of unemployment and underemployment, lower wages, cutbacks in public services, and continued feelings of hopelessness. The benefits of the economy were mostly confined to the upper reaches of the class structure.

Still, criticism was having little effect on state policy. The private centres, still growing in number, began complementing their research activities with short-term experimental programs aimed at countering the effects of certain state policies among selected groups of the poor. An example was design and diffusion of appropriate technology. The Grupo de Investigaciones Agrarias (Agrarian Research Group, GIA), a peasant-support centre, began a project aimed at improving the productivity of small plots; it even started an experimental farm. GIA distributed information about appropriate technology among interested peasants in test areas and designed techniques to facilitate peasant women's household work, such as the use of wind and solar energy for obtaining and heating water.

Another centre, CAPIDE, composed mainly of young anthropologists in the southern city of Temuco in the heart of the Mapuche region, developed support programs for the Native population, stressing training in literacy, health, leadership, and work skills. They also took on the writing of a Mapudungu dictionary, to promote Mapuche language retention.

Another, in Santiago, dedicated itself to women's issues. The Círculo de Estudios de la Mujer, or Women's Studies Circle, engaged in leadership training for domestic servants' unions, carried out sexuality workshops, and evaluated handicrafts workshops as "survival alternatives" for women.

These examples could be multiplied at length, for many centres and many social sectors. The form of advocacy, however, had major limitations: programs often had a welfare character, as they were oriented towards the solution of immediate problems. They also were carried out by small, private organizations, which meant scarce resources for program expansion and very limited coverage of very widespread needs. The centres, in a way, were trying to fill a void left by the massive withdrawal of state services, and attempting to undo damage caused by state policies. Yet the state's capacity for damage was incomparably larger than the centres' capacity for repair. And though the activities were sometimes described as "demonstration projects," it was unclear who was watching the demonstrations.

By 1982, Chile had entered an economic crisis. Years of financial speculation and inattention to investment in productive activities, coupled with declining international prices of Chilean exports, brought the country to the verge of bankruptcy. Loans from international banks came to a sudden halt. Production dwindled, unemployment soared, and the country began living out an economic nightmare.

The economic crisis led to a political crisis. Cabinet changes accelerated: between 1982 and 1985 there were five different ministers of finance, six different ministers of the economy, and six different ministers of planning (Délano and Traslaviña 1989, 204–5). The political opposition, constituted originally by the left and subsequently enlarged by Christian Democrats, now found sectors of the right joining in. Beginning in 1982, protest began to hit the streets. It was met by stepped-up repression. A process of resistance/repression began a cycle of upward and downward waves characteristic in ensuing years.

Economic and political crises opened the way for social scientists' work to become more political. Many opposition members believed that the armed forces would not relinquish power until it was clear what "la alternativa" was. Much attention, therefore, began going into drawing up proposals for alternative state policies under a range of hypothetical new regimes. These proposals were often associated with political parties or coalitions, which felt they were sniffing the scent of a deteriorating regime.

The independent research centres thus became anticipatory advocates for "their" sectors of society in the context of a set of possible political scenarios. It was not known at what moment the policies might leave the drawing boards and be put into action, though it seemed to many at the time that the director of a research centre might become a cabinet minister with little advance warning.

But the optimism was premature. By the mid-1980s it was reasonably clear that the military regime would likely be able to hold to its own set timetable for retaining power and allowing for the possibility of relinquishing it. The latter involved two main future voting events: first, a national plebiscite to be held sometime before March 1989, in which voters could respond "yes" or "no" to the question of Pinochet's remaining in power; and second, in the event of a majority "no" vote, presidential and parliamentary elections to be scheduled within a year following the plebiscite.

A new type of research was launched in this context: surveys of public opinion, including questions on political attitudes and preferences. Although, according to the law, survey research needed prior authorization by a regional military governor, experiences in the early 1980s with privately run commercial (market) surveys had indicated that the law was not necessarily enforced. So a decision was taken to venture into the realm of general surveying, with questionnaires containing political items. The first such survey was carried out by an independent academic centre in 1985, and was followed by many more; eventually six centres were performing this type of research. Questionnaire topics included political parties, the Armed Forces, Pinochet himself, and government policies.

The private centres also participated extensively in the opposition's "NO Campaign" leading up to the national plebiscite, held in October 1988, in which the majority of voters rejected Pinochet's continuation as president. The centres contributed to the overall design of the campaign, public opinion surveying, in-depth psychological studies of target groups of voters, print and broadcast media publicity, and much else (CIS 1989).

Public opinion polling touched off virtual survey warfare, as the results of research conducted by anti- and pro-government organizations were reported by the media. In the months prior to the plebiscite, hardly a week went by without front-page coverage in the newspapers of the latest survey results. Public attention gravitated strongly towards this reportage, and the surveys played a key role in setting the agenda of national political debate. They also received extensive international press coverage. In the process, those private research centres involved in the survey drama came forcefully into Chilean consciousness for the first time.

As Pinochet had lost the plebiscite, presidential and parliamentary elections were set for 14 December 1989. A centrist political leader of the Christian Democratic Party, Patricio Aylwin, became the presidential candidate of a centre-left coalition of parties, running against two right-wing candidates. Aylwin won the election, and took power in March 1990.[9]

The private centre researchers, having spent so much time designing policies in a vacuum, were able to carry out this work in quite a different atmosphere during the 1989 election year. Months before the elections, Aylwin's coalition established working groups of experts covering a broad range of state policy areas. They were charged with designing policy alternatives and recommendations, plus preparation of supporting documentation. Forty-seven such groups, with a total staff of fifteen hundred, worked in a low-profile manner from August to December. By the end of the year their material was ready for presentation to the president-elect and his future cabinet, the composition of which was announced in January 1990. The names of eighty-three key members of these working groups were released to the press (*La Epoca*, 26 December 1989); thirty-five of them (42 per cent) belonged to the opposition research centres.

And thus we see a transition by Chilean academic human rights advocates from impotence to marginal social influence towards having major impact on public policy, a transition comparable in some ways to that of Eastern Europe and the Soviet Union during 1989 (though there academics were not based in private centres).

By the beginning of 1990, a major question loomed over the Chilean centres: what future they might have in a new democratic regime. Their foreign funding had depended partially on solidarity abroad in that they constituted a key element in the opposition to the dictatorship. The new government's ability to fund them was at best unclear, given all the other demands it would have on its limited resources. In broad outline, the centres appeared to face the options of attempting to maintain their independent existence in a more adverse international funding climate, seeking incorporation within universities (or other institutions), or dissolving themselves.

CONCLUSIONS

We wish to propose a typology of the main forms of adaptation/ response on the part of Chilean social scientists vis-à-vis the military regime, from 1973 to 1989. It includes the academic activities of both the occupants of the formal university system and the "informal" world of the dissident research centres. These adaptations, running the gamut between support and opposition, were not mutually exclusive. Any academic could be involved in more than one of them, either because some of the adaptations did not contradict one another, or because one could be a surface adaptation and another a less visible one.

1 Actively *supportive* of the government. This involved joining forces, and included activities such as the design of state policies, inputs into government publicity offensives, and participation in university programs which directly served or helped legitimate the military regime.
2 *Accommodative* strategies, in which academics shifted to non-threatening lines of inquiry which were neither obviously supportive nor oppositional. This was the general tendency among social scientists

who retained or acquired positions in the universities after the coup, at least until the early 1980s.

3 *Critical-analytical* work, attempting to elucidate policy effects and the situations in which the subordinated sectors were enmeshed. Naturally, this work tended to shade into denunciation of what one was elucidating.

4 *Aid-oriented* activities, including many of the outreach sort carried out by the research centres. On the one hand, these could be seen as largely "defensive," i.e. as attending to problems created by the regime. On the other hand, they often had a reorganizational sub-surface, reassociating persons separated from each other by the regime. They therefore often embodied oppositional potential, or assisted those members of the opposition who had already regrouped.

5 Work involving the *development of alternatives*, trying, for example, to facilitate transition back to a democratic form of government. This work included formulation of alternative state economic and social policies, and shaded into the sixth form, below.

6 *Partisan-offensive* strategies, in which research priorities were specifically tailored to the needs of an opposition organization (party, coalition, movement, etc.).

Of these six types of adaptations, it is apparent that only the last four coincide with, or overlap, human rights advocacy.

We conclude with two observations about academic advocacy in its Chilean and its North American contexts:

Despite current political activity, social science in Chile from the second half of the 1960s and the early 1970s to the end of the 1980s underwent a striking transition from *political project advocacy* to *human rights advocacy*. This does not mean that party and ideological attachments no longer played a role in professional activities, but rather that, as the 1990s began, their influence was markedly less than before the military coup. In addition, it means that the greater salience of human rights was guiding research within sets of normative parameters much wider than those of any particular political project.

In North America, perhaps the greatest obstacle to an advocacy role among social scientists is the set of professional norms which academics have raised against themselves (see Spencer below), enjoining "objectivity" and – much more utopian – "value neutrality." In Chile, the obstacle was very different. Far from threatening self-image and professional pride, human rights advocacy put the self at risk, as advocates came face to face with the authoritarian state.

NOTES

1 The participation of Arancibia, Charlin, and Landstreet in this article forms part of a research project sponsored by York University's Centre for Research on Latin America and the Caribbean (CERLAC) and the LaMarsh Research Programme on Violence and Conflict Resolution.

Landstreet thanks the Centre for Latin American Research and Documentation (CEDLA), in Amsterdam, for the collegial support provided while he was Visiting Research Fellow there during part of 1989, and the Chilean branch of the Latin American Faculty of Social Sciences (FLACSO-Chile), in Santiago, where he was an Invited Researcher during parts of 1989 and early 1990.

We also thank the following members of FLACSO-Chile who provided help with specific research issues: Mauricio Culagovski, Angel Flisfisch, Manuel Antonio Garretón, Sergio Gómez, and Carlos Portales. None, however, is responsible for our interpretations. Appreciation goes as well to Edgardo Bousquet, who helped gather documentation, and FLACSO librarians María Inés Bravo and Nancy Moller.

The final revisions to this article were completed in early January, 1990, at FLACSO-Chile, in the weeks following the presidential and parliamentary elections of 14 December 1989, two months before new civilian president-elect Patricio Aylwin was scheduled to replace Pinochet.

2 For inventories of these centres – their staff, organization, teaching and research programs, and publications – at two points in time, see Díaz, Landstreet, and Lladser 1984; Lladser 1986. For descriptive and analytic treatment of them see Frühling 1985; Landstreet 1985; Spalding, Taylor, and Vilas 1985; Brunner and Barrios 1987; Lladser 1989. On the military government's impact on the social sciences as disciplines see Garretón 1983. On military intervention in the universities see Silver and Mery 1975; Elgueta et al. 1978; Puryear 1982; Levy 1986.

3 For a detailed analysis of the relations between democratic and socialist ideas in the context of Chilean politics and the ongoing process of reforms, see Rojas 1984.

4 A standard summary source on pre-coup Chilean politics is Valenzuela 1978. On the military dictatorship see Garretón 1989; Carvallo, Salazar, and Sepúlveda 1988; Valenzuela and Valenzuela 1986; O'Brien and Roddick 1983.

5 For the convenience of those who do not read Spanish, wherever possible we will document the main facts about repression by citing one of the most comprehensive and accessible English-language sources on this topic, C.G. Brown's *Chile since the Coup: Ten Years of Repression* (1983), published by the human rights organization Americas Watch. This book is based largely on Chilean sources, especially the Chilean Human Rights

Commission, of Santiago. The Commission's work, in turn, is based very importantly on information provided by the Vicariate of Solidarity, of the Archdiocese of Santiago, as supplemented by other national sources. See also Frühling 1983, 1985; Arancibia, Charlin and Landstreet 1984, 1987, 1989. In Spanish, see Elgueta et al. 1978; Ahumada et al. 1989; and the periodical reports of the Chilean Human Rights Commission and the Vicariate of Solidarity.

6 On urban poverty see Ortega and Tironi 1988; on life styles of the urban poor, Piña 1987; on poor neighbourhoods and their organizations, Chateau et al. 1987 and Campero 1987.

7 For a general work on Chilean women see CEM 1988; on low-income women, Valdés 1988, and Raczynski and Serrano 1985; on the rise of the Chilean feminist movement, Chuchryk 1984.

8 On COPACHI and the Vicariate of Solidarity, see Ahumada et al. 1989; COPACHI 1975; Smith 1982; Frühling 1983; and CERLAC 1984.

9 Space precludes discussing here the range of constraints – imposed by the junta's constitution of 1980 – under which the new civilian government is operating.

REFERENCES

AHC (Academia de Humanismo Cristiano). 1983. "Relegaciones de Estudiantes Universitarios." Santiago: Mimeo report, Proyecto Boletín de Realidad Universitaria.

Ahumada, Eugenio, et al. 1989. *Chile: La Memoria Prohibida*. 3 volumes. Santiago: Pehuén Ed.

Amnesty International. 1983. *Chile: Evidence of Torture*. London: Amnesty International Publications.

Anonymous. 1975. *Un Año y Medio de Gobierno Militar*. Santiago: Mimeo.

Arancibia, Jinny, Marcelo Charlin, and Peter Landstreet. 1984. "One Decade of State Repression in Chile: A Preliminary Analysis." In A.R.M. Ritter, ed, *Latin America and the Caribbean: Geopolitics, Development and Culture*. Ottawa: Canadian Association for Latin American and Caribbean Studies (CALACS).

– 1987. "Chile." In Jack Donnelly and Rhoda Howard, eds., *International Handbook of Human Rights*. New York: Greenwood Press.

– 1989. "Understanding Data on Human Rights Violations: Issues Arising from a Study of the Chilean Experience." In Peter Blanchard and Peter Landstreet, eds., *Human Rights in Latin America and the Caribbean*. Toronto: Canadian Scholars Press, CALACS, CERLAC, and Latin American Studies Committee of the University of Toronto.

Bengoa, José and Eduardo Valenzuela. 1984. *Economía Mapuche: Pobreza y Subsistencia en la Sociedad Mapuche Contemporánea*. Santiago: Ed. PAS.

Branch, Taylor, and Eugene Propper. 1982. *Labyrinth*. New York: Viking Press.

Brown, C.G. 1983. *Chile since the Coup: Ten Years of Repression*. New York: Americas Watch.

Brunner, José Joaquín, and Alicia Barrios. 1987. *Inquisición, Mercado y Filantropía: Ciencias Sociales y Autoritarismo en Argentina, Brazil, Chile y Uruguay*. Santiago: Facultad Latinoamericana de Ciencias Sociales (FLACSO).

Campero, Guillermo. 1987. *Entre la Sobrevivencia y la Acción Política: Las Organizaciones de Pobladores en Santiago*. Santiago: Instituto Latinoamericano de Estudios Transnacionales (ILET).

Carvallo, Ascanio, Manuel Salazar, and Oscar Sepúlveda. 1988. *La Historia Oculta del Régimen Militar*. Santiago: Ed. La Epoca.

CCHDH (Comisión Chilena de Derechos Humanos). 1984. *Informe Anual: 1983*. Santiago.

CEM (Centro de Estudios de la Mujer). 1988. *Mundo de Mujer: Continuidad y Cambio*. Santiago: CEM.

CERLAC (Centre for Research on Latin America and the Caribbean, York University). 1984. *Vicariate of Solidarity*. Toronto: CERLAC and six cosponsoring institutions. Translated from *La Vicaría de la Solidaridad*. Santiago: Archdiocese of Santiago.

Charlin, Marcelo. 1984. "State Repression and Civil Opposition: The Case of Chile." MA thesis, Graduate Programme in Sociology, York University, Toronto.

Chateau, Jorge, et al. 1987. *Espacio y Poder: Los Pobladores*. Santiago: FLACSO.

Chuchryk, Patricia. 1984. "Protest, Politics, and Personal Life: The Emergence of Feminism in a Military Dictatorship, Chile 1973–1983." PhD thesis, Graduate Programme in Sociology, York University, Toronto.

CIS (CED-ILET-SUR). 1989. *La Campaña del NO, Vista por sus Creadores*. Santiago: Ed. Melquíades.

COPACHI (Comité de Cooperación para la Paz en Chile). 1975. *Crónica de sus Dos Años de Labor Solidaria*. Santiago: Mimeo.

Cortázar, René. 1980. "Distribución del Ingreso, Empleo y Remuneraciones Reales en Chile, 1970–1978." *Estudios CIEPLAN* no.3. Santiago.

– 1988. "Incomes Policies Concertation: Some Relections on Chile." Notas Técnicas, no. 124. Santiago: Corporación de Investigaciones Económicas para Latinoamérica (CIEPLAN).

Délano, Manuel, and Hugo Traslaviña. 1989. *La Herencia de los Chicago Boys*. Santiago: Ed. Ornitorrinco.

Díaz, Harry, Peter Landstreet, and María Teresa Lladser. 1984. *Centros Privados de Investigación en Ciencias Sociales en Chile*. Santiago: Academia de Humanismo Cristiano, CERLAC, and CALACS.

Dinges, John and Saul Landau. 1980. *Assassination on Embassy Row*. New York: Pantheon Books.

Doyer, Jacques. 1985. "Inter-Ethnic Relationships in the South of Chile:

Mapuche Resistance to Domination from Pre-Spanish Times to the Military Regime." MA thesis, Graduate Programme in Sociology, York University, Toronto.

Elgueta, Bernarda, et al. (pseudonyms). 1978. *Cinco Años de Gobierno Militar en Chile: 1973–1978*. Santiago: Mimeo.

Foerster, Rolf, 1989. "Organismos no Gubernamentales y Pueblos Indígenas de Chile." In TCD.

Foxley, Alejandro. 1983. *Latin American Experiments in Neo-Conservative Economics*. Berkeley: University of California Press.

Frühling, Hugo. 1983. "Stages of Repression and Legal Strategy for the Defense of Human Rights in Chile: 1973–1980." *Human Rights Quarterly* 5, no. 4, 510–33.

– 1985. "Nonprofit Organizations as Opposition to Authoritarian Rule: The Case of Human Rights Organizations and Private Research Centers in Chile." ISPS Working Paper no. 2096. New Haven: Institution for Social and Policy Studies, Yale University.

Garretón, Manuel Antonio. 1980. "Universidad y Política en los Procesos de Transformación y Reversión en Chile: 1967–1977." *Estudios Sociales* 26, no. 4. Santiago: Corporación de Promoción Universitaria.

– 1983. *Las ciencias Sociales en Chile: Situación, Problemas, Perspectivas*. Santiago: Academia de Humanismo Cristiano.

– 1989. *The Chilean Political Process*. Boston: Unwin Hyman.

Jadresic, Esteban. 1989. "Salarios Reales en Chile: 1960–1988." Notas Técnicas no. 134. Santiago: CIEPLAN.

Landstreet, Peter. 1985. "Dissident Research Centres in Chile: A Response to the Repression of Social Scientists." *Transactions of the Royal Society of Canada*, series 4, vol. 22, 53–63.

Leiva, Arturo. 1985. "Transformaciones en la Situación Social de la Población Mapuche." Santiago: Comisión Económica para América Latina y el Caribe (CEPAL).

Levy, Daniel. 1986. "Chilean Universities under the Junta: Regime and Policy." *Latin American Research Review* 21, no. 3.

Lladser, María Teresa. 1986. *Centros Privados de Investigación en Ciencias Sociales en Chile*. 2nd edition. Santiago: Academia de Humanismo Cristiano and FLACSO.

– 1989. "La Investigación en Ciencias Sociales en Chile: Su Desarrollo en los Centros Privados, 1973–1988." In TCD.

Martner, Gonzalo. 1989. *El Hambre en Chile: Un Estudio de la Economía Agroalimentaria Nacional*. Santiago: GIA and United Nations Research Institute for Social Development.

O'Brien, Phil, and Jackie Roddick. 1983. *Chile: The Pinochet Decade*. London: Latin America Bureau.

Ortega, Eugenio, and Ernesto Tironi. 1988. *Pobreza en Chile*. Santiago: Centro de Estudios del Desarrollo (CED).

Piña, Carlos. 1987. *Crónicas de la Otra Ciudad*. Santiago: FLACSO.

Puryear, Jeffrey. 1982. "Higher Education, Development Assistance, and Repressive Regimes." *Studies in Comparative International Development* 17, no. 2, 3–35.

Raczynski, Dagmar, and Claudia Serrano. 1985. *Vivir la Pobreza: Testimonios de Mujeres*. Santiago: CIEPLAN.

Rojas, Alejandro. 1984. "The Problem of Democracy and Socialism in the Chilean Political Process from the 1880s to the 1980s." PhD thesis, Graduate Programme in Sociology, York University, Toronto.

Silver, L. and J.P. Mery (pseudonyms). 1975. *Las Universidades Chilenas y la Intervención Militar*. Santiago: Mimeo.

Smith, Brian. 1982. *The Church and Politics in Chile: Challenges to Modern Catholicism*. Princeton: Princeton University Press.

Spalding, Hobart, Lance Taylor, and Carlos Vilas. 1985. *SAREC's Latin American Programme: An Evaluation*. Stockholm: SAREC (Swedish Agency for Research Cooperation with Developing Countries).

TCD (Taller de Cooperación al Desarrollo). 1989. *Una Puerta que se Abre: Los Organismos no Gubernamentales en la Cooperación al Desarrollo*. Santiago: Servicio Editorial.

Valdés, Teresa. 1988. *Venid Benitas de mi Padre: Las Pobladoras, sus Rutinas y sus Sueños*. Santiago: FLACSO.

Valenzuela, Arturo. 1978. *The Breakdown of Democratic Regimes: Chile*. Baltimore: Johns Hopkins University Press.

Valenzuela, J. Samuel, and Arturo Valenzuela, eds. 1986. *Military Rule in Chile: Dictatorship and Oppositions*. Baltimore: Johns Hopkins University Press.

Vergara, Pilar. 1986. *Auge y Caída del Neoliberalismo en Chile*. Santiago: FLACSO.

VS (Vicaría de la Solidaridad). 1982. *Informe Anual: 1981*. Santiago: Archdiocese of Santiago.

HOWARD ADELMAN

The Policy Maker and the Advocate: Case Studies in Refugee Policy

INTRODUCTION

"Human rights" emerged from the "nationalities question" in the nineteenth century with the introduction of the anti-genocide, anti-racist, and civil and political rights conventions. The Universal Declaration of Human Rights was proclaimed by the United Nations on 19 December 1948. A number of conventions implemented this Declaration. They are the Convention for the Prevention and Punishment of the Crime of Genocide, the International Convention on the Elimination of all Forms of Racial Discrimination, the Covenant on Civil and Political Rights, and others prohibiting slavery and protecting indigenous and tribal populations. Human rights are defined *within* the authority of the state and as a limit on that power and authority. Traditionally conceived, human rights do not include the right to live in a state which protects human rights. The respective conventions only say that, given the state in which the individual lives, that state should protect human rights. Human rights really depict the responsibilities and limits of the powers of states. Ironically, they do not address the more fundamental issue of whether a human, qua human, has the right to live within the confines of a political entity which will *protect* his or her human rights.

There is also a difference between saying that the state, within which an individual lives, has the obligation to protect human rights of individuals, and saying that the state has the obligation to *protect* individuals who do not belong to a state which provides such protection.

Under Human Rights Conventions the right to have a state which protects you is more fundamental than whether the state within which you live, in fact, provides such protection. Yet surely, if it is a human right not to be abused by a state within which you live, it is even more fundamental to belong to a state which has such obligations and responsibilities.

If an individual no longer belongs to a state which protects his human rights, he or she has the right to claim the protection within the state where he currently resides, and that state has the obligation to consider that claim under the Geneva Convention for Refugees. However, the Refugee Convention itself does not spell out that process. The Refugee Convention is about protection and international obligations. It is not about human rights. It is about the *victims* of human rights abuses when they have fled the jurisdiction which abused them.

The Convention on Refugees, passed in 1951, and the subsequent 1967 Protocol define a refugee as a person with a well-founded fear of persecution because of race, ethnicity, religious affiliation, membership in a political group, etc. Countries signing the Convention and Protocol agree to provide protection for such refugees and ensure that they are not sent back to the country from which they fled. Since the Refugee Convention is not a Human Rights Convention, it does not deal with the rights of individuals in relationship to the states to which they belong and the obligations and the limits of state power and authority in dealing with those individuals. Instead, the Refugee Convention deals with the predicament of individuals who are no longer within the authority and power of those states. Yet, given the definition of a refugee, there is some coincidence with human rights. Certainly, the Inter-Church Committee for Refugees describes *Refugee Determination* (the process by which a country signing the Convention processes a refugee claim) as an issue of protection, human rights, and international legal obligations. Refugee determination, in so far as it guarantees due process for hearing a claim, *is* a human rights issue. In fact, the Supreme Court of Canada has ruled that the Immigration Department in Canada on one occasion abused the human rights of claimants by not allowing an oral hearing for such claimants. The quasi-judicial process structuring a claim for refugee status – the refugee determination process – must meet human rights criteria.

Nevertheless, when the earth is divided up among the jurisdictions of different state authorities and there is no place to go where one can be outside those authorities, the responsibility of states to individuals who no longer live within *any* jurisdiction that guarantees protection of their rights becomes a fundamental issue. Advocates for refugees argue that every human has human rights within the state in which he or she resides *and* has the right to reside in a state which will protect his or her human rights.

THE DILEMMA OF THE ADVOCATE

We in Europe and North America live in states which, by and large, respect human rights. But there are different political theories and ideologies for structuring the governance of those states consistent with the protection of human rights. In the liberal-reform vision of government,[1] politicians decide, bureaucrats implement, and "non-government advocates," driven by a vision of a better world, or stirred up sufficiently by the plight of a particular group, make representations to politicians to change policy. The politicians set the goals, the bureaucrats find the instruments to achieve them, and the reformers translate those heartfelt pleas by intelligent analysis into policy recommendations for a suffering or deprived group. The twentieth-century liberal-conservative vision[2] is somewhat different. Governments legislate in order for individuals in the non-governmental sector to achieve their goals; government is a vehicle to facilitate the advancement of the interests of its own citizens. Public policy facilitates private initiative and enterprise. The doers are in the private sector. The lobby of a legislative chamber is but the assembly room where the various competing private interests can confront their "political servants" so that the legislators can better adjudicate those interests. In a Marxist-Leninist form of government, the state holds or controls the monopoly not only on the production of goods and services but also on the production and distribution of ideas. Since the government by definition (though clearly not in reality) is the people, individuals or groups who ascribe to themselves the responsibility for challenging this state monopoly are considered to be practising a form of treason. Marxist-Leninist states do not permit advocacy or lobbying.

Advocacy for refugees presumes a twentieth-century "liberal vision" (reform or conservative) of government: with some reservations, government may foster universal rights and obligations. Liberal government also serves particular interest groups, sometimes at the expense of other interest groups. There is, thus, an inherent conflict between the universal obligations of a liberal state and its particular sensitivities to serve interest groups. Liberal government promotes human rights issues, but only where they are congruent with majority interests. Further, one minority at least, law and order professionals, see their particular interests as one with the obligations of states to keep order and very much more important than any human rights issue. The result is that refugee rights have no natural constituency, even in liberal governments, except where refugees belong to ethnic groups with a significant minority presence in the polity. In this sense, promoting refugee rights has a close kinship to ecological and nuclear issues and to the protection of the way of life of small numbers of indigenous peoples. As in these issues, the locus of advocacy tends to veer towards the extra-parliamentary.

One may argue that, in the long term, accepting refugees is in everyone's self-interest, for accepting refugees reduces the instability of the world in general and also provides a significant creative, and, eventually, economic input into the society. But the principle of sacrifice for a better good is part of a traditional ethos, not part of the nature of technocratic decision making. The dilemma of the advocate for an "enlightened" refugee policy is that these "traditional" arguments have little appeal for the majority of the citizens. If the arguments about long-term benefits are presented, they are too abstract and probabilistic, and are formulated in universal value terms. If the arguments are adapted to a utility format, then they lack authoritative weight and have little appeal to particular interests.

In addition, there are communication problems inherent and unique to refugee policy. First, there is *no necessary connection* between a small "l" liberal ideology and the acceptance of the premise that every human being has the right to reside in a state which provides protection. Secondly, though the polis may be structured as a small "l" liberal polity, the form may be liberal but the members of that polis may be overwhelmingly conservative. Citizens may assess governments on whether or not they protect citizens' personal self-interests. Further, many of those who disagree with government policy may be radicals.[3] Refugee policy in the context of a large conservative constituency, a small "l" liberal structure, and a significant minority of radicals in the opposition camp will produce many problems.

Add to this a dilemma about the role advocates play as experts on refugee issues. Experts are supposedly "objective" and dedicated to bringing reason and rationality into the political process. Yet, as the case studies will illustrate, refugee advocacy relies less on rational discourse than on media imagery. Expert analysis contained in briefs is replaced by the stories on public television. Further, the stories which have an impact are not those with an information content, but those which trigger predispositions already present in the audience. Advocates do not convince people, or even raise their consciousness, but trigger the right response. In the case of refugees, this means triggering sympathetic concern. This evocation of a sympathetic emotional response is necessary to counter the opposition, since the rejection of refugees is based upon defensive mechanical responses to perceived threats of "invading hordes." The tension between the emotional and cognitive modes of advocacy only emerged, as we will see, when the politicans, bureaucrats, and non-governmental organizations or groups (NGGS) were out of synchrony on the fundamental values behind the decision – that is, it emerged over normative rather than deliberate decisions.

DECISION THEORY

Different issues produce different contexts of interpretations, which suggests that there is no one mode of triggering sympathetic concern in each of the parties involved – politicians, civil servants, and NGGS. We use NGG instead of the traditional NGO designation, since NGG includes non-government organizations but also refers to less organized and institutionalized groups in the private sector. One issue and one set of circumstances will yield one mode of communication as more appropriate. Depending on the *type of decision* entailed in the policy process, the three elements in the process – the NGGS (non-governmental organizations/groups), the bureaucrats, and the politicians – shift roles. In each case, successful policy making requires coherence among all three elements. Essential to that coherence is the employment of the appropriate communicative mode by each party to suit that particular form of decision. Three different types of decision are apparent in refugee issues. I have labelled them implementation (opportune or crisis) decisions, deliberative decisions, and normative decisions. Implementation decisions are decisions *to do*. We know what to do. We know, implicitly or explicitly, why we are doing it. We simply must decide *to do* it, to implement what we have decided is the right thing to be done, limited and propelled by the circumstances with which we are faced. The decision is practical in the literal sense, to put into practice what we already know is best. That implementation requires a particular form of communicative competence and coherence of both aspects of the public sector (politicians and civil servants) with the NGGS.

In contrast to implementation decisions, deliberative decisions determine what is the best thing to do. The problem is not simply deciding to implement what is best, but deciding what is the best. In deliberative as in implementation decisions, there is no disagreement about values and motives. The disagreement is about the conclusions to be derived given the values and motives and the knowledge available.

Decision Making and Advocacy Initiatives on Indochinese Refugees
Admitted to Canada, 1978–80.

The Content of the Decision (numbers and assignment of responsibility)			Advocacy Initiatives and Direction		
Govt. sponsored	Non-Govt.	Total	Politicians	Civil Servants	Non-Govt. (NGGs) + Public
PHASE ONE 5,000		= 5,000	Decides ←	Advocates Totals ← ⌐	Inactive Public Assent
PHASE TWO 8,000	+ 4,000	= 12,000	Decides	Advocates Involvement ⌐	Active Assent/ Inactive → Dissent
PHASE THREE 8,000 + 21,000	+ 21,000	= 50,000	Decides ←	Advocates Limits ← ⌐	Active Assent/ Active Dissent
PHASE FOUR 20,000	+ 30,000	= 50,000	Decides ←	Advocates Reconciliation ⌐ ⌐	NGGS Protest →
PHASE FIVE 30,000	+ 30,000	= 60,000	Decides ←	Direct Action ⌐ ▲	NGGS Advocate

The third type of decision is a normative one involving a fundamental expression, determination, or shift in values. The way in
which we envision the world – our metastructure of values – is what
is at stake, not simply deciding what is the best thing to do, or
deciding to do what you already know is the best. What is involved
in this third case is a fundamental change of heart which will result
in a structural change in the way in which politicians, civil servants,
and the private sector interact. It is in this latter area where the real
test of communicative competence and coherence emerges.

The following case studies will concentrate on the first and third
of these types of decision making. The first case study deals with

five stages of decision making on the number of Indochinese refugees to be brought into Canada and the sector to which responsibility for them was to be assigned. Those five stages and the analysis of the roles of the various parties in what was essentially an implementation decision are summarized in the chart which precedes the analysis.

CASE STUDIES

Case 1: The Number of Indochinese Refugees to Be Admitted into Canada[4]

In the spring of 1979, the Canadian government planned to take 5,000 Indochinese refugees into Canada (phase 1, in table). In June, that policy was amended to increase the number of government-sponsored refugees from 5,000 to 8,000 and to target an additional 4,000 refugees for private sponsorship (phase 2). In July, the numbers were altered again. Over and above the 8,000 to which it was already pledged, the government decided to sponsor one additional refugee for every refugee sponsored by the private sector, with an overall goal of bringing 50,000 Indochinese refugees into Canada during 1979 and 1980. (phase 3). That meant the government was planning to sponsor 21,000 refugees in addition to the 8,000 to which they were already committed, provided the private sector (NGGs) sponsored 21,000 refugees.

By the end of September 1979, the NGG target was already exceeded. The NGGs had arranged sponsorships for about 30,000 and not just 21,000 refugees. If the government matched its commitment, then it would sponsor 38,000 Indochinese refugees (30,000 to match the private sector in addition to the 8,000 to which they were already committed); the total refugee intake would have been 68,000, 18,000 above and beyond the 50,000 original target.

Even if the government interpreted its commitment as simply matching the original target of the NGGs, it had agreed to sponsor 29,000 Indochinese refugees (21,000 to match the original target of 21,000 for the NGGs, and the 8,000 to which they were already committed); the total refugee intake would have been 59,000, 9,000 above and beyond the original target. This is particularly important since the government in its pledges to the NGGs reiterated over and over that the NGG initiative would not detract from the government's commitment. The Tory government revoked its commitment and decided to limit the overall commitment to 50,000 by cutting the government commitment from 29,000 to 20,000 and permitting the balance to be taken in by the NGG sector (phase 4). This was followed, in the spring of 1980, by the new Liberal government increasing the government commitment by 10,000, restoring in effect the matching commitment, and setting the overall target at 60,000 rather than 50,000 to be taken in during 1979 and 1980 (phase 5).

The widespread impression is that the policy changes, both for the increases and limitations on refugee numbers, were each in turn a result of public pressure on the politicians, i.e., a product of NGG advocacy. The media conveyed a view of governmental decisions as belated responses to the increasing momentum of public pressure, advocacy by the media and by groups committed to refugee intake. This impression is partly wrong, for the process of decision making was far more complex. When the government was committed to the intake of 5,000 Indochinese refugees (phase 1), the decision was primarily that of civil servants engaged in the professional application of planning norms in the allotment of Canada's international commitments and the distribution of that commitment among various refugee-producing areas. It was, of course, endorsed by the politicians and concurred in by the lack of public protest.

The first decision in which a definite policy initiative was involved was the increase in numbers in phase 2, a decision announced in June of 1979. Given the front-page articles and the editorials on the plight of the Boat People that flooded the newspapers in May and June of that year, it is not surprising that the public viewed this as government response to public pressure. In fact, the new Tory government had been alerted by its civil service to increasing pressure from the international arena requiring a larger Canadian role. The civil servants obtained the consent of the new government to approach the churches to sign "umbrella" agreements whereby churches would take initiatives to organize private sponsorships of refugees by their members.

By March of 1979, only the Mennonites and the Christian Reformed Church had agreed to participate in the program. While other churches, such as the Roman Catholic and United churches, took the matter under consideration, the Anglicans were openly hostile to the scheme. Their articulated conviction was that the whole enterprise was a plot by the Tory government to dump its responsibilities for assisting refugees onto the private sector. The public at large were unaware of behind-the-scenes attempts by the government to mobilize the NGG sector on humanitarian issues. There were many attempts to put pressure on the government to assume greater responsibility, including my own attempt in the latter part of June to organize a petition to the minister, who was my federal MP, to urge the government to take in more refugees. The minister, hearing of the petition, sent two top civil servants to a Sunday morning meeting to suggest, with great diplomacy, that it might be more effective if the group actually sponsored refugees rather than writing petitions. The group agreed. The consequence was the birth of Operation Lifeline, the largest organization in Canada involved in stimulating NGG sponsorship of Indochinese refugees.[5]

The effect of large-scale NGG involvement was beyond the Tory government's expectations. For example, in the first two weeks of the campaign to encourage NGG sponsorships (in early July), the initial chapter of Operation Lifeline had already exceeded its full summer's target; there were already over fifty chapters of Operation Lifeline that had been organized in addition to other similar types of organizations, such as Project 4000, organized by Mayor Dewar's office in Ottawa.

In phase 3, the funding formula shifted from a straightforward ratio of 2:1 Govt:NGG to a matching formula of 1:1 Govt:NGG beyond the 8,000 refugees to which the government had already committed itself. The overall target figure of 50,000 refugees was presumably determined by the interaction of technical studies of the feasibility of handling the increase without falling short of the stated target.[6] It was not the result of media and private pressure on a reluctant government.

The fourth phase in the series of decisions on numbers occurred when the government reneged on the matching formula. NGG sponsorship had soared by the fall of 1979 to almost 30,000. And the government found itself over-extended. The minister for external affairs, Flora Macdonald, had pledged $15 million in aid for Kampuchean overseas relief, instead of the $5 million authorized by Cabinet. The other $10 million had to be found. Further, the government did not have the funds in its budget. At the same time, the civil servants did not believe there was a capacity in place to take in 70,000 refugees by the end of 1980, which was by now the minimum level of government obligations. Finally, there was a fear of a public backlash by those Canadians who opposed large intakes of visible minorities.

Though a civil service proposal to the politicians attempted to resolve this problem by extending the time period into 1981, the minister ignored that proposal and decided to renege on the matching formula. The government decided it would only sponsor the difference between NGG sponsorships and the total target of 50,000 refugees – a clear breach of the commitment that private sponsorship would not detract from the government action but only enhance it. The breach of faith incurred the wrath of many NGG refugee sponsors who felt betrayed. Shortly after, the government was defeated on very different, and, to the Canadian people, more important issues. The number of refugees to be sponsored was not an issue in the following election. In addition, the NGG analysis indicated that an election debate would be counterproductive, for there was a large potential for generating a backlash opposed to immigration.

When the Liberals replaced the Tories as the government (phase 5), contacts between individuals in the NGG sector and politicians led to an increase in the overall target from 50,000 to 60,000 by renewing government obligations to the 29,000 refugee figure originally envisioned.

Analysis of Case 1

Civil Servants and Politicians. Advocacy involved a mix of initiatives and the nature of that advocacy shifted both in content and direction. In the first phase, the civil servants recommended the totals which the politicians decided to adopt. In the second phase civil servant advocacy was primarily aimed at the NGG sector. In the third phase, the civil servants were most concerned with determining the practical limitations – travel space available, manpower overseas, etc. – and advising politicians of these limits. In the fourth phase, the civil servants were involved in advocating a mode of reconciling government policies and practical limitations with commitments to the private sector, a role ignored by the politicians, which resulted in a breakdown of the team effort. In the fifth phase, civil servants worked with NGG representatives to find a technical and practical means of reconciling the ruptured alliance in order to restore the original commitment.

Public and Non-Government Groups. The role of the public also shifted between assent, commitment, and protest. At first assent was tied to inaction. In the second phase, a portion of the public and NGGs became actively involved, but the major support institutions continued to be passive, indicating dissent by inaction although their involvement was invited. By the third phase, new NGGs came into being and the major NGGs had become involved, but the anti-refugee sector was then aroused to protest – somewhat ineffectively: for the NGGs committed to refugees, the battle became to ensure that the anti-refugee voice – a majority voice – remained ineffective. In the fourth phase, when the politicians reneged on the previous commitment, the refugee-committed NGGs became the protestors. Their protests did not become a media issue, given the potential for a much larger backlash from the relatively ineffective and inactive segment of the non-governmental sector opposed to refugees. But the government breach of faith thrust the committed NGGs into the role of refugee advocates, a role unnecessary until the breach of faith occurred. In the fifth phase, the pro-refugee NGGs worked quietly with the government to devise a formula which would restore the principle of the original commitment.

Operation Lifeline. Though Operation Lifeline was conceived by the group that met in the minister's constituency and agreed to sponsor refugees, none of the parties involved knew that it would rapidly become the largest organization in Canada sponsoring refugees. The goal was simply to provide a witness for a private effort in the constituency. There was no real debate in the initial meeting about whether to sponsor refugees. It was the media which gave birth to "Operation Lifeline." An opportunity suddenly emerged to take action in an area that the media had indicated was crying for action.[7] The media provided the symbols and the name Operation Lifeline – to symbolize salvation. The name matched the previous symbols about refugees as victims, risking their lives to escape from Vietnam, then again risking their lives in leaky rafts and crowded unseaworthy boats.

Experts, initially from the government, but shortly thereafter from the NGGs themselves, provided detailed information in the form of a 60-page booklet on how to go about sponsorship. An uncertain and insecure public wanted to act, but needed technical tools to initiate the action. Communication expertise was necessary in structuring the organization, expressing goals through radio and TU interviews, and mobilizing people at public rallies, of which there were two or three per night in the various constituencies in greater Metro Toronto.

The churches, which were initially hesitant, quickly joined the bandwagon and signed umbrella agreements to organize refugee sponsorships and provide some financial security for the refugees. In this phase, the coherence of NGG initiative, communicative expertise, media, government officials, and politicians meant the refugee program could take off with little resistance.

But the fact was that most Canadians were opposed to the intake of Indochinese refugees.

The highest support reached for intake occurred in phase 1, when front-page stories appeared day after day about the plight of the Boat People, and "wrenching the hearts" of the viewing public. At a time when the government was only committed to take in 5,000 refugees, the support level for intake was at 49 per cent of the public polled. When the target was raised in phase 2, public support slipped to the low 40s in percentage terms. When the government made its bold commitment of 50,000, the support slipped to the low 30s in percentage terms. Over 50 per cent of those polled were overtly opposed to the new policy.

The Backlash: Anti-Refugee Advocacy. It was at that point, phase 3, that dissent became public in full-page advertisements paid by the National Citizens' Coalition (NCC). The NCC published its own "poll" on the issues. Though its questions were misleading, the results were not dramatically different from those which emerged from more neutral and detached confidential surveys commissioned by the government.

The NCC damaged its own credibility by the racist overtones and the exaggerations of its advertisements and by false predictions of how many relatives would follow the initial group. Nevertheless, the dissenting opposition now had a voice which gave expression to the fears and prejudices of Canadians, and these outnumbered those impelled to act by their humanitarian concerns. NGG leadership in Canada – whether political, religious, business, labour, academic, or professional – was by now overwhelmingly for the refugee sponsorship program. The National Citizens' Coalition gave voice to a plurality of Canadians who held no such roles.[8]

Though the credibility of the NCC was damaged by its misleading advertisement, the fear that the NCC fed remained. And though the NCC was wrong about the reasons for the fear, it was not wrong about the belief that a large number of people were opposed to the new refugee policy. Only mobilization of business support to oppose, undermine, and effectively halt the NCC campaign prevented a full-fledged backlash.

Case 2: The Status Determination Process for Refugee Claimants

The issue in this case was not how to get on with a program to which everyone was committed, but how to determine the value framework for dealing with refugee claimants. A fundamental vision of Canada was at stake, involving, on the one hand, absolute sovereign control in the selection of new citizens, and, on the other hand, Canadian obligations to a Convention on refugees in the international arena.

Under the Refugee Convention, to which Canada is a signatory, the Canadian government surrendered a small aspect of its sovereignty to undertake an obligation to allow individuals having a legitimate fear of persecution in their country of origin to make claims for entry into Canada. Once they had escaped that country of origin, such a claim could be made on the grounds that, if returned to their home country, claimants had a legitimate fear of persecution because of race, religion, membership in a particular group, etc. The long-held Canadian view of Canada as an immigrant-receiving country put the total responsibility for deciding which individuals would be selected to join the Canadian family into government hands. We determined those who were allowed into Canada. Today individuals from all over the world fly to Canada and claim refugee status. The gates of entry are no longer under the absolute control of government. Further, those refugees have rights once they have arrived. In the light of the Supreme Court decision mentioned above, refugee claimants are entitled to the rights of citizens under the Charter of Rights, specifically the right to an oral hearing in front of an official who adjudicates the refugee claim.

In this case, the relative positions of NGGs, civil servants, and politicians are very different. Church leaders, solicitors, and others concerned with the rights of potential Convention Refugees push to expand the protections accorded to refugee claimants lest any possible legitimate refugee be returned and face persecution or death. Civil servants, on the other hand, see the potential for Third World "economic" refugees to use the rights of refugees as a window of opportunity to migrate to Canada, thereby doing an end-run around the queue of immigrant applicants seeking entry through legitimate means. Further, they also see a loss of control. As more refugees are produced and can find the means to arrive in Canada, they believe Canada will lose control of the numbers we take into this country. Civil servants see "the dike being breached," and feel an obligation under Canadian law to restrict entry. In the Canadian civil service structure of values, the civil servants do not regard Canada as a country of first asylum for refugee claimants, except in the most marginal of ways. Canada is a refuge for those who flee refugee-like situations; refugee claims are not and should not be a significant part of immigration intake. We must *control* the intake of immigrants and limit any compromise to Canadian sovereignty to a relatively very small number of cases under the Refugee Convention.

There is a conflict between those charged with responsibility and imbued with the values of sovereign control with respect to refugee claimants and those in the NGG sector who place primary emphasis on international obligations. The latter argue for the protection of human rights of all individuals, not just Canadians, and advocate the fairest possible procedures for refugee claimants.

In such cases politicians do not simply have the role of facilitating the expression of a consensus, or implementing what has already been decided by interaction of civil servants and NGGs, but of adjudicating value conflicts. Do we give the benefit of the doubt to potential refugees and accord claimants rights and privileges in order to ensure that every potentially legitimate claim is given a proper hearing? Or do we view refugee claimants as illegitimate queue jumpers and devise a system which will try to winnow out legitimate claims from the ill-founded ones? Such a winnowing process would reject those legitimately in need and fearful of their lives along with those who seek to better their economic opportunities. Or even more strictly, do we only allow those refugee claimants to make a claim in Canada who could not have made a claim elsewhere, so that Canada remains a country which *chooses* refugees and not a country chosen by refugees in which to claim refugee status?

The government may side with the civil service and risk the wrath of a concerned citizenry. Or it may identify with concerned citizens and have to override reluctant civil servants wedded to an older view of the world order. Royal Commissions and Parliamentary Committee studies will not resolve the issue. Part of the problem is that such studies are often used either to stall the debate or to misconceive decisions as deliberative when they are about fundamental norms and values.

There were two phases to refugee advocacy conducted on this issue. Advocates found that the government was being lobbied by three different groups. The first represented a number of individuals in the government caucus (Brian Mulroney's Tory government succeeded the Liberals in 1985). They were small "c" conservatives who believed that a government represented the self-interest of its own citizens both as a collective whole and in the subgroups that constituted that citizenry. Their viewpoint was put forth in the part of the Nielsen Task Force report which dealt with the topic of "Immigration and Citizenship." The report advocated that the government cease direct sponsorship of refugees and that future refugee determination for Convention refugees take place abroad. In effect, the spontaneous arrival of Convention refugees would be eliminated, whereas responsibility for sponsorship of humanitarian refugees would be entirely shifted to the NGGs.

The second group dovetailed with the Nielsen Task Force. They advocated much greater control and denial of opportunities for access for spontaneous arrivals. This second group largely consisted of civil servants, motivated not so much by a small "c" conservative ideology as by a concern with monitoring control over admissions within a bureaucratic framework; their ideology is of sovereign control over who could become members of the Canadian polis.

The third group consisted of virtually all of the non-governmental groups (NGGS) concerned with refugees. These included most of the mainstream churches, the Canadian Jewish Congress, the Inter-Church Committee, Amnesty International, a committee of lawyers of the Canadian Bar consisting of refugee and immigration lawyers, most of the ethnic groups, and many, if not all, of the support groups who worked with refugees in the resettlement area. They advocated a refugee determination process which would be both efficacious in discouraging abusers and fair to genuine refugee claimants.[9]

At first advocacy consisted of briefs to the ministers, meetings with the minister, and discussions with reporters and columnists specializing in refugee issues. One case involved taking the government to court to ensure the right of a refugee to an oral hearing; the court upheld the position of the NGGS.

With the introduction of new regulations on refugees in February of 1987 and the tabling of Bill C-55 in that year, advocacy shifted to the public arena. It became clear that the small "c" conservatives, in tandem with the civil servants, had come up with legislation that ran against the recommendations of every prior study. It provided prescreening for any refugee claimant from a refugee-producing country who had arrived via a "safe" third country where the refugee claimant could have made a claim. Since the USA, which rejected over 97 per cent of Salvadorean and Guatemalan claims to refugee status,[10] would not likely be classified as an unsafe country, the NGG community argued that the new legislation would effectively reject genuine Convention Refugees.

Aside from the usual petitions and briefs, media advocacy demonstrated that opposition to this bill concerned a large, well-informed middle class. One of the events that set a tone for this form of advocacy was the Third Seder held on behalf of refugees in one of the largest synagogues in Toronto. A reenactment during Passover Week of the Seder ritual was rewritten as a theatrical event focusing on the refugee issue. The audience included representatives from most religious and refugee groups, as well as a broader TV audience through videotape news clips. While a brief providing reasoned arguments was distributed in kits to everyone attending, the main intention of the theatrical event was to identify government policies with the historical persecution of Jews. The image proposed was that of the "Egyptians": those enacting policies of the government were restricting the right of the refugees to seek freedom in a land and country that would protect them.

A broad coalition of Canadian groups, which now included trade
union and other organizations not normally identified with the refugee cause, began a national week of protest against the new legislation. The opening of the week began symbolically with some
"water theatre" and a group of refugees in a sailboat in Toronto
harbour to mark an anniversary of the refusal of the Canadian
government to admit a boatload of Jews escaping Nazi persecution.[11]
"Theatre" conveys the message in non-technical language of freedom
versus oppression, acceptance versus rejection, and the risk of torture and death.

The refugee debate was now cast in simple symbolism. The government had been successful in selling the bill as an anti-abuser and
not an anti-refugee bill. The community concerned with refugees
had unequivocally to communicate that the bill was an anti-refugee
bill and that there was a great deal of public opposition to it. Following the National Week of Protest, the government did not push
second reading of the bill, which was held over until the fall session.
It is uncertain whether the delay was a result of the advocacy or
because of other pressing government business or both. But the
refugee support community claimed the delay as a small but significant victory against "regressive legislation."

After Parliament adjourned, a new event occurred which provided
strong symbolic support to those who wanted a bill giving absolute
control to Canadian officials over refugee entry. One hundred and
seventy-four Sikhs arrived by boat on the shores of Nova Scotia and
claimed refugee status. The symbolic advocacy of "water theatre" in
Toronto was effectively undercut by a real event which reinforced
the position of the other side. The result was an urgent recall of
Parliament and the introduction of an even more Draconian piece
of legislation – Bill c-84. Bills c-55 and c-84 were both passed in
that emergency session.

Symbolic victories for advocates, unfortunately, are of only short
duration and are only as good as the last media image.

CONCLUSIONS

Sometimes the politicians have the responsibility of facilitating actions by formulating a position which will harness the energies of
government and NGGs into a common enterprise. In such instances,
it may appear as if the public has pushed and shoved the government
in a specific direction when, in reality, it is frequently the government
which has lobbied, urged, and provided direction for the public.
However, in cases of fundamental divisions over the metaframework

of values of our society, the situation is quite different. If government officials manipulate public opinion and ignore, obfuscate, or stall on the value concerns of committed citizens, the results are alienation and weakening of the communicative network through which non-governmental and governmental sectors are required to communicate and cooperate. In turn, if those individuals in the NGG sector malign the intentions of the civil service, misrepresent the issues, or exaggerate the crises and value differences, they may possibly win their case but they injure the whole system of adjudicating conflicts.

Similarly, the media cannot simply be instruments of hype or disinterested (perhaps bored) bystanders and purveyors of conclusions. They must serve as the focus for debate between traditional and reform groups competing for endorsement of particular political policies in the public arena. Even when incompatibility exists in the decision-making structure, the overall process must retain a coherence and, at least, an implicit set of rules for adjudicating decisions so that a congruence of all three sectors (the politicians, the civil servants, and the private sector) can be maintained.

The dilemmas of advocates as "experts" and advocates as symbolizers of oppression through the use of media can best be examined in the different contexts of these incidents and through different functions which advocates perform. If McQuail's list of campaign requirements is taken as a guide (McQuail 1983, 79–84), the functions of *informing* and *interpreting* seem, at least on the surface, to be consistent with the role of advocate as expert. The expert provides the information and interpretation to allow the decision maker to make a more rational decision. The aims and activities of the various interest groups within the government and outside of it *opposed* to the position being advocated all form part of the information base. The expert provides information about the effects of placing a priority on certain actions rather than others, and about the consequences that can be expected concerning different priorities.

The same is true of the interpretive role. Traditionally, interpretation meant rational explanation – that is, showing how the information provided fell into a rational pattern of either customary decision making or general lawlike behaviour. Nevertheless, as interpreters, experts involved in this type of advocacy find themselves providing feedback or interpreting responses to shifting alliances. The expertise used will advance the cause of one side and weaken the position of the other.

The objectivity of experts is clearly not that of non-interfering observers but is an objectivity which recognizes the necessity for feeling and commitment. As interpreters, advocates are continually confronted with choices – whether to remove themselves at certain points to return to a neutral position, or to surrender their commitment in favour of pushing the issue. Expert-advocates try to walk the fine line, but at certain points the choice must be made.

If the dilemmas are chronic with respect to the role of the expert in providing information and interpretation, the dilemmas become acute when the voice of the advocate is wedded to *expression* and *mobilization*. For here the "expert" is not simply helping decision makers decide what is the best thing to do, but activating people to do it. In these functions, the expert becomes a media spokesperson, giving a voice to the beliefs, values, ideologies, and principles of the advocacy group and providing a coherent philosophy for that group. To this media function must be added skills in activating interest, mobilizing support, and guiding the activities of the group in its attempts to persuade others and to raise funds for its activities.

Can these activities be called "objective" in a liberal-reform society? Yes. Because the various activities of the group and its mode of fundraising have a profound effect on how the advocacy group *appears*, *what* message is communicated, and how it is communicated. Abstract truth will only realize its meaning in the relatively mundane activities of the advocacy group. Nevertheless, the expert involved in advocacy is faced with a tension between the universal values and abstract knowledge on the one hand and the social specificity and varied contexts in which the symbolic appeals take place on the other. It is the expert's responsibility to be the conscience of the advocacy group to ensure that emotion and mobilization do not betray ideals.

NOTES

1 In the nineteenth-century liberal vision of government, the role of government is, in one sense, more restrictive and, in another, more expanded than in the conservative vision. The function of government is twofold. On the one hand, the legislative and adjudicative powers are defined, not by the property or broad interests of the individual, which are rather extensive even when restricted to property interests, but only by those interests which are considered rights. As John Stuart Mill has pointed out, those laws must also ensure that the burden of defending the society and its members from injury are shared fairly. The introduction of the principle of equity and burden sharing with respect to obligations and the redefinition of interests in terms of rights in fact led to the twentieth-century welfare state as the definition of rights expanded and the principle of burden sharing applied to wider and wider

conceptions of defending the members from injury. In its widest conception, Jacques Maritain defines the state as "an agency entitled to use power and coercion, and made up of experts or specialists in public order and welfare, an instrument in the service of man" (Maritain 1956, 13).

2 In a traditional conservative view, according to John Locke, the function of government is: 1 to establish the rules of the game or public laws by which people can act to preserve and increase their persons and property; 2 to provide an independent judiciary to interpret and adjudicate those laws; 3 to establish a monopoly on power to enforce those laws; and 4 to preserve and protect the collectivity from invasion from abroad and from any injury to the persons or property of citizens. A *progressive* conservative vision broadens the enterprise of the private sector to include all initiatives for change rather than merely property acquisition, and redefines the role of government to provide the necessary stability to deal with change. In the words of de Jouvenel (1957, 300), "this task of adjustment and stabilization is the essential duty of the sovereign."

3 The radical view presumes that there is a human good, a good which the individual shares with humanity in general, and that there are universal laws of humanity to express the spirit of this goodness. Schleiermacher in *The Monologen* makes a great deal of this notion of the individual spirit as a direct expression of a universal human spirit. The presupposition that all individuality is an expression of a universal human spirit requires language to be a creative expression, to have its own unity of form and expression independent of traditional speech patterns, creating new uses, rules, and literary forms rather than expressing itself in a form of persuasion or as an address where the meaning and form are derived from the rules of speech from language as it has already been used. Gadamer (1975, 152–93) also has a useful analysis of romantic hermeneutics.

4 Cf. Adelman 1980 for a more detailed description of this series of policy shifts.

5 The media was to dub this organization the leading *advocate* of the increased intake of refugees, ignoring totally the repeated messages to the media that, in fact, the whole *idea* was a government and not a NGG initiative, even if the NGG sector was crucial to the concrete implementation.

6 The original proposal put to Ron Atkey was the following. At that time, if half of the ridings in Canada sponsored half the number of refugees to which the NGG sector had already committed itself (sixty-six sponsorship groups), and if the average number of refugees sponsored by each group was five ((66x5x.5) x 130), then the NGG sector would sponsor at least 21,000 refugees and most likely many more. If the government made its new initiative a matching formula whereby it would increase

its sponsorship of two refugees for every refugee in the NGG sector, then more than 21,000 privately sponsored refugees could be virtually guaranteed. The minimum number of government-sponsored refugees would then be 50,000 (42,000 + 8,000).

7 A *Globe and Mail* stringer happened, by accident, to be at the initial meeting. The stringer thought it would be an interesting story for the *Globe*. Dick Beddoes, a *Globe* columnist at the time, picked up the story, named the group "Operation Lifeline," and published a phone number of the group's contact person. The group responded to the inundation of phone calls by taking the initiative to *become* experts on Indochinese refugees and the methods of sponsorship, and began to publish and make available materials to other chapters of the "organization" based on its new-found expertise.

8 A few individual spokespeople did emerge, such as a former moderator of the United Church who had spent many years of missionary services in China, and who felt Asians should more properly stay in Asia.

9 A small group within the larger NGG community, the Society of Friends, had little concern with differentiating between Convention refugees and those who arrived in Canada as a result of economic rather than political conditions.

10 In the Canadian system, 40 per cent of those claims were found to be valid.

11 The key to attracting the attention of over thirty media representatives was the leak given to Canada's largest newspaper of the presence of one of the few survivors of the *St Louis*, who came up from the U.S. specifically for the occasion. The *St Louis* was a ship carrying 930 Jewish refugees from Nazi Germany who were refused entry to Canada in 1939.

REFERENCES

Adelman, Howard. 1980. *The Indochinese Refugee Movement: The Canadian Experience*. Regina: L. Weigl Educational Publishers.

Gadamer, Hans-Georg. 1975. *Truth and Method*. New York: Seabury Press.

Jouvenel, Bertrand de. 1957. *Sovereignty: An Inquiry into the Public Good*. Cambridge University Press.

Maritain, Jacques. 1956. *Man and the State*. Chicago: Chicago University Press.

McQuail, Denis. 1983. *Mass Communication Theory: An Introduction*. Beverly Hills: Sage Publications.

Mill, John Stuart. 1947. *On Liberty*. New York: Crofts and Co.

Schleiermacher, Friedrich Ernst. 1869. *Monologen, eine Neujahrsgabe*. Leipzig: Bockhaus.

TIM REES AND CAROL TATOR

Advocacy and Race Relations

The underlying premise to advocacy activities in the field of race relations is that racism in any form is not to be tolerated. The fundamental rights and freedoms that Canada holds to as a liberal democracy include the commitment to full and equal participation of all citizens in the cultural, social, economic, and political life of the country. The ideal that the circle of Canadian life should embrace all Canadians equally includes the principles of equality of access, equality of opportunity, and the equality of all cultures.

These principles have been encoded in multicultural policies of both federal and provincial governments as well as in many other laws and statutes. At the same time, societal abhorrence of racial discrimination is reflected in various legislative forms including human rights acts, labour codes, and the Canadian Charter of Rights and Freedoms.

Effective advocacy entails having an impact on the nature and extent of discriminatory practices. Advocacy activities can be directed, first, at improving the legislative framework or removing the more discretionary intrusions on the part of various sectors and institutions in society which effectively discriminate against racial minorities. Secondly, advocacy activities may contribute to a non-racist environment and culture by seeking general consensus of the justness of this ideal. Or thirdly, and more particularly, advocacy may be focused on defending and protecting the rights of individuals against racial discrimination.

This article, drawing from the particular experience and activities of one community organization, the Urban Alliance on Race Relations in Toronto, is an attempt to assess those strategies that can be pursued to eradicate racial discrimination in Canada.

As our understanding of the nature of the problem of racial discrimination has evolved over the last decade, so too has our perception of appropriate solutions. Experience has shown that there is no single approach or strategy universally applicable when confronting racism. Racism wears many masks and its diverse forms are institutionalized within the major systems and structures of society, including education, media, employment, and government itself. Sharing the facts of racial discrimination is a process of broadening the base of support. It is not enough for victims of discrimination to pursue the struggle for justice and equality. The problems of minorities are in reality the problems of the majority. Even more clearly the solutions rest within the hands of the majority. Consequently the vehicles for information dissemination that the Urban Alliance has developed, including its own quarterly journal *Currents*, are not only intended for community volunteers but also support the growing level of professional competence and skills required to create the kinds of institutions responsive to the needs of the multiracial society. The broad promotional activity of sharing knowledge and skills therefore has a number of different objectives and is targeted to a range of audiences.

THE URBAN ALLIANCE ON RACE RELATIONS

The Urban Alliance on Race Relations of Metropolitan Toronto came into being in 1975. It was the result of an increasing concern on the part of a group of people from a wide diversity of racial and cultural backgrounds about an increasing number of racial incidents, and of a perception of growing racial tension in the city. The founders of the organization had no clear picture of how serious or pervasive racism actually was. What they did recognize was that visible minorities were deeply concerned about racial assaults on the streets, in subways, and in parks; and increasingly disturbed by the defacing of South Asian places of worship, fire-bombing of businesses, and vandalism of homes.

Adults and children whose skin colour was either black or brown were the prime targets of this harassment. What did these incidents signify? How widespread were they? Were they really symptomatic of a much deeper problem? In 1975 we were not sure. There were few studies, and therefore almost no data existed in Canada on the subject of racism. We knew little about the victims or the nature of the problems they were experiencing.

The mandate that the Urban Alliance adopted reflected our limited understanding of the problem. The major thrust was to develop strategies and programs which would promote racial harmony, tolerance, and understanding. In implementing this rather abstract goal, a significant proportion of activities were directed at "public education." We held conferences, forums, workshops, and seminars with all kinds of voluntary associations, religious institutions, and service clubs. However, we soon began receiving requests from "front-line" workers, people in organizations and institutions who were facing a new and very different constituency.

The dramatic changes in the composition and complexion of Canadian society, particularly in Metro Toronto, were presenting difficulties to people whose responsibility it was to deliver services to the public. A racially and culturally pluralistic society was posing new challenges to teachers, police, social workers, health-care specialists, and others. What did these front-line workers hope to gain from these training workshops that we were asked to provide? Some wanted an opportunity to gain greater sensitivity and skills in dealing with clients who now frequently came from different cultural backgrounds than the workers themselves. Many of the participants felt threatened and insecure in their interactions and relationships with people whose language, values, and norms were often unfamiliar.

The primary aim in these workshops was directed at changing attitudes. The training sessions focused on helping practitioners to understand cultural and racial differences, as well as commonalities, and thereby to modify biased and discriminatory behaviour. The assumption which both trainers and trainees shared was that there is a definable body of information which can be transmitted and which will help practitioners understand and deal more effectively with minority communities.

While the participants may have learned a little from us, those of us leading these sessions certainly increased our understanding of the problems of front-line workers. It was not simply a matter of changing perceptions and attitudes of workers. Frequently these individuals were operating in ambiguous, uncertain, and unsupportive environments, both within their own agencies and outside of them. They had been trained and equipped to perform a job, to provide a service; however, they now discovered that their roles were no longer the same. They lacked the knowledge and skills necessary to adapt: in a very real sense, they lacked the technology to understand the problems they were confronting and to solve them. Moreover, in many cases, the organizational settings in which they functioned had little comprehension of the concerns of their workers. In most of these agencies (in both the public and private sectors) the decision makers, including trustees, directors, managers, and supervisors, had little understanding of how cultural and racial diversity might affect the delivery of their services. These organizations saw no real need to change their policies, programs or their allocation of resources. Generally speaking, the burden of change was placed solely upon the shoulders of front-line workers within the system; the system itself remained unaffected and unchanged.

SYSTEMIC DISCRIMINATION

In the period between 1978 and 1981, several studies of racism were published.[1] The Urban Alliance began to engage in its own research on policing, education, human rights in Ontario, and media. All of these studies contributed to a growing body of both objective data and subjective experience which indicated that the main structures and systems of society were directly responsible for racial discrimination.

This evidence, in turn, influenced the nature of the activities of the Urban Alliance. In the very early days of the organization, racism was viewed as essentially a human relations problem in which individual bias and bigotry were the key operative factors. In responding to this kind of analysis, advocacy activities were largely devoted to changing those attitudes. But gradually there was a recognition that, however well-designed those "sensitivity training" sessions were, however skilled the trainer, they would do little to reduce racial discrimination. As the body of knowledge and expertise in race relations grew, it was apparent that change would not occur through changes in individual attitudes. Racial discrimination was woven into the policies and practices of the major structures and systems in society. Even if individuals responsible for translating policy into practice were not themselves prejudiced, the established and conventional modes of organizational operation often had an adverse and discriminatory impact on people of colour.

"Training," in all its various interpretations, had been the major focus of efforts to reduce racism. It was becoming increasingly evident that we had to reevaluate the relevance of such training in dealing with the systemic forms of racial discrimination. So the Urban Alliance began to focus on identifying and pursuing advocacy strategies that would more directly affect the policies and practices of institutions. Like all community-based advocacy groups, the Urban Alliance operated with limited resources, but with enormous energy and commitment. Based upon the needs and concerns articulated by minority groups, the Urban Alliance pursued several fronts simultaneously: educational institutions, media, police and social services, and employment.

CHANGING LEVELS OF INSTITUTIONAL RESPONSE

The involvement of the Urban Alliance with institutions such as boards of education and radio stations (described below) was therefore aimed at establishing the kinds of corporate, consultative, monitoring, and employment practices that are equitable and responsive to the needs of minorities. To a large extent these kinds of cooperative relationships and liaison with formal institutions were first initiated by the institutions themselves. For the Urban Alliance, simple entry into these institutions was considered to be a major accomplishment, evidence of an open and responsive system. At the same time, it is instructive to assess how far these institutions were prepared to adapt their policies and practices as a response to advocacy. A rough categorization of response facilitates discussion of change over time. In a 1981 report, Young and Connelly propose four categories of institutional response to race relations, each category representing a "level" or threshold which moves up and down in time.

The first category or level Young and Connelly propose is that of the *pioneers*. Pioneer institutions are those which have been the first to create new committees, new positions, and new machinery, and have redefined the norms of policy development to the point where "race relations implications" are a normal facet of any issue under discussion. In the second category are the *learners*, institutions who have accepted that major adaptations have to be made and have adopted some general policy statement affirming their commitment to a multiracial society and/or its goals as an equal opportunity employer. Very rarely is any more substance put to this generalized commitment. The third category are the *waverers*, who may acknowledge the issues a multiracial society poses for them but, by resorting to many of the myths previously described, would argue that the topic is beyond their powers, and no changes can or should be made. The last category are the *resisters*, who refuse to accept that the existence of a multiracial population has any implications for the institutions.

Notwithstanding the simplicity of this categorization, the majority of institutional responses in Canada a decade or so ago could be categorized as "resisters" and "waverers." Hardly any agency could be identified as a "pioneer." As indicated by chart 1, there is a very flat-looking pyramid.

In the latter half of the 1980s, the shape of the pyramid changed somewhat.

Chart 1

Institutional Response to Race Relations circa 1970

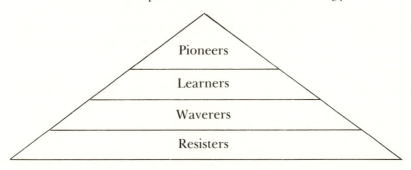

Chart 2

Institutional Response to Race Relations circa 1990

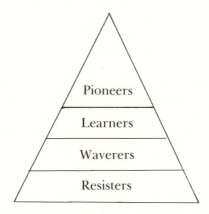

There are considerably fewer today who would articulate a "resister" position. While one might identify a few more "pioneers," the vast majority of agencies and institutions can be categorized as "learners" and "waverers." The purpose of race relations advocacy is to move institutions up this ladder of categorization – that is, to support the work of the "pioneers," to help the "learners" learn, and to make the "waverers" resolute.

The advocacy experience with the radio station CKFM depicts a process of moving a "waverer" to "learner" to "pioneer" in the broadcasting field. The experience with the boards of education describes a "learner" fleshing out generalized commitment with the substance of a race relations policy. Advocacy was a process of providing technical assistance to develop their capacity to respond to the needs and aspirations of minorities. The advocates were required to identify both the problems and the solutions – the specific practices appropriate to the institutional context.

On the other hand, our experiences with the *Toronto Sun* required another style of approach. Advocacy activities that are intended to expose and oppose racism may include marches, rallies, demonstrations, and public meetings. They may also include supporting and aiding community coalitions to sustain political pressure. Such confrontational tactics are generally associated with institutions which fall into Young and Connelly's category of "resisters."

EDUCATIONAL INSTITUTIONS

While rooting out prejudice and discrimination is the responsibility of no one public agency, the institution with the greatest responsibility in this area is the educational system. Whether justified or not, the public has placed great faith in the power of education to solve societal problems, and to create a more racially harmonious, tolerant, and just society. In reality, those who actually work with the system realize that unless sweeping changes take place which penetrate all aspects of educational practice, our society's racist culture will continue to be transmitted to our children.

In defining the problem the first issue was to acknowledge that the boards of education were, by and large, unaware that their operating techniques and their criteria for judgment were often functionally discriminatory against racial minorities. Racial discrimination manifested itself in several areas, including the curriculum, which was filled with inaccurate and biased information, as well as misrepresentations and stereotypes of minority groups. There was an almost total absence in the curriculum of the important economic, social, and cultural contribution of groups other than the British and French to this country's growth and development. Stereotypes and the distorted depiction of minority groups as outsiders, aliens, and exotics were incorporated into many school texts.

Another area of critical concern within the educational institutions was the hiring and promotion practices of teachers and administrators, which had resulted in an abysmal absence of non-White staff in senior positions of responsibility. There were almost no principals, no administrators, and virtually no trustees.

Of equal concern was the perception that visible-minority students were being streamed into non-academic, lower-level programs as a result of culturally biased placement tests, inadequate psychological assessment instruments, and the racially biased attitudes of educators themselves. In one municipality in Metro Toronto, an analysis revealed that 60 per cent of the student body of a vocational and technical school was Black.

A further concern was the number of racial incidents taking place within the school and playground. Frequently, those incidents were simply ignored by school staff. However, they were in fact part of a cycle of experiences which undoubtedly contributed to the lack of self-esteem and self-confidence felt by children from minorities which recent studies have demonstrated.

Finally, we were seriously concerned about the lack of knowledge and skills of educators. Both the basic pre-service training of teachers and the in-service training opportunities were totally inadequate, with respect to anti-racist education.

In three boards in the Metropolitan Toronto area, the Urban Alliance provided consultation on a sustained basis in a variety of forms beginning in 1977. The goal was to help the boards recognize their responsibility in developing their own internal capacity to deal with the problems of racism. It is important to stress that, in the initial stages of the work with the boards, the Urban Alliance, like other community groups, could only do what the boards determined as appropriate in meeting their needs. In most cases this was limited to providing workshops and sensitization sessions for teachers and students. Gradually we were able to develop programs for principals, and later we were asked to provide consultation to administrators.

In two of the boards, subcommittees were established to look at the question of race and ethnic relations. These committees consisted of internal staff, but they were given the freedom to consult others outside of the board, which they did. In the third board, community and resource people from outside the system actually sat on the committees together. Both those from outside the system and some within advocated one major change which would serve to incorporate all other aspects: a comprehensive policy on race and ethnic relations. The purpose of this policy was to provide for each board a step-by-step process for achieving a non-racist school environment and system. After much consideration and a good deal of resistance, each of these boards, at different times, set out to design and create such a policy. For the Toronto Board, it was 1979; the North York Board of Education's policy was approved in 1983, and the Metro Separate School Board's in 1984. During this phase the community's advocacy role became a crucial one. Drafts of the policy were submitted first internally, then shared with the community. Input in the form of briefs and position papers was presented, including critical analyses of the draft policies. Countless hours were spent first with committees and later at board meetings, persuading reluctant trustees of the importance of approving these documents. It is important to note that those educators who were directly involved in the process emerged with a strong commitment to changes of policy and became powerful allies.

Once the policies were in place, the next and perhaps even more difficult stage began, and still continues: the implementation of the policies. Each board had to grapple with the dozens of recommendations contained in the report, struggling to determine what are the appropriate mechanisms for translating the policy into a living reality for students and staff within a board. Policies alone are not enough. How do you ensure the cooperation and support of those charged with the responsibility of implementation, a group which actually includes hundreds of people within each board? How do you acquire from trustees adequate financial and human resources to integrate the policy into the system when the number one priority today in boards of education everywhere is fiscal restraint? What is the role of the Ministry of Education in all of this? Where does its responsibility lie? Thus far, advocacy efforts within education have not targeted the ministry itself, and this is a gap that will need to be addressed.

MEDIA

Like the educational system, the media represent a powerful influence over both attitudes and behaviour. As major transmitters of cultural standards, myths, values, roles, and images, the electronic and print media affect people at every socio-economic level. The media set norms, create stereotypes, and establish priorities. In recognition of the powerful and pervasive effect of this institution, the Urban Alliance developed an ongoing program of education and advocacy directed at the various industries within the media.

We began with the world of advertising. The first task was to identify the nature of the problem. After a long period of monitoring advertising in both the print and broadcast media, we found an almost total exclusion of visible minorities. On the rare occasions when individuals from non-White groups were used, they were often the subject of negative stereotyping, dressed in their "native costume" or eating their favourite "ethnic food." They were rarely portrayed as Canadians, engaged in the normal activities of everyday life such as brushing one's teeth, driving a car, wearing fashionable clothes, buying houses, furniture, etc. The subliminal message contained in these advertisements was that this is a society made up of people whose skin colour is White, and only they are capable of participating in the good life. Visible minorities are invisible, and therefore do not belong.

A number of strategies were followed in order to bring about change in the industry. Members of the Urban Alliance and other organizations developed a small advocacy group made up of individuals from a number of different racial and ethnic groups who, as leaders in their respective communities, were very knowledgeable and articulate. Carefully designed meetings were held between this group and senior levels of management in the major advertising companies. The group began networking with various industry representatives who held important positions with the various associations within the advertising community. The Urban Alliance and the group sponsored conferences and seminars for the community which focused on not only giving people information about the problems, but providing them with advocacy skills in relation to the media.

Simultaneously we began working with government, at both the provincial and federal levels, to lobby for government advertising and communication which were more reflective and representative of the multiracial composition of Canadian society. Policy guidelines have since been established by both the Ontario government and the federal government.

A mail-back campaign was organized when efforts with major retailers failed to yield any measurable results. Several companies were targeted, all of whom regularly produced large numbers of flyers and catalogues. Communities across Metro Toronto were contacted and asked to mailback those brochures when they failed to adequately reflect the thousands of non-Whites who live in and around Toronto. They were asked to attach a note to the president and advertising manager explaining their actions. Letters were sent to the target companies informing them of the campaign and the reason for it. A press release was distributed to the media announcing the campaign. A simple monitoring process was developed.

In assessing the impact of this strategy, we consider it to have been quite effective. Significant numbers of non-Whites, particularly Blacks, are being used on a regular basis in advertising. In the company which had the poorest record, promotions and catalogues have shown dramatic signs of change and now better reflect the multiracial reality of the city. Whether these gains will be sustained is difficult to say. However, the changes which have taken place give us reason to be somewhat optimistic, and clearly demonstrate that communities, when working together, do have considerable power and potential to influence major institutions.

Another example of the use of advocacy within the media occurred with a radio station in Metro Toronto, CKFM. This station, which ranked among the top in popularity among Toronto FM listeners, was also considered an outstanding example of good corporate citizenship, sponsoring many charitable events. Among its announcers was a man who had achieved international eminence as an authority on jazz. One morning after the jazz programme he hosted had ended, he inadvertently left the sound system on while talking on the phone. He was then overheard on air by thousands of listeners referring to the upcoming Caribana parade (an annual event presented by the Black community) as "four million niggers jumping up and down." This blatant racist comment created a groundswell of protest not only from Blacks but from other visible minorities as well. Initially CKFM emphatically denied any responsibility for the incident, but the station ultimately realized that the issue would not go away. An advisory board was established, made up of several members of the Urban Alliance as well as other community people. Over the next two years, the advisory committee and the station developed a very constructive working relationship. A number of changes were implemented affecting all aspects of the company, including policy, programming, and even hiring practices. The enormous respect and trust which has developed between the senior management of CKFM and its community advisory board provides a unique model and important vehicle for understanding the positive role of community advocacy.

Another example of advocacy in the media took place in response to a concern by the community about racism in a particular newspaper, the *Toronto Sun*. For a number of years the *Toronto Sun* had been accused of treating various minority groups in a negative, derogatory manner. In particular, it had been accused of biased, inaccurate, and unbalanced portrayals of ethnic and racial minorities and Native people. Groups representing the Arab, Moslem, and Native communities tried several different approaches with the *Sun* to try to get them to address their concerns. Meetings with publishers and editors and submissions to the Ontario Press Council and Ontario Human Rights Commission produced no results. When the *Toronto Sun* began publishing a series of columns on South Africa, the Anti-Apartheid Coalition of Toronto was outraged by the racist views expressed by several columnists and editors. They communicated their indignation to the publisher. They appeared before the Toronto Mayor's Committee on Community and Race Relations seeking intervention against the *Sun*. During the same period of time, the *Sun* printed an article which the Anti-Apartheid Coalition considered an outrageous attack on Blacks. The paper continued to deny and ignore allegations of racism as they had always done. What became clear was the need for a systematic and comprehensive analysis of the *Toronto Sun*. The Urban Alliance had been considering doing such a study for years. We now viewed this initiative as imperative, and a researcher was contracted. Based on literally hundreds of clippings from the *Sun*, the researcher, Effie Ginzberg, sought the answer to the following question: "Is there prejudice and racism in the *Toronto Sun*'s columns, articles and editorials?"

The report was published and released at a press conference. Although the *Sun* categorically denied the findings of the study, they agreed to meet with several groups including the Coalition and the Urban Alliance to discuss these findings and their implications. The only immediate result was that the publisher agreed to monitor his paper very carefully, and to provide an open door for individuals and groups wishing to express concern about any future articles.

In the time which has passed since the publication of the content analysis, there has been a significant improvement in the paper's coverage of race relations issues and visible minorities. Although there are still occasional articles which are extremely offensive, many of the writers who were the most virulent have toned down their rhetoric or no longer write about these subjects. Thus we can see from this case study that the combination of advocacy and research can provide a powerful catalyst for social change in the area of race relations.

EMPLOYMENT

The problems posed by racial discrimination in employment have been identified as the most formidable challenge confronting visible minorities. Over the last ten years, the Urban Alliance has attempted to analyse the nature of the problem and identify strategies to reduce the pervasive and systemic barriers which continue to deny people of colour equal access in the workplace. Briefs have been submitted and presentations made to various task forces, parliamentary committees, and commissions at municipal, provincial, and federal levels of government, identifying the employment process as the one which is the most riddled with bias and discrimination against visible minorities.

One of the major difficulties encountered by the Urban Alliance was the absence of concrete data on the extent and nature of employment discrimination. This lack of systematic, direct research was the concern of many other groups besides the Urban Alliance. In submissions to the Special Parliamentary Committee on the Participation of Visible Minorities in Canadian Society, in 1983, many organizations and individuals raised their concerns about the poor statistics and data base since a good data base is essential in developing any kind of integrated, comprehensive, and consistent approach.[2]

To respond to this abysmal lack of concrete information, the Urban Alliance and the Social Planning Council of Metro Toronto undertook a large-scale study which would directly test racial discrimination in employment, using the technique of field-testing. In the first phase of the study, teams of job applicants, matched with respect to age, sex, and educational and employment histories were sent to answer advertisements for jobs as listed in the classified section of a major Toronto newspaper. Each applicant carried a résumé which had been carefully constructed to meet the requirements of the job being tested.

The job applicants were as similar to each other as possible. The majority of them were, in fact, professional actors who assumed the various roles required for the different jobs tested. The only major difference between the testers was that of race. Racial discrimination was said to occur when the White applicants received a greater proportion of job offers than the non-White applicants; when the White applicants were called back for a second interview in greater proportions than the non-White applicants; and when the White applicants were treated fairly and courteously while the Blacks were accorded rude, negative, and sometimes blatantly hostile treatment. We called these latter forms of behaviour "differential treatment." In the 201 workplaces tested, racial discrimination took place in almost one-quarter of all job contacts tested in this study.

The second way in which discrimination was tested was to find out if job applicants using different non-Canadian accents and "ethnic"-sounding names would be treated differently by employers over the telephone. Accordingly, four job seekers (actually eight, since we surveyed both male and female jobs), including a West Indian, an Indo-Pakistani, a White immigrant "ethnic," and a majority Canadian, phoned a series of jobs listed in the newspaper. Occupational groupings surveyed in both the in-person direct field test and the telephone test included both blue-collar and white-collar occupations. In total, 237 jobs were tested, and in 52 per cent of these calls, there was some form of discrimination present.

The results from the two phases of the study revealed an extremely high rate of discrimination at the point of entry or selection in the employment process. The overall ratio of discrimination was three to one. Whites had three job prospects to every one for Blacks. The findings of this study are documented in the report *Who Gets the Work* (Henry and Ginzberg 1985).

The second phase of the study examined large businesses and corporations employing more than fifty employees. The purpose of this study was to collect sound qualitative and quantitative data on the attitudes and practices of a representative sample of Toronto employers, on issues relating to the hiring and management of a multiracial work force. Personal interviews were conducted with key personnel decision makers in each organization. The questionnaire covered a variety of policies, practices, and attitudes directly and indirectly related to racial minorities. Questions were directed at areas of recruitment, hiring, promotion, training, and termination.

The findings of this study, *No Discrimination Here*, showed that employers had, to a significant degree, overtly racial views of minorities. A total of 28 per cent, almost one-third, feel that non-Whites in general do not have the ability to meet job performance criteria, compared to Whites; 13 per cent perceive non-Whites as threatening, particularly where non-Whites gain promotion over Whites; 7 per cent expressed outright contempt for non-Whites.

Results of the survey suggest that current personnel recruitment, selection, training, and termination policies are informal and subjective enough to provide ample opportunity for exercising racial bias. Furthermore, interviews with respondents revealed that many employers overlook or discount racial tensions in their work force or blame minorities for these problems. About half (49 per cent) of all non-White complaints to management about Whites resulted in disciplining the non-White complainant!

Employers surveyed view the creation of race relations policies as a negative outcome, although 82 per cent have no special policies in this area. Even though almost half could not name a single measure that Affirmative Action might include, 78 per cent of respondents did not want any policy changes forcing them to eliminate discriminatory practices.

GETTING GOVERNMENT AS ALLY

The political system in Canada is obviously in a critical position to play a leadership role in all human rights issues, especially in promoting racial equality. The importance of securing government as an ally in the pursuit of improved race relations is that it alone can change legislation and thus affect practices across institutions. As service provider, government is responsible for many of the key services that determine the quality of life. Through making structural changes, it can allocate greater resources, and through policy and program changes, it can ensure that minority needs are more equitably met. The public sector is the largest single employer in the country. As such it can take the lead role in implementing employment equity programs. As a purchaser of services and goods, government also has the capacity to influence the employment practices of the private sector. Yet the experience of the Urban Alliance is that in many respects the government can be categorized as a "learner" in the field of race relations. The legislative and policy commitments are often in place, but governments, whether federal, provincial, or municipal, do not clarify the objectives of policy and do not carefully assess the scope and limits of potential government intervention.

One of the techniques government has used to slow down and limit the process of change is to encourage community participation in the decision-making process. In reality, this has meant the establishment of a profusion of parliamentary committees, task forces, advisory councils, and so forth that are forever consulting with the community. The community has been consulted to death, bogged down with the task of preparing yet another brief. This whole array of consultative mechanisms has created institutional barriers that place minorities yet another step away from the real decision-making process.

Advocacy groups exist because of deficiencies in the formal institutional systems of provision. Advocacy activities are directed at the promotion of changes within these institutions, and this will always be fraught with tension and conflict.

Tension is certainly a factor when efforts are directed at seeking government intervention. Advocacy groups who have no formal ties with government may strengthen their campaigning role, but may weaken their resource base. Government is always in a position to marginalize such activities through its control of information, expertise, and material resources. In terms of the potential influence over the formation or changing of public policy, advocacy groups constantly have to compare the relative effectiveness of confrontational tactics and direct cooperative linkages.

At the same time there is always a danger in race relations that any initiative will result in a mere gesture or token which is a substitute for long-term change. The political solution for race relations in the 1960s was to throw money at the problem. In this age of austerity, the solution is often to hire a minority person, with no resources and no decision-making authority, to assume all responsibility for change within an institution once a policy has been accepted. There is a tendency to assume that, once a staff person has been appointed or a committee struck to implement a race relations policy, the job is done. Unfortunately, this is not the case. The "race relations" coordinator appointed by government as an outcome of advocacy is often isolated from the rest of the system, and is almost always overwhelmed by the task he or she must perform. To this person alone is delegated the task of reducing or dismantling institutional barriers and discrimination.

Racism cannot be solved by one person, or even one committee. The solution is an institutional process which requires the active commitment and participation of all those in positions of power and authority within the institutional setting. With these ideas in mind, the Urban Alliance has taken a definite stand for affirmative action or employment equity. In June 1985, the government brought in Bill c-62 as the legislated response to a call for affirmative action or employment equity. The bill was viewed as totally inadequate by all the target groups. The legislation only required the mandatory reporting of work force data and not the implementation of employment equity programs; it contained no provisions for enforcement and no penalty for failing to implement these.

As a result of their overwhelming disappointment with this long-awaited legislation, organizations representing women, the mentally and physically disabled, visible minorities, and labour formed a coalition to lobby for substantive amendments to the bill. The Urban Alliance, which had first brought together visible minority organizations into a coalition, then proceeded to help orchestrate the formation of a much broader coalition, one which incorporated the other target groups. For almost a year, these groups worked closely together developing strategies and briefs, holding press conferences, meeting with politicans and bureaucrats, and organizing letter-writing and telephone campaigns to MPs.

The coalition did not succeed in getting government to make any substantive changes in Bill c-62. Nevertheless, the principle of employment equity is now enshrined in public policy. Perhaps more important than the bill itself was the fact that this piece of legislation provided the catalyst for a new form of advocacy in Canada. For the first time, the victims of discrimination are acting as a cohesive, united, and powerful group which government will ignore at its own peril. The alliance which has been created among women, the physical and mentally disabled, and visible minorities is an extremely significant development. Together these groups represent more than 50 per cent of the electorate and will no doubt shape the process of social change in this country from now on.

NOTES

1 One of the first was Henry's (1978) study of racial attitudes in Metro Toronto, which confirmed what we had already come to suspect: that a large percentage of the population was extremely racist, and an additional 35 per cent had racist tendencies. After 1978, there was a considerable expansion of research activity, including Pitman's (1978) study of racism in Toronto; Ubale's (1982) analysis of discrimination experienced by the South Asian community; Head's (1975) research into the inadequacy of social services to racial minorities; Reitz's (1981) and Goldlust and Richmond's (1974) data on discrimination in the workplace, and others.

2 Buchignani (1983) concluded that two basic types of analyses were urgently required. The first requirement was actual controlled tests of discrimination in such things as hiring and securing rental accommodations carried out through such strategies as the use of actors. This type of research would reveal those key areas of economy and society requiring more intensive investigation.

REFERENCES

Abella, Rosalie S. 1984. *Report of the Commission on Equality in Employment.* Ottawa: Supply and Services Canada.

Armour, M. 1984. *Visible Minorities, Invisible Currents: Readings in Race Relations.* Toronto, Urban Alliance on Race Relations.

Billingsley, Brenda, and Muszynski, Leon. 1985. *No Discrimination Here? Toronto Employers and the Multi-Racial Work Force.* Toronto: Urban Alliance on Race Relations.

Bolaria, B. Singh. 1983. "Study of Employment Agencies." Toronto: Canadian Civil Liberties Association.

Bowerman, J. 1980. "East Indians in Alberta: A Human Rights Viewpoint." In K. Victor Ujimoto and Gordon Hirabyashi, eds., *Visible Minorities and Multiculturalism: Asians in Canada.* Toronto: Butterworths.

Buchignani, Norman. 1983. "Some Comments on the Elimination of Racism in Canada." *Canadian Ethnic Studies*, 15, no. 2 Cadieux, R. 1980. *The Representation of Women and the Various Minorities in Broadcasting.* Ottawa: Canadian Human Rights Commission.

City of Toronto. 1982. "Equal Opportunity Employment Utilization Study." Toronto: City of Toronto.

Eng, S. 1984. "Visible Minorities in Advertising." *Currents: Readings in Race Relations*, 2, no. 2: 11–15.

Ginzberg, Effie. 1985. *Power Without Responsibility: The Press We Don't Deserve.* Toronto: Urban Alliance on Race Relations.

Goldlust, John, and Anthony H. Richmond. 1974. *Multivariate Analysis of Immigrant Adaptation.* Toronto: York University.

Head, Wilson. 1975. *The Black Presence in the Canadian Mosaic.* Toronto: Ontario Human Rights Commission.

Henry, Frances. 1978a. *The Dynamics of Racism in Toronto.* Ottawa: Secretary of State.

– 1978b. *The Forgotten Canadians: The Blacks of Nova Scotia.* Toronto: Longmans.

Henry, Frances, and Effie Ginzberg. 1985. *Who Gets the Work? A Test of Racial Discrimination in Employment.* Toronto: Urban Alliance on Race Relations and the Social Planning Council of Metropolitan Toronto.

Hughes, David, and Evelyn Kallen. 1974. *The Anatomy of Racism.* Montreal: Harvest House.

McDiarmind, Garnet L., and David Pratt. 1971. *Teaching Prejudice: A Content Analysis of Social Studies Textbooks.* Toronto: Ontario Institute for Studies in Education.

Mukherjee, A. 1984. "How to Adjust the Educational System." *Currents: Readings in Race Relations* 2, no. 3:41–3.

Muszynski, Leon, and Jeffrey G. Reitz. 1982. *Racial and Ethnic Discrimination in Employment.* Working Paper 5, Social Planning Council of Metropolitan Toronto.

Pitman, W. 1978. *Now Is Not Too Late: Report on Race Relations in Metro.* Toronto: Metropolitan Toronto Council.

Ramcharan, Subhas. 1982. *Racism: Non-Whites in Canada.* Toronto: Butterworths.

Reitz, Jeffrey, et. al. 1981. *Equality and Segregation in Jobs.* Toronto: Centre for Urban and Community Studies, University of Toronto.

Robertson, P. 1980. *Some Thoughts about Affirmative Action in Canada.* Ottawa: Ministry of Employment and Immigration.

Scott, P. 1983. "Debunking the Myth: The American Experience with Affirmative Action." *Currents: Readings in Race Relations* 1, no. 1:19–22.

Sivanandan, A. 1984. "Challenging Racism: Strategies for the 80's." *Race and Class* 25, no. 2:1–13.

Thomas, B. 1984. "Principles of Anti-Racist Education." *Currents: Readings in Race Relations* 2, no. 3:20–4.

Ubale, Bhausahab. 1982. *Working Together: Strategy for Race Relations.* Toronto: Ontario Human Rights Commission.

Urban Alliance on Race Relations. 1984. *Advocacy and the Media. Currents: Readings in Race Relations* 2, no. 2.

Wilson, G. 1983. "Racism-Related Problems, Research and Strategies." *Council on Interracial Books on Children* 14, no. 7 8–14.

Winks, Robin W. 1971. *The Blacks in Canada: A History.* Montreal: McGill-Queen's University Press.

Young, K. 1982. "Local Authorities and the Promotion of Racial Equality." *Policy Studies* 3, no. 1.

Young, K. and Naomi Connelly. 1981. *Policy and Practice in the Multi-Racial City.* London: Policy Studies Institute Report no. 598.

PART TWO: SOCIAL EMPOWERMENT AND THE ADVOCATE

Social Empowerment and the Advocate

The following case studies present an identifiable process of advocacy and empowerment whose circularities of dialogue, learning, analysis and evaluation follow this scheme:[1]

1 *Understanding*: preliminary presentation of alternative construction of social reality ... Opening of dialogue.
2 *Investigation of themes*: alienation, powerlessness, dependence, confusion, anxiety ... unconscious assumptions in favour of the dominant ideology.
3 *Action*: informed participation, inter-organization negotiation or advocacy, collective struggle.
4 *Learning*: Grasping the meaning of conflict, understanding the need for strategic engagement, learning from each other.
5 *Evaluation*: observing consequences of action, developing self-concept as participant and advocate.

The focus of Heyworth's study of social empowerment is the relation between the university and the community in which the university is situated. Most members of such a community, among which are many minorities and educationally disadvantaged, perceive the university as being part of the dominant power structure. While the universities wish to demonstrate their social responsibility, successful demonstration of this depends upon the way in which the university perceives its relationship with the community.

Heyworth notes that many universities define social responsibility in terms of a one-way relationship, that is, of *responsibilities to* the community. Rarely, if ever, do they think about a two-way relationship between the institution and the community. The proposition that the community itself might be knowledgeable is generally absent in the major writings on the question.

Empowerment requires the university to be open to learning from the community itself. The advocate assumes that the community involved has a view of education which is valid for itself, and that – with encouragement – people will share their perceptions and experience in order to establish practical norms for education and institute a means for maintaining the dialogue.

It is clear from Heyworth's analysis that the steps needed in building a two-way relationship and the constant feedback necessary to maintain dialogue require a better understanding of the methodology of reflection-in-action (see also Morgan below). Once people learn to act together under these circumstances, understanding will take place and learning will have been achieved. Marshall shows that a similar proactive dialogue is required in the field of labour studies and industrial relations. Trade unionists have concluded that conventional academic researchers ignore their legitimate concerns. Worse still, academics often direct their research towards projects which aid management policy and practice. Not only do academics fail to evaluate the usefulness of the knowledge they are producing, but applicable information is seldom transmitted to practitioners in the trade union movement. This situation has justifiably been labelled the "corporatist" approach to social science research. As Marshall indicates, the corporatist approach in labour and industrial research is skewed towards an "Administrative Point of View." This includes the fiction that research embodies "value neutrality," a fiction that hinders advocacy in fundamental dimensions.

Marshall calls for an alternative perspective to guide research and method on labour issues. He calls it a Labour Point of View. A Labour Point of View must be distinguished from a lurch into syndicalism. It signifies a working relationship which enables labour to be effective both in its immediate interests and in the long term. A Labour Point of View advocates alternatives to the pervasive corporate world view, by investigating themes that are of central interest to labour – for example, understanding the need for strategic engagement – and giving meaning to the history of labour-capital conflict. In effect, researcher and labour leader learn from each other. A Labour Point of View enables labour to build upon the skills and insights of scholars for purposes of policy making. It also enables consciousness raising among those engaged in labour action – negotiators, leaders, or workers. Though progressive academic researchers do not have the credentials for leading labour unions, the practical aspect of information gathering is useful in the education of union officials and workers alike.

Dippo raises some structural issues of class underlying work skills and job training. "Work," considered as an abstract category, is nearly always under the control of "the owners of work"; that is to say, employers maintain that they have the unqualified right to specify what work the employee must carry out. This drives a social and psychological wedge between work as objective action and reflection on the work process, as self-knowledge and skilled appreciation. Existing "Job Skills" training manipulates the very categories and modes of thinking which reflective workers might use in order to reach an understanding of the relation between themselves as workers and the products of their work. Within the context of the classroom, the curriculum materials Dippo has developed provide a formal opportunity for students and teachers to reexamine the history of their own work practices and explore those alternative forms of work practice that make sense.

None of the articles report on the fifth step of the empowerment process – "*Evaluation*: observing consequences of action and planning for next action; developing self-concept as participant and advocate." Evaluation requires longitudinal studies of empowerment, and in academic research, longitudinal studies of this sort are rarely reported on. Each of the case studies expresses a fundamental criticism of academic research. Why are these authors concerned that academic research, being theory-oriented, is a block to the advocacy process? A total of 82 per cent of all social research in Canada is carried out in the universities. The universities house basic research equipment and are almost the only source of independent research and theoretical thinking.

The government sector has social researchers, but direct research and development in the human sciences in Canada is very small indeed. Social research at the federal government level is a secondary activity. Of the overall in-house expenditures on research at the federal level, 75 per cent goes to natural sciences and only 25 per cent to human sciences. Of this 25 per cent, only a tiny proportion (2.7 per cent in 1983–84) is actually devoted to research and development in the social sciences.[2] Concentration of social research in the universities in Canada has definite consequences both for the social system in which researchers find themselves and for the type of research which is taken up. The major characteristic of such research is that it is undertaken within largely autonomous institutions and serves the purposes of academic departments within scholarly disciplines. Academic research, therefore, is largely undertaken for theoretical purposes, and therein lie some of the dilemmas of advocacy research in Canada.

By contrast, advocacy in the United States is intimately tied to the requirements of political lobbying. Lobbying is increasingly becoming a way of running government in the United States. Overall the number of lobbyists in Washington is estimated to be more than 10,000. Lobbyists outnumber u.s. congressmen by about 19:1. Of the total number of lobbyists, about 1,250 represent individual companies; 2,500 represent foreign governments or state governments or municipalities; and another 4,000 a mix of trade unions, professional associations, and the like. The range of special causes represented varies from the National Rifle Association to the Wilderness Society. Among these are a mixture of organizations, some of which are simply part of a business lobby under another name. All special-cause advocates not only lobby u.s. Congressmen, but also, as might be expected, make ongoing presentations of the issues to many other groups. The category of "advocate" thus embraces an occupationally diverse group of people, involving government, private sector enterprise, the military, and the universities.

The United States Congress passed the Federal Regulation of Lobbying Act in 1946, imposing a number of requirements. Lobbyists must register before they begin their activity. They must report each quarter, under oath, money they have either received or spent in pursuit of lobbying. They must report in specific terms to whom they gave money, for what purpose, and for the promotion or defeat of what legislation. They must list the name and address of each person who has made a contribution of $500 or more for lobbying purposes, and keep receipts for all expenditures of $10 or more. And lobbyists must list any publication of any type – newspaper, periodical, magazine – in which they had articles published as part of their overall promotion. All this information is then published in the Congressional Record (Johnson 1985).

Canada also has a growing flock of lobbyists and "paid government consultants," but the much stronger pull of party politics in Canada has inhibited the growth of the United States phenomenon until recently. The Canadian government passed a bill requiring lobbyists to register in 1988. The Lobbyists Registration Act came into force in September 1989, but it does not regulate lobbying; it simply requires that lobbyists register their names, the names of their companies, and a description of the issues on which they lobby, so that the public can be aware of who they are. The act does not require disclosure of what they are paid or whom they meet in government back rooms. The spread of interests at the time of writing is unknown.

NOTES

1 A much more elaborate scheme, presented in somewhat different order, is to be found in Rose and Black 1985, 61.
2 Bureaucratic budget needs swamp actual research on social policy and planning, since more than half of the total budget devoted to human science activity goes to three agencies – Statistics Canada, the National Museums, and the National Library. Moreover, the federal government has actually reduced the number of people doing in-house social research during the past few years (by 55 per cent since 1976) (Science Council of Canada 1985, 51, 246).

REFERENCES

Johnson, William. 1985. *Globe and Mail*. Toronto. 20 December 1985:A5.
Rose, Stephen, and Bruce Black. 1985. *Advocacy and Empowerment: Mental Health, Care and the Community*. London: Routledge and Kegan Paul.
Science Council of Canada. 1985. *Social Science Research in Canada: Stagnation or Regeneration?* Ottawa: Ministry of Supply and Services.

ELSPETH HEYWORTH

"Town"/"Gown" and Community Relations: Case Studies of Social Empowerment

Relationships between "town and gown" have been the subject of debate for many centuries. The forms they have taken vary with time, place, and the particular university or community. Today, in North America, community projects and activities initiated by universities are paraded on every campus. Nevertheless, their underlying rationale is less clear. The major preoccupation for the university continues to be with effects of the economic crisis, while doubts and perplexities are expressed in a general groping after social legitimacy of community projects.

In all this uncertainty, the concept of advocacy serves only to complicate matters. For if an advocate is one who pleads for, defends, recommends, or supports another, then advocacy raises some troubling questions in university-community relations. Not only are there potential issues of paternalism – advocacy for whom? and by whom? – but there is also the much-cherished principle of neutrality. In many universities this principle equates with autonomy, objectivity, and academic freedom. With advocacy, not only is the purity of research at stake, but so is the autonomy of the university. For when advocates are researchers in the university on behalf of the community outside it, as is often the case in community outreach, then the assumption is that the wall between the inside and the outside is permeable. And so the question of advocacy becomes part of the larger issue: what are the desirable or appropriate relationships between the university and the community?

SERVICE: THE NEED FOR A CLEAR PREMISE

Universities today seldom operate the Settlements which were once meeting grounds between the educated middle classes and the illiterate – viewed then as the degenerate poor. Instead they sanction a growing number of projects and programs designed to promote access to university facilities or services, or to provide field experience for students. Public lecture series, continuing education courses, and various *ad hoc* activities are ways of promoting access. Nevertheless, members of the public may remain confused or uncertain whether individual requests for a library card, for a student to act as volunteer tutor, or for a faculty member to speak at a community meeting – or even for an opportunity to swim in the university pool – will be granted or not. The public may not know to whom they can direct those requests. Sometimes they hit lucky; sometimes they do not. The most important questions for the public, such as requests for assistance with significant social issues, may never be asked. The public may have difficulty formulating them, especially if they are not certain that they are appropriate questions, or if they have any right to ask them.

Universities may share the public's perplexity, but seldom do they acknowledge that modes and models of interaction between universities and communities depend entirely on the philosophy which underlies their relationship. This article will argue for a rigorous philosophy to guide interaction, based on an understanding of education as social empowerment. This is not a neutral stance. Yet, acting on this premise, the university can challenge social inequality and strive to play a liberating role in the education process. It can promote the development of a critical understanding of social problems, and of the possibilities for overcoming them.

This stance depends on democratic reciprocity; that is to say, those outside the university have much to teach as well as much to learn. It also includes positive discrimination for those who may not yet believe that they have a social contribution to make – groups of women, visible minorities, and those of low socio-economic status. These groups have been seriously underrepresented in both the generation and dissemination of knowledge. The stance also demands a strong advocacy role for these groups within an institution like the university, which has for so long been a part of the dominant power structure. Advocacy in this sense is cooperative, in the manner Rees and Tator describe above, rather than confrontational.

It is precisely because higher education has traditionally focused on individuals and their educational growth, rather than paying attention to potential education of socially defined groups, that societal obligation has taken a back seat. The implementation of the belief that the vigour of our free institutions and our national life depends upon educated women and men at every level of society may appear in rhetoric to be the role of the university, but this is not often the case. An underlying premise of democratization must be sustained if a fruitful, two-way relationship between universities and society is to develop. Lack of this leads to a climate of mutual distrust. At the same time, acceptance of this premise by university administrations is by no means a foregone conclusion. The university has come to evaluate itself in relation to the community by other criteria than that of social legitimacy. Changing the universities' self-conception of their social responsibility is often a long and difficult task.

Nevertheless, there have been some remarkable changes in the last few years. A rash of publications exploring the need for stronger relations with communities have appeared, each giving different justifications. There are three major themes: the rationale of service, which has become recognized as an overall mission of the university; the rationale of social responsibility for community interaction; and the rationale of the taxpayers' dollar. Examining the motivation of programs designed to bring universities and communities together, these publications distinguish between programs governed by motives of access and those governed by motives of outreach (Fuller and Heyworth 1984, 3). A further set of categories are those of democratization, economic efficiency, and more relevant teaching techniques. These are the criteria of the United Nations Office of Economic and Cultural Development (OECD). I shall discuss all of these criteria in the following sections, but clearly the lines drawn between some of the categories are both fuzzy and peppered with self-interest.

The clearest attempt to dissect the rationale of service can be found in Crosson's *Public Service in Higher Education: Practices and Priorities*. Crosson puts forward four rival propositions as to how the "service role" is best fulfilled: through ideas of value, through social criticism, through social problem solving, and through social activism. Research and teaching are seen as forms of "service" in all these propositions. In grappling with ideas of value, Crosson argues that universities should not be content merely to reflect upon tensions existing in society, but rather should ensure that values are "dealt with, criticized, refined, reordered and brought to the attention of individuals and other institutions" (Crosson 1983, 14). At the other end of the spectrum, that of social activism, she states that the primary purpose of a university is seeking the truth and if that purpose leads the university into social or political activism, so be it.

Discussing the barriers to the fulfilment of this mission, Crosson finds that while public service is deemed to be an important function, it is a distinct third – after teaching and research. At the moment the ability to perform service is based upon a retention of boundaries between university and society. Public service cannot change in importance until it is eliminated as a separate category, and subsumed under research and teaching. Only when service to the public is regarded as part of the transmission of knowledge and the pursuit of truth will it become a central mission.

One of the difficulties in Crosson's work is that she does not sufficiently question the use of the term "service." She does not, for example, distinguish the function of "service for" a community from that of "service with" community members. She falls into the same sort of arguments about social responsibility: responsibilities "to" the communities are not distinguished from mutual relations with the community. Crosson is not alone in this failure to draw a distinction. Social responsibility "to" a community, or social need "for" university-community relations, is a theme that senior university administrators find most congenial in their writing on the question.

A former president of Harvard University argues "the need for social relevance" based on social justice and ethical responsibility. Bok tries to avoid the "shrivelled view of education" in which a university accepts no responsibility for the social conscience of its members, but stresses that social criticism can be preserved only if universities refrain from taking stands on political issues. Bok outlines a clear obligation to serve, but adopts a cautionary tone. He suggests the need to avoid commitments which would imperil research and teaching.

Bok writes as an administrator concerned with the repercussion of activities closely connected to research and teaching functions. He does not discuss reward systems for faculty who might work in less traditional ways, but does suggest that "if professors have lost some of their objectivity by trying to shape the society they purport to describe, they have also gained something in experience and first-hand knowledge" (Bok 1982, 74).

The concept of neutrality has brought more confusion than clarity, because it is so easily taken to mean that universities should seek to carry on with no institutional values or moral commitments. Bok believes that the reverse should be true. He suggests a few concrete measures worth taking to implement this reversal, including the tutoring of underprivileged children, the provision of legal services to the poor, and programs to identify jobs for students to work with "those less fortunate than themselves." He complains that these initiatives often proceed with little support on the part of the administration and he suggests that other ways should be sought to strike at "the evils of society" (Bok 1982, 309).

Howard Clark shares Bok's unease about institutional neutrality. As vice-president of Guelph University, he points out that views of university neutrality on all political, economic, and social issues hamper expression of institutional opinion. Guelph University has officially accepted that a liberal education ought to develop "moral maturity" in a student. If this is an educational objective, then the university can hardly remain morally indifferent itself. Clark's defence of this possible erosion of university neutrality is based on the concept of humanity: "the university must always remember that it is a human institution in a human world" (Clark 1984, 3).

The president of the University of Manitoba stays with the theme of social responsibility. Nevertheless, Farquhar (1983, 2) moves away from addressing the broad constituency of scholars and professionals, and directs his attention more fully to the local community. He states that all universities influence the communities in which they are located, and in turn are influenced by them. He stresses that if universities are interested in paying attention to the quality of life of the communities in which they reside, then this emphasis should be particularly important for those located in communities where the need for improvement is greatest.[1]

Despite varying terminology, there is no hint in any of these writings of a university grounded in a two-way or mutual relationship between the institution and the community. Each of these senior administrators may suggest that communities can provide some real-life experience. They certainly acknowledge that universities should provide some public service in order to justify taxes which the community pay. None put forward the view that communities and universities might be joint searchers for "the truth."

Only a United Nations Report, *The University and the Community*, offers the sustained argument in favour of these ideas. It makes a leap from "service to" a community to "relationship with" communities. In doing so, this OECD report opens up a discussion of democratization in the university setting. It notes that increase in the numbers of students going to university in recent years has not resulted in a larger proportion from low-income families. Second, it suggests that stronger links between universities and communities will help ensure that a university does not cater solely for a privileged group. In its discussion of ways in which the university can participate with the community, the OECD Report emphasizes the importance of flexibility and intellectual modesty on the part of the university.

It suggests a reciprocal opening up of resources, and that the university refrains from assuming a relationship in which it alone identifies problem areas (United Nations, OECD, 1982).

COMMUNITY OUTREACH

There are many within the university who support the type of action suggested by the OECD, and throughout Canada and the United States individuals and groups have striven to translate the notion of social responsibility into pragmatic terms. Usually these groups speak of the need for "community outreach," but the concept is a slippery one. Its definition requires care in defining purpose, explicit identification of target populations, and the search for a viable methodology.

To Fuller, outreach implies that the university engage the community in on-campus and off-campus activities beyond traditional pursuits of formal education and research (Fuller 1983, 5). In his terms, outreach implies a proactive stance for promoting mutually beneficial relationships between the university and the community; the university should be an integral part of the society in which it resides, as well as more responsive in the disposition of its resources. Fuller sees outreach as knowledge-sharing, with the university disseminating existing knowledge and providing specialized training functions for the community. Activities of outreach would include business and industrial research, continuing education, and technical assistance.

It has not been difficult to persuade the university of the need for relationships of this kind of outreach, because of the ability of target groups to respond with clear and appropriate requests. But a definition of outreach which includes reciprocity as a premise for university-community relationships must go beyond this. The community outreach concept bases education on social empowerment and democratization. It draws closer to these themes when its activities are marked by the following traits (Schwager 1985, 2):

- they are undertaken with the community as an equal or senior partner, i.e. the community has control and ownership of the project;
- the community partner is generally not a traditional university client, such as a senior level of government or a larger business corporation;
- the activities are undertaken for purposes of social development or social emancipation;

- in general, the activities are not undertaken for the direct profit of the university.

The need to serve as wide a constituency as possible requires that groups must have special encouragement to make sure they use university resources available to them. Schwager suggests that less privileged groups be assisted in their quest for social emancipation.

Moral imperatives, however noble, do not constitute strong arguments in a period of shrinking resources. Schwager therefore points out that community outreach activities can also serve important academic purposes. These include opening up of new fields of academic endeavour; the establishment of research opportunities in the community; the creation of training opportunities for graduate students; the possibility of creating new job opportunities for academics and other staff; and the acquisition of new resources to aid teaching and research.

Within this definition of community outreach, several universities in the United States – especially the land-grant institutions – and some of the universities in Canada have initiated outreach projects. The Rural Development Outreach Project at Guelph, for example, secured funding for a six-year experiment designed to link it with rural "communities of interest" through endogenous research, graduate placement, and specialized research services. The Guelph project enabled some conclusions about the best way to pursue rural development outreach. Outreach towards the "common citizen" excludes sophisticated "knnowledge users." It always involves an interdisciplinary approach, but produces more than mere engagement of faculty in community activities. Outreach is professional in the sense that there is a need to use specific methods and theory. Finally, outreach has an essential feedback component (Auger and Cebotarev 1981, 28–9).

Laurentian University collaborated with Guelph and soon became aware that communities were expecting more than formal services, or commitment of faculty. Weekly meetings of an outreach group led to heightened awareness of how naïve faculty had been, prior to the project, about the need to discharge their responsibilities to the community. The outreach group struggled through a process of clarifying the distinction between their role as researchers and their role as community participants. The group soon defined itself as "broker" with the task of building links between the community and the university. As I shall show, York University came to some of the same conclusions about the need for coordination and the need to develop links when community issues were thrust upon it.

All these universities are struggling with similar issues: how can universities build bridges between themselves and communities which are acceptable to both? The main danger in outreach, as in all community-based research, is that outreach projects can set themselves up as the saviours of the community. As Turner puts it: "How do we help communities learn that we are available and how do we proceed in working with them in a manner that is not seen as us telling them what to do?" (Turner 1983, 9).

PATERNALISM AND EMPOWERMENT

The community's discomfort with the university's paternalism, or its acting as community saviour, arises from a dichotomy between the university as "giver" and the community as "taker." This, in turn, is linked to the premise of "service to" the community. The whole issue can only be resolved if that premise is altered to a reciprocal relationship "with," which, in turn, establishes different practical relations between town and gown.

Part of the issue of paternalism arises from the nature of universities, enfolded as they are within the dominant power structure. Knowledge and education are indeed powerful. The powerless are frequently uneducated, as well as being disadvantaged in other ways. Social empowerment does not take place when those who have always been givers simply continue to give in bigger and different ways. Empowerment requires a fundamental change of relationships. However powerless, community groups are never merely empty vessels waiting to be filled with knowledge. Empowerment must be a relationship of equality, based on an understanding of reciprocal ties of different strengths. Outreach may be part of a process that leads to this new relationship. In addition, relationships that more easily facilitate faculty undertaking advocacy with community groups can lead to an alteration of the giver/taker equation.

There are many pitfalls and institutional blockages in this reordering of relationships, and I will examine some here on a step-by-step basis. A first step in social empowerment requires identifying existing activities which take place between university and community. As pointed out above, research and service activity is usually initiated by individuals within the university. A community frequently finds difficulty in defining its own research needs. It needs assessments – even search conferences – as a means of identifying issues and problems (Craig, Morgan, et al. 1983, 2:470).[2] The disadvantages of such assessments are that they may result in a list of community "needs" which are static, linked to a particular point in time. The alternative is an evolving or process-based assessment. This rests on the view that a collaborative relationship is a long-term project requiring a long-term assessment, one that depends on the community's knowledge of potential resources evolving, while the availability of university expertise increases. Longer-term assessments may permit community groups and individuals learn how to access university resources as they feel the need of them. Eventually, they should not rely on the university's initiative in this sphere (Wolfe 1983, 21).

Of the many difficulties inherent in this method of "evolvement," the most obvious are disjunctions in timing. Universities need to plan ahead. Outlines for courses or research plans are formulated months in advance. Communities, on the other hand, frequently find it difficult to plan. Their expression of need is often an all-at-once affair. After a long incubation period, a group in the community may suddenly gain the strength to start working on a community health centre, for instance. Theoretically, this type of project is ideal for collaborative relationship, drawing on expertise in the university as well as on the experience and knowledge of the particular community. Yet time sequences may make collaboration impossible. The frustrations experienced on both sides in an unsuccessful collaboration of this nature may cause both partners to be more wary about entering collaborative relationships on subsequent occasions.

Various means to combat this dilemma have been tried. One attempted solution has been to let a special body in the university take up these issues. The University of Manitoba founded an Institute of Urban Studies to address specific community needs. In the United States, the University of Missouri Centre for Community Development lists among its objectives the need "to increase the exchange of knowledge and ideas in an interactional process between the University and the citizens of the state within their communities."

These institutional forms, and the Guelph Project, have all been mutually beneficial to community and university. Nevertheless, a specialized project or institute is almost always in danger of becoming peripheral to the university's main mission. It can reinforce the opposition of those within the university who see themselves as "serious" researchers and can relegate the issues of university-community relations to the "social tinkering" of one small group on the "margin" of research.

An alternative to the creation of special centres lies in the university encouraging researchers to become partners in community research. Community advocacy involving academics falls into this category. The University of West Virginia set about this project by creating an exhaustive inventory of all faculty research areas, special skills, and other interests. A Centre for Voluntarism then acts as a broker between community needs and the university. Successful broking ensures that outreach has been accomplished both internally and externally in order to develop a pool of resources on both sides. A second model is employed by the Action Learning Group at York University. This works on altering the attitudes towards research by those already practising it. Action Learning is based on the principle that no group or theory has a monopoly of insight or knowledge. The capacity for intelligent and responsible action is widely, rather than narrowly, distributed. Action Learning seeks to dissolve boundaries which inhibit the fusion of distributed knowledge. It seeks both to empower through learning and to integrate understanding through action.

The principles of Action Learning are certainly those of reciprocity, democratization, and pluralism. The practice is that a group of people, mainly from the university setting, jointly discuss their projects and gain strength from each other through joint project implementation. Action Learning sees the need to be proactive in order for this to occur, but circumstances should dictate whether this happens in an evolutionary and continuous way or in a revolutionary and discontinuous way (Craig, Morgan, et al. 1983, 1:1). Usually the members of an Action Learning project share common values, but the question of who identifies projects in the case of disadvantaged groups, and how this comes to be either evolutionary, or revolutionary, remains problematic.

The benefit of having research defined by the community, on the other hand, is that researchers can be on the cutting edge of new issues. Those issues which are most relevant and productive for reciprocal relationships emerge slowly. Different institutions and different communities want to design programs which reflect their unique histories, environments, traditions, and priorities. At the same time, such flexibility allows people in the community to initiate ideas and feel commitment to the resulting program. For example, the University of Wisconsin has formed an Urban University – Urban School Alliance designed to increase the numbers of university entrants coming from schools with a high proportion of working-class and Black students. This Alliance opens up resources in the universities and sends professors out to the schools in an attempt to redress the balance.

Projects and activities like these are not difficult to organize. The important decision is to keep them in line with the underlying principles of interdependence and empowerment. Many apparently ad hoc activities, such as courses in micro-computing or fine arts, can be open for community residents, and can be well justified on the grounds that residents who gain familiarity with the campus may then begin to use other resources. Thus a relationship begins to evolve that is far more complex than the mere service type.

Creating interdependency in the major teaching and research areas of the university is more difficult. Research conducted in a collaborative manner may mean finding faculty members willing to donate time to the sensitive and delicate practice of working with communities. This type of work demands new roles and a range of skills not usually included in the education and training of a researcher: those of facilitator, trainer, mediator, organizer, communicator, liaison person, leadership developer, and public participation expert (Wolfe and Fuller 1983, 23). Meeting these demands is likely to be poorly rewarded by universities when "pure research" still commands the highest respect.

Finally, if these obstacles are surmounted and collaborative research takes place, neither side can then relax. Intrinsic to the practice of social empowerment is the need for feedback; and for feedback to be useful to the community, it must be translated into non-academic language. Thus, the process of building a truly democratic, two-way relationship depends on the constant flow of information from both sides. Methods and subject matter evolve out of real engagement and connectedness, and only when people learn and act together can empowerment take place.

THE YORK UNIVERSITY CASE

University administrators are prone to expect that town-gown relations evolve through rational choice of objectives, followed by implementation of appropriate activities with appropriate groups. Reality turns these expectations on their head. The university is frequently not an initiator in its dealings with the community, and instead finds itself reacting to events. The relationship between York University and its neighbour, the Jane-Finch community, is an interesting example of a university forced to react.

York University is situated on a newly developed, densely populated high-needs area, whose phenomenal rate of growth can be measured by a single observation: Jane-Finch was farmland when York University opened its main campus doors in the late 1960s. The fact that an instant city with traditional urban problems was created in a semi-rural suburban area has made Jane-Finch a popular phenomenon for study. Its varied racial and ethnic mix, its high proportion of low income earners, the existence of public housing, and the presence of new immigrants have also drawn the attention of the mass media.

The unusual characteristics of this community and its proximity to the university resulted in the Jane-Finch area becoming fertile ground for "research." This was not funded or contract research, with the careful regulations which accompany research applications involving the use of human subjects. The community soon became flooded with students looking for projects. With no continuity or feedback assured, Jane-Finch residents began to feel "used and abused." A group of feisty women from the community eventually marched to the office of the president of York University and made it clear that their community did not like being treated as a social laboratory. They were tired of donating their precious unpaid time to interviews and never receiving information on the data gathered or being invited to become involved in the research projects. An outcome of this protest was a proposal to set up a joint community-university board, the York-Community Connection, which could explore programs of mutual benefit to both.

What is significant about this experience is that the area was disadvantaged and desperately required resources. Jane-Finch residents had engaged in intense advocacy with local and provincial governments to gain benefits, but the university had done little or nothing on their behalf during this intense advocacy campaign. In fact, apart from the damaging "studies" done by students, the university (with notable individual exceptions) had taken no interest in its neighbouring community until this period of advocacy. Ironically, when Jane-Finch became labelled as "an undesirable place to live" the university began to see it as a socially significant area to investigate.

By this time the community had already managed to conduct much of the research that it needed for its campaign. The university, from the community point of view, was no source of research expertise relevant to its needs. Instead, the only benefit the community could see in having a university on its doorstep was in its provision of material facilities. The university was courted for its swimming pool, its gymnasium, and its tennis courts. Fortunately, there were individuals in the university who thought it not too late to undertake an institutional rethinking, and the issue became a part of York University's Commission on Goals and Objectives for the University. This commission, struck by the president of York, examined York's physical and social isolation and made a series of recommendations based on the view that "universities and their larger societies are critically interdependent" (York University 1977, 86–7). However, other recommendations in this report, having nothing to do with the Jane-Finch question, created deep divisions within the university. The Commission report was quietly shelved.

Yet the issue did not die and continued to catch fire on and off over the next five years. The Social Work Department at Atkinson College began to develop a pool of resources in the student body to meet the needs of community groups. This "Training through Service" program carried forward the notion that the community should identify its own needs and that mutual trust between it and the university should be developed through consultation. But when the department hired new faculty, the program was dropped. Once again residents of the local community intervened. They deluged the dean with letters of complaint. The residents felt let down by the university. As a result the dean and the administration decided to recreate the Community Relations Office originally proposed in the York Commission on Goals and Objectives.

Once hired, the community relations coordinator set about meeting the substance of residents' complaints. One program requested was a bridging course for low-income, low-educational-level mature women who wished to enter university. Another was an attempt by ninety-seven self-help groups in the community to collaborate on collective action. The bridging course worked because its content was decided upon by the community, as were details of time, location, and recruitment. The extent of community involvement created a commitment of common support. In the process, community residents began to have some sense of the university, formerly an intimidating institution to them, as being "our university." In addition, joint planning was a process of real empowerment for the women which, in turn, aided formal class learning, as well as skills of negotiation and analysis.

The case of the ninety-seven self-help groups involved a different use of the university. The community relations coordinator had been able to identify some common community issues, one of which was destructive competition for funding. The coordinator and the community leaders agreed that a series of meetings should address this issue. Residents did not want to invite representatives from large institutions to these meetings, as they felt they might be intimidating. They agreed instead that facilitators from the university could help to guide delicate negotiations between groups and that students could help guide documentation and research. An Action Learning class and some faculty members agreed to be involved. As the project went on it became on the one hand an exercise in the refinement of analysis appropriate to a university training for the students, and on the other hand a new perspective of the university for the community.

Both instances illustrate how community groups, initially powerless, gain strength through the process of reciprocal involvement. They are cases in which "advocacy with" leads to mutual benefits. On the basis of this experience I have designed a model of university-community interaction whose details can be found in the appendix to this article. Of particular importance are the criteria for choice of interaction. The model assumes that there are benefits of equal value to be gained by both community and university. It assumes that the interaction will generate new knowledge about the social issues being addressed. It assumes that the interaction will develop relationships different from those engaged in by the community with other institutions. At the same time the university is able to allow its members to play a "neutral" role in the community, without the institution itself becoming neutral to the whole stake of university-community relations. The model points out that other institutions cannot afford to take some of the risks involved in these endeavours.

CONCLUSIONS

The thesis of this paper is that a university needs to concentrate more on the invisible groups of society, and that this can only take place within a broad atmosphere of social interconnectedness. Democratic principles of knowledge-generation need to be accepted before this can take place. Taking responsibility inherent in knowledge means a combination of both knowing and doing. Guarantees of tenure and academic freedom provide an atmosphere of "genial anarchy" in a university, which can allow individual faculty members or even entire academic departments to engage in "doing" through advocacy on public issues. Yet, if we are to move beyond these valuable but particular contributions to the commitments of universities as institutions, then the approach of genial anarchy must be reworked.

Universities have to examine their basic philosophy of "service." A service role based on the concept of neutrality is not sufficient. There must be an active search for new methods of interaction "with" communities and the wider social world of which the university is a part. Advocacy with groups outside the university frequently results in forging new forms of relationship. Although the pitfalls of this approach are many, the process of engagement is rewarding for the university. Not only can it help achieve social empowerment, but the process underlines to its participants the importance of both knowing and doing in the synthesis of knowledge. As Morgan states in another article in this volume, the process is a type of learning equal in importance to the formal characteristics of research. In short, outreach projects which stem from advocacy with local communities are an aspect of "double loop learning."[3] The "double loop" is the means through which action taken becomes the source of further knowledge.

APPENDIX 1

A Community Relations Model

Different institutions will want to design programs in community relations which reflect their unique traditions, environments, and priorities. The model at York reflects the newness of both the university and the community: both have developed at an astonishing rate and are in a constant state of transition. This transitional state should be conducive to a model of university/community interaction that emphasizes process more than outcome, the method of building a relationship with a community more than specific predesigned programs.

In the attempt to develop the focus for activities and the strategies to be used, the following elements have been developed as the Community/University Interaction Model for York University's Community Relations:

Purposes: Criteria for choice of interaction

1 *Sharing benefits*: The model assumes that there are benefits of equal value to be gained by both the community and the university.
2 *Knowledge potential*: The model assumes that the interaction will generate new knowledge about the community and about the social issues being addressed. The benefits to the university include the opportunity for keeping abreast of issues as they happen and for research into subject areas of contemporary relevance.
3 *Unique relationship*: The model assumes that the interaction will develop relationships different from those engaged in by the community with other institutions which have a more direct stake in the community. Elements particular to the composition of the university, such as tenure, allow its members to play a "neutral" role and to participate in innovative activities with community members. Other

social institutions cannot afford to take some of the risks involved in these endeavours.

Ethics and responsibilities: Underlying Values

1 *Holistic analysis*: identifying and filling gaps in the university's current efforts to meet its social responsibilities to its local community. The means of filling these gaps include interdisciplinary research which applies reflexively to whole problems rather than to pieces or symptoms;

2 *Long-term approach*: providing continuity and consistency, with a long-term commitment to continued interaction;

3 *Appropriate and real expertise*: providing a match between that required by the community and that which can be delivered by the university; the value of collaborative research emerges when both partners recognize the legitimacy and limitations of their respective expertise and experience;

4 *Dual accountability*: consultation and agreement on adjustments to projects and programs, directed by the continuous feedback of ongoing evaluation.

APPENDIX 2

The philosophy is one of social development, based upon education as empowerment, on the need for access to the resources of education and the need for positive discrimination to redress long-standing gaps. Increased access to the university and an improved public image are by-products.

Modes of Interaction

1 *Access*: to facilities and other services, including university admission.

2 *Programs*: training, extension, practicum, field experience.

3 *Projects*: social research and other activities using outreach methodologies with social development goals.

Methods: Implementation of Values

Bottom-up rather than top-down methods. Thus, relationships are developed from the base of grass-roots and real involvement, with knowledge from the source contributing to that development.

Evolving methods of identifying issues, programs, and activities. The needs assessment and survey methods of community research usually assess need at a static point in time. The emergence of collaborative relationships requires a longer-term and broader-based assessment, one that depends on the community's knowledge of potential resources and expertise available through the university, rather than on a one-time survey. This long-term methodology also teaches communities how to access appropriate university expertise on their own, and when needed, rather than just on the university's terms or initiative. A further benefit to emerge from this process is a sensitivity, gained by the university and its members, to the range of cultures found within the community.

Partnership relationships. A partnership with community groups and with other institutions working in the area is an effective way of operating, and one that requires mutual understanding, sensitivity, and respect. A partnership relationship also requires each side to follow through with commitments made to the other, and to have some choice on the type of commitments being made and on the individuals who will be involved.

Evaluation. Ongoing evaluation, together with group evaluation, from various bodies in the community and the university will be sought. The York Community Connection provides a consistent monthly check, but an annual review of long-term goals should employ a broader range of relevant people who would assess the merits of potential activities for the future on the basis of need and from the vantage point of reflective evaluation of completed and ongoing activities.

Information flow. Information needs to go out in a number of forms, such as written, oral, and audio-visual, in order to ensure community knowledge and understanding of university resources and the means through which access to them can be secured. Channels for inward information flow need to be developed and sustained. In addition to sharing information, the university must remain accountable to the community with respect to research carried out within the community. Mechanisms for providing feedback on research results must be established and maintained.

NOTES

1 A similar but less forceful position is taken by the president of McMaster University (Lee 1984, 2).

2 A search conference assists organizations to plan with a context of societal trends, desirable futures, and practical choices.

3 "Double loop learning" was a term first introduced by Gregory Bateson as a result of therapeutic work with patients suffering from incapacities in their mental logic or ordering of events. It describes the ability of people to "learn to learn."

REFERENCES

Auger, A., and E.A. Cebotarev. 1981. "Towards an Outreach Service at the University of Guelph." RDOP Executive Group. Position Paper no. 1.

Bok, Derek. 1982. *Beyond the Ivory Tower.* Cambridge, Mass: Harvard University Press.

Cebotarev, E.A., ed. 1983. *Development Praxis.* CRRS Applied Series, University of Guelph.

Clark, Howard. 1984. "Social Issues and the University." *University Affairs.* University and Colleges of Canada.

Coward, Harold G. 1983. "The University and the Community: Partners for the Future." University of Winnipeg, Institute of Urban Studies, *Occasional Papers* no. 3.

Craig, Jack, Gareth Morgan, and David Morley. 1983. *Cooperating with Community Agencies.* Action Learning Seminar volumes 1 and 2. San Francisco: Jossey-Bass.

Crossson, Patricia H. 1983. *Public Service in Higher Education: Practices and Priorities.* Washington, DC: Association for the Study in Higher Education.

Dickson, Alex. 1977. "How Every School and College Can Become a Citizenship Training Centre." *Community Development Journal* 12, no. 1.

Farquhar, Robin H. 1983. "The University of Winnipeg's Role as an Urban University." University of Winnipeg, Institute of Urban Studies, *Occasional Papers* no. 2.

Fuller, Tony. 1983. "What Is University-Community Outreach? Some Types, Prospects and Problems." Unpublished.

– 1984. "Ontario Universities: Options and Futures." In *Report of the Commission on the Future Development of the Universities of Ontario.* Government of Ontario.

Fuller, Tony, and Elspeth Heyworth. 1984. "Social Responsibilities of Universities: Gaps and Potentials for Leadership." Unpublished.

Glaser, Barney, and Anselm Strauss. 1967. *The Discovery of Grounded Theory: Strategies for Qualitative Research.* Chicago: Aldine Publishing Co.

Gollattscheck, James F., Ervin L. Harlacher, et. al. 1976. *College Leadership for Community Renewal: Beyond Community-based Education.* San Francisco: Jossey-Bass.

Hall, Budd, Arthur Gillette, and Tandon Radesh. 1982. *Creating Knowledge: A Monopoly?* New Delhi: International Council for Adult Education, Society for Participatory Research in Asia.

Heyworth, Elspeth, Jackie Wolfe, Tony Fuller, and Walter Schwager. 1984. "Use of Collaborative Research to Address Community Needs." Unpublished.

Lee, Alvin. 1984. "Universities and Society." Speech to the Financial Executives Institute of Canada. Toronto. Unpublished.

Lees, Ray, and George Smith. 1975. *Action-Research in Community Development.* London: Routledge and Kegan Paul.

Mustafa, Kamal, and Yusuf Kassam. 1982. *Participatory Research, an Emerging Alternative Methodology in Social Science Research.* New Delhi: Society for Participatory Research in Asia.

Naisbitt, John. 1984. *Megatrends: Ten Directions Transforming Our Lives.* New York: Warner Books.

Nash, Bernard E. n.d. "The Ethics of the University Engaging in Community Development." In *Background History of the Center for Community Development.* Columbia: University of Missouri.

Schon, Donald. 1983. *The Reflective Practitioner: How Professionals Think in Action.* New York: Basic Books.

Schwager, Walter. 1985. "University Community Outreach: Opportunities and Obligations." Unpublished.

Teather, David C. 1982. *Towards the Community University: Case Studies of Innovation and Community Service.* London: Kegan Paul.

Thomas, Alan M. 1983. "Learning in Society." Ottawa: Canadian Commission for UNESCO. *Occasional Paper* no. 41.

Toffler, Alvin. 1981. *The Third Wave.* London: Pan Books.

Trist, Eric. 1979. "New Directions of Hope: Recent Innovations Interconnecting Organizational, Industrial, Community and Personal Development." Unpublished.

Turner, Francis J. 1983. "The Emerging Role of Regional Universities in Community Service." Conference on Universities and Communities, Laurentian University. Unpublished.

United Nations, Organization for Economic and Cultural Development (OECD). 1982. *The University and the Community.*

Wolfe, Jackie, and Tony Fuller. 1983. "Geography and Community in Collaborative Research: Prospects for Mutual Learning." Sixth Annual Applied Geography Conference, Toronto. Unpublished.

York University. 1977. Commission on Goals and Objectives.

STAN MARSHALL

Developing a Labour Point of View: Advocacy and the Labour Movement

A quick perusal of the literature in work and industry, industrial relations, and labour studies readily confirms that the current trend is towards some form of Quality of Working Life (Cunningham and White 1984; Nightingale 1982) coupled with an appeal for all parties involved – employer, employee, and government – to change radically their attitudes towards collective bargaining. Employers have to become more willing to accept union contributions; employees have to become more cooperative and "confine adversarial tactics"; and the government has to adopt "a more positive attitude toward employers and unions" in order to facilitate trust and harmony between the two (Haythorne 1983, 354).

Industrial conflict introduces a large degree of uncertainty into the managerial task. Where industrial action has been institutionalized through trade unions and dispute resolution mechanisms such as mediation, conciliation, and arbitration, some of the uncertainty can be eliminated or, at the very least, accurately predicted. But illegal strikes, work-to-rule actions, and slow-downs are disruptive tactics which management cannot accurately control or predict. Hence, the recommendations of many management consultants for the cultivation and inculcation of cooperative organizational cultures are increasingly common and attractive to managements (Peters and Waterman 1982). Under such conditions it is hoped that the "problems" of industrial conflict can be avoided.

Nevertheless Quality of Working Life Programs (QWL) are not convincing for unionists, whose guard goes up when "trust" and "cooperation" are proffered by employers.

General Motors wants to cut my pay. That doesn't surprise me. G.M. has always wanted to cut my pay ... Management doesn't talk to workers or care about how its workers feel – until now, that is, when it wants us to sacrifice ... General Motors expects two things of a worker: come to work and do what you are told. Once there was a time when G.M. had customers standing in line and couldn't produce enough cars to satisfy the demand. The profits rolled in, but did the company offer to share them with their workers? Not on your life; ... now [the president of General Motors] comes to me when times are hard and asks for sacrifices, and I say to him, "You should have come a little earlier when times were good and we could have gotten to know each other. If you had, I would be more willing to help. (a G.M. worker as quoted in Douglas, 1982)

The shortage of lockers and wash-up facilities was another matter close to our hearts. There was a notion in the minds of management that sorting was clean work, so postal clerks, with the exception of a few favourites, had to leave their street clothes, hats, overshoes, work jackets, aprons, lunch boxes et cetera on open racks. The borrowing and filching, especially when the armies of Christmas casuals came in, drove people to distraction. The CPEA [Canadian Postal Employees' Association] raised the demand for private lockers repeatedly until supervisor George Morley finally said "o.k., you tell me where we're going to put them". This was what we were waiting for, so we showed him a forgotten space that was perfect for the purpose. Two days later it was filled with letter sorting cases. This was the kind of thing that made postal workers laugh bitterly whenever management talked about the advantages of good faith and consultation. (Davidson and Deverell 1978, 50–1)

The resolution of the "problem," then, is a direct threat to labour organizations qua organizations, and a direct threat to free collective bargaining. Much of the current tensions between labour and QWL research can be traced to this threat of diminished free collective bargaining.

Researchers in other areas of industrial relations and labour studies are also aware of tensions that exists between them and the labour movement. Trade unionists charge that labour researchers both ignore the legitimate concerns of trade unionists and actively direct their research towards aiding *management* policy and practice. Scholarly research is perceived by trade unionists to be a management tool used against unionists in collective bargaining, and in restructuring work relations. Consequently, the relationship between academic researchers and the labour movement is a strained one. Further, unionists charge that labour research is often of an esoteric sort which bears little relation to the practical concerns of unions because it is published in "obscure academic journals." Geoff Bickerton, research officer for the Canadian Union of Postal Workers, admonishes academics for their "virtual failure ... to critically evaluate the direction and practical application of the knowledge that they are producing" (Bickerton n.d., 3).

The impetus for this paper stems largely from a desire to bridge the gap between labour research and practical labour concerns. For this reason it is addressed primarily to the group of social scientists who act in some sense as "advocates" for labour but find their work being criticized as being irrelevant, or even detrimental, to the labour cause. In this essay I hope to show how the development of a Labour Point of View (LPV) is a central first step in breaking down the barriers between academic research and labour practicality. Towards this end four major areas need to be considered.

First, it is necessary to consider the obstacles which keep these two communities at odds. Particular obstacles include the presence of an ideology, an Administrative Point of View (APV), which stresses "management" problem solving and decision making as opposed to "labour" decision making and strategizing. The propensity of many industrial relations researchers to decry industrial conflict as a "social problem" which is to be resolved at any cost is a very real barrier to the formation of an alliance between the academic community and labour.

Second, this paper will consider Bickerton's comment on the direction and practical application of the knowledge labour researchers are producing. More bluntly put, are labour researchers asking questions in which labour might be interested? I shall argue that a critical evaluation of this orientation in the context of advocacy reveals an underlying bias, influenced by the APV. This bias leaves unionists rightly sceptical.

Third, assuming that advocacy is a legitimate role for labour and industrial relations research, how is this to be accomplished? Can the obstacles now separating the academic or researcher and the active trade unionist be overcome in order to forge a new alliance which is mutually alive, rewarding, and satisfying? This task is ultimately the most important one facing the advocate for labour.

Last, many advocates for labour are prone to vanguardist and/or syndicalist tendencies in the sense that they advocate the use of the trade union *as a vehicle* for the achievement of other goals – for example, socialism, equality of the sexes, or equality of races. While these goals in themselves are noble and, indeed, desirable, they become problematic when they are advocated as goals for trade unionists by those who are themselves not part of the labour movement. As such the impetus for social, political, and economic change does not arise from within but is imposed through external change agents who claim a greater expertise and/or vision. I shall argue that the perception of trade unions as the vehicles for *particular political or social* goals produces a situation in which the working class is denied any capability "of comprehending its own experience and leading itself" (Aronowitz 1973, 441).

My thesis therefore is that labour researchers in contemporary capitalism need to develop a new perspective, a Labour Point of View. Developing this LPV needs to be on the agenda of every advocate for the labour movement.

THE ADMINISTRATIVE POINT OF VIEW

Many business schools have been more than happy to pick up the task of teaching issues in the workplace as managerial problems to be solved by managers. This particular perspective is referred to as the Administrative Point of View (APV). At some schools this is a most important part of the business student's socialization into the business community. The University of Western Ontario Business School, a major business school in Canada, states that one of their three objectives is "to help the student acquire an administrative point of view" (University of Western Ontario 1984–5).

The specifics of the APV are quite straightforward. Business schools naturally see their constituency as business and seek no apology for engaging in research which contributes to the abilities of managers. The APV is a perspective which emphasizes "decision making" and "problem solving" for managers. "The successful manager must know people, *must see events in perspective*, must develop flexibility in thinking; in short, he requires a general education" (University of Western Ontario 1984–5, emphasis added). An examination of the course descriptions at this major business school provides an indication of how firmly this perspective is entrenched. Thirty-five of fifty courses descriptions directly mention managerial problem solving, or decision making, as a key feature of the course. In several others this objective is implicit rather than explicit.

At the graduate level the perspective is no less pronounced. Problem solving and decision making are still the primary foci, and the school's attempt to function as an academic arm of support for the business community is made strikingly specific.

The School of Business Administration is known for its practical approach in teaching men and women the skills of management. [Programs are offered to people] who wish to improve their effectiveness as managers. [D]evelopment of behavioral and analytical problem-solving skills is seen as important as the acquisition of knowledge of how a business functions.

The school works closely with the business community. The case writing, research and consulting activities of both doctoral students and faculty ensure that knowledge flows freely from the school to practising managers and from managers to the school. (University of Western Ontario 1978)

It is safe to say that business schools are the "home of the APV" and the instance put forward here represents that perspective.

Nevertheless, managerial orientation in the form of problem-solving is present in more subtle forms in other research on industrial relations. For example, programs such as QWL are designed to deal with *organizational* problems, *managerial* problem solving, and *organizational* decision making. The word "organization" carries no ideological distraction and implies objectivity, favouring neither management nor labour. Indeed, it implies that both management and labour are equal "stakeholders" in the organization (Nightingale 1982).

Much of the Quality of Working Life literature is of this genre, especially that of Eric Trist and the Tavistock Institute, which pioneered the "socio-technical" approach to organizational management. This approach is not as unabashedly managerial in its APV orientation. Its goal is to combat the detrimental effects of the modern industrial workplace through the implementation of innovations which meet both social and technical requirements of the organization (Trist 1984, ix–xiv; 1981). Genuine QWL is to be a "win-win" situation, with management reaping the benefits of increased productivity through a stable labour force, lower absenteeism, and increased worker satisfaction, while workers benefit from a less rigid and repressive workplace.

The issue to be addressed here is not whether QWL works or doesn't work, for there are plenty of examples on both sides, but how QWL is influenced by the APV. I will argue that QWL addresses issues in which management is interested at the expense of issues in which labour is interested for two main reasons.

First, no organization is distinct from the actions and goals of its human participants. We cannot legitimately speak of "organizational responses" or "organizational needs" as distinct from the responses and needs of those who control the processes of the organization. Second, all "stakeholders" in the organization do not have equal power to influence decision making.

In the QWL literature the rhetoric is one of "organization" but the initiatives are ultimately those of management. *Organizations* do not respond to circumstances, but *managements* and *workers* do. The second question raised above then becomes significant. Who in the organization has the power to take initiatives? The answer is that both management and labour can take initiatives, but the nature of the initiative is qualitatively different for each. The initiatives of workers take the form of pressure tactics, but their influence is not sufficient unilaterally to implement organizational change. Labour can only place pressure on management to make organizational changes such as protection in the areas of job security, working conditions, and wages and benefits. Management, on the other hand, *can* make unilateral changes in organizational structure and in the nature of the labour process. In unionized workplaces this does not often occur because of the workers' disruptive potential; nevertheless, no structural change can occur without management agreement.

Clearly, the power of the "stakeholders" is by no means equal, yet QWL proponents seem not to be aware of this power differential. To acknowledge its existence places the entire ideal of QWL cooperation in doubt.

Although the expressed commitment is to QWL as a *program*, the technique of implementing QWL reveals a presence of the APV. Don Wells (1982), in an evaluation of two plants using a form of QWL, notes that in each case the first phases introduced employees to *problem-solving* techniques. In one plant this was referred to as "Corporate Decision-Making" (CDM) and was designed to teach workers "how to choose production-related problems from their own work environment" (Wells 1983, 92).

QWL consultants conducted seminars in order to familiarize workers to CDM "in a way designed to do '*a lot of climate setting*', as one plant executive described it" (Wells 1983, 94, emphasis added). Problem-solving and associated decision-making techniques were being presented and taught to workers in a way in which workers were "to internalize criteria of decision-making which were consistent with management's overall productivity goals" (Wells 1983, 37). An internal management memo makes this technique and goal explicit: "Our specific goal was to build business teams trained in both behavioral and technical aspects of problem-solving to deal with those issues that were inhibiting business success" (as cited in Wells 1983, 139).

If one compares these techniques and mandates to those of the APV stated by the Business School at the University of Western Ontario, the similarity is striking. The APV appears to be alive and well in QWL programs. Cooperative decision making does occur, but within a very limited predetermined range of production-related problems.

A critical look at sympathetic evaluations of contemporary QWL successes and failures does nothing to dispel this contention. The evaluations most often consider such outcomes as individual motivation, turnover patterns, teamwork, economic performance. Their hope is that future results on profit performance, cost improvements, new business developments and readiness, and creative-innovative climates will be forthcoming as the project progresses (Ondrack and Evans 1984, 127–32).

The evaluation from a union perspective usually is incorporated in the discussion of union-management relations or the structure and degree of union participation in decision making. In some cases organizational design issues are paramount (Dresner and Younger, 1984; Adams and Kyle 1984), and in all cases the commitment to QWL as a long-term project rather than a "quick-fix" solution is stressed. What is absent is any analysis of the impact of QWL on the work force directly. What changes affected the workers the most or the least? Resolution of concerns and problems expressed by the workers, the impact of QWL on group cohesiveness or worker solidarity, and the impact on workers' abilities to influence the decision-making process either individually or collectively are also not analysed. What was the impact on union structure? How did the role of shop stewards change under QWL? These are questions not asked because the APV limits evaluation to outcomes of managerial concern. Such outcomes may or may not be consistent with "progress" for workers, but if the necessary questions were not even asked it is necessary to develop an alternative perspective. What follows are some thoughts on developing such an alternative, a Labour Point of View.

DEVELOPING A LABOUR POINT OF VIEW

Much of the previous section of this paper may sound like an apologia for the selling out of the sympathetic faction of the academic community. It is not. It is merely intended to denote the kinds of pressures on industrial relations researchers, the subtle influence of ideology in the selection of research matter, and the strength of the managerial orientation (APV) in that ideology. Despite these pressures, there is a body of literature which is highly critical of corporate research on "managing" workers. Rinehart's (1984) study of employee participation groups at a General Motors plant and Swartz's (1981) discourse on types of workers' participation are particularly good examples. These outline the implications of cooperative programs for labour. Rosen (1983, 373) observes that workers themselves still remain highly sceptical in as much as "their future is too risky and vulnerable to trust even good-faith management proposals or plans that are not validated by experience."

Both unionists and progressive academics seem to agree that some sort of alliance, a working relationship between academic researchers and trade unionists, is desirable in order for labour to be effective in both its immediate and long-term interests.

Research should be viewed as a necessary element in the process which enables workers to understand their struggles in a broader context. In a very real sense, information is ammunition necessary to help workers counteract the massive and pervasive "corporate world-view" embraced by virtually all of society's agencies of socialization. (Bickerton n.d., 5)

... labour generally lacks both the internal analytic capability of charting and assessing economic-policy choices, and the access to skills and insights of the larger community of progressive scholars and analysts. The contrast is striking between this state of affairs and the well-endowed, well-developed centres of policy analysis that now serve the conservative and corporate communities. To correct this imbalance will require a commitment of resources and a development of a dialogue, between labour leaders and the academic and scholarly community, that has not been made. (Rosen 1983, 376)

This call for alliances of progressive groups critical of the existing set of power relations is not an unusual one. It has been made many times (Bickerton n.d.; Johnston 1978; Deaton 1972). Of course, the most pressing question is how these academics, sympathetic to the labour cause, can forge a working alliance with labour.

It is often assumed that an alliance means a *direct* role for each of these groups in each other's immediate struggles – i.e. some attempt at formal and internally coordinated decision making, strategy planning, and action. Convergence of diverse groups (environmental, minority rights, consumer rights, civil liberties, disarmament, feminism, labour, etc.) does occur occasionally but is generally short-lived. Rather than waiting for an alliance which will produce one cataclysmic event to end inequalities and injustice, it seems a far better strategy to develop parallel attacks which can be mutually supportive. Through such parallel development, relevant information can be readily shared and utilized to the extent that each group is equipped to do so. This calls for a qualitatively different approach to the formation of alliances.

I would like to take labour research and its potential for empowering the labour movement as a case in point. Even though progressive academic researchers of labour issues have neither the credentials for leading labour nor the mandate to do so, it is left to them to form a parallel community which can contribute expertise in the form of ideas and analysis. We have to assume that labour is interested enough in developing their own internal capabilities to such a degree that they can take those ideas, analyses, and information and use them to their own best advantage. Without these parallel developments in labour, obstacles between labour and academia will remain intact and hostilities will persist.

The development of a parallel support network for labour can begin on a number of fronts. Advocacy can be maintained in the form of critical analyses of labour issues and labour relations that result in ideas and information generated for the consumption of unions. Advocacy in this form does not mean directives, or even recommendations, to labour, but a partnership in a common view of social, economic, and political relations.[1]

Information generated through research, conducted with the LPV in mind, can be very useful in the empowering of union officials and workers alike. Labour history and social history can contribute to workers' awareness of their own biographies and of the continuing struggles of their class. Political economic analysis can provide frameworks for understanding how and why existing power relations are as they are. Industrial relations research can offer an analysis of current legislative and collective bargaining issues and procedures. Sociological research into such areas as attitudes of the general public to unions and unionism can potentially provide unionists with information vital to their policy making and their public relations programs. This is essential to give unions as large a base of public support as possible.

The LPV recognizes the adversarial nature of labour's past struggles. Attempts to rid our industrial relations system of conflict have the consequence of threatening the rights of workers and their organizations. Conflict in our society is not an unnecessary evil perpetuated solely by the intransigence of greedy, militant unions. Conflict is not a social problem to be resolved, but an indicator of much deeper social, political, and economic ills. It is not the conflict *per se* which needs to be investigated and treated, but the underlying conditions in which such conflict flourishes.

Similarly, the LPV means resisting the temptation to support programs such as QWL when its rhetoric of "trust," "cooperation," and "participation" is used to equalize the power structure in the capitalist workplace. Working-class experience indicates that such an equality is not possible within the present set of power relations. Thus researchers must be aware of the history of conflict in labour-management relations and must be prepared to recognize the centrality of such conflict – for without it we deny the working class their only resource in political and economic matters.

USING APV TO STRENGTHEN LPV

There are few current examples of the LPV; it is not a well-developed or firmly established perspective in labour research. Ironically, the relationship between business researchers and the business community through the APV provides some insights into how labour researchers can establish a successful relationship with labour. In this section, two specific examples of LVP research will be considered. In the last section I will consider several concrete recommendations as to the necessary relationship between LPV and practical labour concerns. Both sections exemplify the basis for successful advocacy.

Wells's (1983) evaluation of QWL and its associated processes is an excellent example of research encompassing an LPV. It was carried out with the active involvement of workers, including their consultation on the design of the questionnaires. Wells has formulated his research report so that it can be used for union education purposes. He even offers an outline for educational sessions to be conducted *by* unionists. In a letter introducing the case studies Wells states his intentions openly: "This report is intended to help you and other unionists deal with Quality of Working Life (QWL) proposals or changes in the workplace. The emphasis is on the development of practical and realistic union responses." More specifically, his intentions are to evaluate the impact of QWL; to consider the connection between QWL and other related changes in the workplace; to consider the implications of QWL for the balance of power in the workplace; and to assess how unionists may respond in their own best interests (Wells 1983, 6–7). These are the very questions not addressed in other evaluations of QWL as typified in Cunningham and White (1984).

Some of the findings reported by Wells are instructive. Workgroup cohesion was high *within* workgroups using QWL but cohesion *between* workgroups was low in both of the plants under study (Wells 1983, 48–56, 124–9). The significance of these findings is not readily apparent without some interpretation. As long as the objective is cooperation, the outcome of increased cohesion would be a desirable one from an administrative point of view. As Wells suggests, "increasing workgroup cohesion becomes a management objective, part of the enhancement of workgroup identity in pursuit of common goals with management" (1983, 56). However, in situations where conflict between labour and management exists, increased work-group cohesion means "an increase in mutual support and protection [for labour] against management" (1983, 56).

As long as cooperation is a common goal for both groups then cohesion as an outcome of QWL presents no problem. Indeed it may be beneficial for the formation of resistance to management intransigence should it arise at workgroup level. However, there is a downside for labour. The QWL process is usually implemented in phases, with only a few workgroups participating initially and often with a slightly different focus for each group. This uneven implementation and application of QWL has an outcome of low cohesion *between* workgroups and reduces future "plant-wide solidarity ... the cohesion of workgroups in opposition to management" (Wells 1983, 56).

Wells also found that the structure of union representation and collective bargaining would be altered under QWL. Some of the functions performed by the union would be performed within the corresponding QWL structure. This structure now becomes the site for the resolution of workers' complaints and grievances which normally would be resolved through the negotiated grievance procedure. The shop steward system in many unions is a strong one because of stewards' central role in the settlement of these disputes. In QWL, rather than representing workers in the grievance process, stewards increasingly are thrust into the role of disciplining workers who do not conform to QWL goals (Wells 1983, 85). Union officials and leaders, often criticized as performing the contradictory functions of representation and management control agents (Rinehart 1975, 153), increasingly are placed in the position of controlling behaviour.

The nature of decision making in QWL situations is ideally made bilaterally, but Wells found that genuine participation was not evident. Under QWL, workers gained some participation in "specific low-level issues mainly concerning the way workers are motivated to perform their jobs." Major decisions "concerning investment, finance, product design, research planning, and marketing strategies" – all with a significant impact on workers' lives – still remained firmly as management's prerogatives (Wells 1983, 83). Even the implementation of QWL was firmly under management control in conjunction with their consultants. Management controlled the "climate-setting" and the nature of problem solving, the pace of diffusion of QWL throughout the plant, and the composition of the membership of the workgroups selected for QWL (Wells 1983, 144–5).

Studies such as Wells's break through the rhetoric of the APV and give workers an indication of what changes they can realistically expect to encounter so they can gauge their own responses accordingly. In considering the implications of his findings for labour, Wells has offered a number of suggestions for the direction which labour responses may take.

Unions may need to adopt a public relations response to the overtures of QWL in as much as QWL places considerable responsibility for the current "hard times" on workers' lack of productivity and militancy.

... the implication [is] that hard times are essentially a problem of labour relations. This is likely to reinforce the public's penchant for scapegoating workers and unions. At the same time, it places unionists in a bind: unionists who support QWL may be seen as tacitly admitting that the implications about workers are true, while those who oppose QWL are likely to be seen as reactionary. The name alone – "quality of working life" – makes it sound as if unionists would be insane to turn down this new nirvana of work. (Wells 1983, 156)

Regardless of whether unionists accept or reject QWL, they had better prepare both themselves and the general public for the type of problems QWL is designed to solve and for the likely outcomes.

In order to prevent the complete undermining of union functions, unions need to expend considerable resources on promoting unity *among* union leaders, and *between* the leadership and the rank and file (Wells 1983, 156). In this way QWL is less likely to supplant the collective agreement and the union's representation function. Such action may inhibit a potentially divisive situation within unions, and solidarity is less likely to be replaced by a structure with few negotiated guarantees. The dangers associated with low cohesion between workgroups can be alleviated by ensuring that the union retains a strong representation function.

The significance of Wells's study lies in its analysis of the implications of QWL for a key feature of union success – solidarity. Unionists need to have this type of information in order to enter into discussions of QWL, with well-thought-out positions regarding its impact on labour relations.

THE LPV IN ACTION

Lessons learned from the business schools and the APV are also instructive in providing a description of practical techniques which may serve to bridge the gap between academic research and labour. All the tehniques listed below have been followed with some success by business researchers in bridging the gap between APV and the business community.

1 Pursue parallel publishing streams. Theoretical and empirical work can be written for the consumption of both scholars and practitioners. Business academics often publish in scholarly journals such as the *Journal of Industrial Relations* or the *Journal of Marketing Research* with a second version written for the consumption of managers through such vehicles as the *Harvard Business Review*, the *California Business Review*, the *Sloan Management Review*, or the *Business Quarterly*. The information is presented in a less academic format, pointing out the relevance for practitioners. To some extent this parallel publishing approach is carried out in other areas of sociology – e.g., in either the *Family Coordinator* or the *Journal of Marriage and the Family* depending upon the target audience. In the area of industrial relations such a strategy is less in evidence, although Panitch and Swartz (1983) published abridged versions of their work "on permanent exceptionalism" in the *CAUT Bulletin* and in *Labour Files* (both practitioner-oriented) as well as in *Labour/Le Travail* and in Thompson and Swimmer (1984). Sass (1977; 1979; 1980a; 1980b) has also provided both a scholarly version and a lay version of his work on the politics of occupational health and safety.

2 Employ more case studies of real-life situations facing trade unionists. Case writing in business schools serves the purpose of educating students about the necessity for developing skills in decision making and problem solving. Cases with an LPV would serve to educate students about the issues and problems facing unionists in decision making. The idea here is to let students know that the case is not just theory but an actual situation which a union or group of unions has faced. The task for the student is to assume a labour point of view and to analyse the factors in order to make a decision best serving the interests of the workers involved. In this way the student must at least recognize the labour perspective.

Cooperation from trade unions is essential in case writing. They must be willing to provide information so that the case can be written in a manner which accurately portrays the problem. The union would be offered the opportunity to read the case and the accompanying note on teaching method. The union would have the option of not releasing the case should it not accurately reflect the real-life situation.

3 Programs for workers and unionists must be established at universities. These programs may be credit or non-credit, but in either case the mandate must be to help unionists do their job more effectively. Summer or evening courses could be established to ac-

quaint unionists with the latest trends, theories, research, and techniques in labour relations. Cooperation with unions could result in unionists receiving educational leave to pursue such studies on an accredited basis. Universities are already engaged in a cooperative effort with corporations to provide what may be called an "executive MBA." Programs of this sort are offered at Concordia University, the University of Toronto, York University, and Simon Fraser. A labour parallel would benefit both universities and labour unions.[2]

4 Research associated with such programs as outlined above should have as its mandate the improvement of labour representation of its membership. Research grants solicited from labour should be clearly demarcated to meet this objective. Funds donated by labour should be administered by a board with seats allocated to representatives from labour. In this way labour has some control over "tied" funding, fostering a cooperation between researchers and labour in the pursuit of a common mandate.

5 Credit within the university needs to be given to researchers doing work within the labour community. Many business schools give some recognition to faculty members who consult for business or sit on boards of directors. The magnitude of this credit may be variable. It is not necessary to weight it equally with scholarly publishing or teaching. However, in business it is encouraged because it represents some direct contact with the constituency it seeks to serve. In sociology contact with the labour community should be encouraged in a similar fashion; i.e., it should be considered a *merit* and not a *demerit* as it may be by those who assume that sociology should be value-free.

CONCLUSION

The above are all policies for developing an LPV and, in turn, are policies for the mutual reinforcement of an established LPV. In the preceding pages I have attempted to isolate several key obstacles to the development of an alliance between researchers, academia, and labour. The APV and its prevalence in mainstream industrial relations research has been examined in its role as an orientation which is both overtly and covertly supportive of managerial goals. In order for labour to be represented adequately in their relations with management, an LPV must be adopted by labour advocates. It is only through the LPV that we can ask and answer questions of relevance to the labour movement. In particular it represents the only way academics can even hope to approach the labour movement on a common ground.

NOTES

1 Within the academic community, we must be aware that attacks on progressive academics are still possible under conditions of academic freedom. Tenure is one of the privileges of academic life which makes
advocacy and critical analysis possible, though it is often under attack
(Bercuson et al. 1984; Matas 1984). Researchers of unpopular ideas and
political issues can find themselves compromised by the threat of dis-
missal if the ideological component of their research does not meet the
criterion of transparency.

2 A second example of the LPV in action is provided by the Labour College
of Canada. This college, co-sponsored by the Canadian Labour Congress, McGill University, and the University of Montreal, is
housed at the University of Ottawa and provides an academic arm for
the labour movement. It does not offer university credit courses but
does provide trade unionists with an academic-style educational program. Its objective is "to develop leadership by increasing the ability of
unionists to understand, analyze and deal with the problems and issues
confronting them in the workplace, in their unions and in the community" (Labour College of Canada). It provides courses in economics,
labour law, political science, industrial sociology, and labour history. The
courses are designed with an LPV and foster a greater commitment to
the labour movement. Instructors are recruited primarily from academia
throughout Canada. Such a college represents a partial counterpart to
the business schools and their associated APV, albeit on a much smaller
scale with far fewer resources.

REFERENCES

Adams, Don, and Dean Kyle. 1984. "A Program for Organization and Job
Redesign." In J.B. Cunningham and T.H. White, eds., *Quality of Working
Life: Contemporary Cases*, 203–30. Labour Canada.

Aronowitz, Stanley. 1973. *False Promises*. New York: McGraw-Hill.

Bercuson, David J., Robert Bothwell, and J.L. Gratanstein. 1984. *The Great
Brain Robbery*. Toronto: McClelland and Stewart.

Berger, Peter L., and Hansfried Kellner. 1981. *Sociology Reinterpreted: An
Essay on Method and Vocation*. Garden City, New York: Anchor Books.

Bickerton, Geoff. n.d. "The Role of Industrial Relations Research." *Labour
Files* 1, no. 1:3–5.

Christensen, Sandra. 1980. *Unions and the Public Interest*. Vancouver: Fraser
Institute.

Cunningham, J.B., and T.H. White. 1984. *Quality of Working Life: Contemporary Cases*. Ottawa: Labour Canada.

Davidson, Joe, and John Deverell. 1978. *Joe Davidson*. Toronto: James Lorimer and Company.

Deaton, Rick. 1972. "The Fiscal Crisis and the Public Employee." *Our Generation* 8, no. 4 11–51.

Douglas, Martin. 1982. "GM versus Its Workers." *New York Times*, 15 February 1982.

Dresner, Barbara, and Jonathan C. Younger. 1984. "Designing Everdell." In J.B. Cunningham and T.H. White, eds., *Quality of Working Life: Contemporary Cases*, 77–105. Ottawa: Labour Canada.

Haythorne, George Vickers. 1983. "Canada: Industrial Relations – Internal and External Pressures." In Solomon Barkin, ed., *Worker Militancy and Its Consequences*, 325–57. 2nd edition. New York: Praeger Publishers.

Johnston, Paul. 1978. "The Promise of Public Sector Unionism." *Monthly Review* 30, no. 4: 1–17.

Labour College of Canada. 1985. *1985 Residential Program*. Ottawa.

Marchak, M. Patricia. 1981. *Ideological Perspectives on Canada*. 2nd edition. Toronto: McGraw-Hill Ryerson.

Matas, Robert. 1984. "University Deans Stunned by Attack of Bank Executive." *Globe and Mail* 16 October 1984:1–2.

Mills, C. Wright. 1959. *The Sociological Imagination*. New York: Oxford University Press.

Nettler, Gwynn. 1980. "Sociologist as Advocate." *Canadian Journal of Sociology* 5, no. 1:31–53.

Nicolaus, Martin. 1972. "The Professional Organization of Sociology: A View from Below." In Robin Blackburn, ed., *Ideology in Social Science*, 45–60. Fontana.

Nightingale, Donald V. 1982. *Workplace Democracy*. Toronto: University of Toronto Press.

Ondrack, D.A., and Martin Evans. 1984. "QWL at Petrosar: A Case Study of a Greenfield Site." In J.B. Cunningham and T.H. White, eds., *Quality of Working Life: Contemporary Cases*, 107–36. Ottawa: Labour Canada.

Panitch, Leo, and Donald Swartz. 1983. "The Economic Crisis and the Transformation of Industrial Relations in Canada." *CAUT Bulletin*, December 1983:21–5.

– 1984a. "Towards Permanent Exceptionalism: Coercion and Consent in Canadian Industrial Relations." *Labour/Le Travail* 13:133–57.

– 1984b. "From Free Collective Bargaining to Permanent Exceptionalism: The Economic Crisis and the Transformation of Industrial Relations in Canada." In Mark Thompson and Gene Swimmer, eds., *Conflict or Compromise: The Future of Public Sector Industrial Relations*, 403–35. Ottawa: Institute for Research on Public Policy.

– n.d. "From Free Collective Bargaining to Permanent Exceptionalism." *Labour Files* 2, no. 1:3–14.

Peters, Thomas J., and Robert Waterman, Jr. 1982. *In Search of Excellence*. New York: Warner Books.

Reasons, Charles E., and Williams D. Perdue. 1981. *The Ideology of Social Problems*. Sherman Oaks, Calif.: Alfred Publishing Co.

Rinehart, James. 1975. *The Tyranny of Work*. Don Mills, Ont.: Academic Press 1975.

– 1984. "Appropriating Workers' Knowledge: Quality Control Circles at a General Motors Plant." *Studies in Political Economy* no. 13:75–97.

Rosen, Sumner M. 1983. "The United States: American Industrial Relations System in Jeopardy." In Solomon Barkin, ed., *Worker Militancy and Its Consequences*, 359–77. 2nd ed. New York: Praeger Publishers.

Rudolf, Frederick. 1965. *The American College and University: A History*. New York: Vintage.

Sass, Robert. 1977. "Occupational Health and Safety: Contradictions and the Conventional Wisdom." *Labour Gazette*:157–61.

– 1979. "The Underdevelopment of Occupational Health and Safety in Canada." In Wm. Leiss, ed., *Ecology Versus Politics in Canada*, 72–96. Toronto: University of Toronto Press.

Sass, Robert. 1980a. "Work at the Centre." *Canadian Dimension* 14, no. 17:27–30.

– 1980b. "Stress the Tolerated Bedfellow." *Canadian Dimension* 14, no. 17:30–33.

Swartz, Donald. 1981. "New Forms of Worker Participation." *Studies in Political Economy*, Spring:55–78.

Tagliacozzo, D.L., and Joel Seidman. 1967. "Rank and File Union Members." In E.W. Bakke *et al.*, eds., Unions, *Management and the Public*, 162–7. New York: Harcourt, Brace and World.

Thompson, Mark, and Gene Swimmer, eds. 1984. *Conflict or Compromise: The Future of Public Sector Industrial Relations*. Institute for Research on Public Policy.

Trist, Eric. 1981. *The Evolution of Sociotechnical Systems: A Conceptual Framework and an Action Research Program*. Toronto: Ontario Quality of Working Life Occasional Paper no. 2, 1981.

– 1984. Preface to J.B. Cunningham and T.H. White, eds., *Quality of Working Life: Contemporary Cases*. Ottawa: Labour Canada.

University of Western Ontario. 1978. *The Ph.D. Program at Western's Business School*.

– 1984–5. *Calendar*.

Wells, D.M. 1983. *Unionists and "Quality of Working Life" Programmes*. Toronto: Humber College Centre for Labour Studies.

D O N   D I P P O

Critical Pedagogy and Education for Work

Educators who take account of theories of reproduction and resistance have criticized both the form and content of a wide variety of curriculum materials on the grounds (a) that they serve to legitimize and reproduce dominant ideologies (Anyon 1979; Osbourne 1980; Taxel 1979), and (b), that they do not lend themselves to methods of inquiry which encourage either dialogue or debate (Giroux 1982).

As I shall demonstrate, conventional approaches to career education based on "talent-matching" provide yet another example of a politically inappropriate and pedagogically inadequate curricular form. For those of us concerned with the provision of a more critical kind of work educaton, the problem becomes one of moving beyond critique to formulating alternatives to current pedagogical practices and producing resource materials which would support such an approach. What we want to encourage are school programs that promote the development of those analytical skills and technical competencies which help students gain some measure of control as they enter into and participate in the social relations of the economy.

In this regard, John Dewey provides a useful starting point. As early as 1916 he wrote:

Any scheme for vocational education which takes its point of departure from the industrial regime that now exists, is likely to assume and to perpetuate its divisions and weaknesses, and thus become an instrument in accomplishing the feudal dogma of social predestination ... But an education which acknowledges the full intellectual and social meaning of a vocation would include instructions in the historic background of present conditional training in science to give intelligence and initiative in dealing with material and agencies of production; and study of economics, civics, and politics to bring the future worker into touch with the problems of the day and the various methods proposed for its improvement. (Dewey 1966, 318–19; see also Braverman 1974, 445–6; Browne 1981, 453; Gorz 1972, 487–9)

The development of a strategy for the production and use of work education materials which speak to this possibility is the central concern of this article. I will not, however, be proposing a particular course of study in the form of curriculum guidelines, nor will I provide specific lesson plans. Rather, I will begin with a critique of technocratic rationality, dominant in existing forms of "career development." Next, I will formulate an alternative rationality from which to develop curriculum materials and teaching strategies which might serve pedagogical rather than administrative interests. The formulation of such an alternative is an essential prerequisite to the actual development of materials and teaching/learning strategies.

A rationality appropriate to such a pedagogical intent would be one based on the social and political organization of knowledge whereby *knowledge* is recognized as a social product and *knowing* as a social process. Within such a view knowledge is never neutral and all claims to knowledge are seen to carry political commitments which have historical grounds and practical implications. This rationality seeks to uncover interests embedded in taken-for-granted ways of thinking, in this case thinking about work. It is in this sense that the rationality is "critical."

Critical rationality proposes social transformation, and social transformation is not an objective one would expect to find in curriculum guidelines or lesson-plan books. Indeed, it is reasonable to ask who would be able to take materials and curricular aims based on notios of social transformation and put them to use in a classroom? (See Simon 1983; Simon and Dippo 1987.) The view of sceptics (to say nothing of publishers) is surely that "Teachers only want lesson recipes in cookbooks." Yet work with teachers using our materials in cooperative education in Ontario tells us quite clearly that the sceptics are wrong. Teachers don't want cookbooks in work education. What they do want are suggestions that deal with real teaching/learning concerns of practical and theoretical importance. This leads to my third argument. While social transformation is rarely an explicit aim of teachers' everyday classroom practice, a deep-seated concern with providing "good education," and a genuine interest in working for students in producing "really useful" knowledges (Waugh 1982), skills, and abilities, provides the grounds and possibility for the development of a critical pedagogy of work education. As advocates,

our task has been to provide continuing support for critically oriented, experientially based programs of work education, and to continue developing resource materials which expand the educational
potential of this alternative approach.

"CHOOSING" A CAREER

Since the beginnings of the economic crisis in the early 1980s, suc-
cessive federal governments have announced "new" job-creation and
job-training programs directed at youth employment. At times these
have been "stand alone" efforts like the billion-dollar "First Chance"
program, intended to provide work experiences for up to one
hundred thousand unemployed youths a year. At other times youth
training and employment programs have been put forward as a part
of more comprehensive employment initiatives, as Job Entry and
Community Futures are part of the Canadian Jobs Strategy.

Less spectacular perhaps, but certainly more significant in terms
of numbers of people affected, have been federal initiatives to combat unemployment through "career development." Since its incep-
tion in 1977, the Department of Employment and Immigration has
been a primary source of career development programs and materials aimed at helping people "choose suitable careers." These programs and materials are used by counsellors at Canada Employment
Centres and have wide currency within both secondary school guidance departments and non-profit counselling centres. Looking over
these materials, one is struck by the variety of forms and packages
that they take: straightforward textual presentations, kits and resource boxes, filmstrips and games, videotape banks and on-line
computerized guidance programs. Yet close inspection reveals a
striking uniformity of approach: career guidance is based on the
assumption that "choosing a career" is the best way of expressing –
and indeed understanding – the relationship between people and
the work that they do. "Choosing" is the common organizing principle used to help students establish themselves in the work force.
And the process of "choosing" has been uniformly organized into a
procedure of "talent-matching." Quoting from one of the counsellors' guides: "The Index to Canadian Occupations and the Occupational Exploration Questionnaire are designed to help clients to
explore the world of work and choose career goals. Users can find
suitable careers by choosing characteristics that they feel describe
them or the kind of work they want. Occupations that fit several
(but not necessarily all) of a user's chosen characteristics probably
best suit that person's career needs" (Canada 1979, 1)

Generally this talent-matching procedure involves four steps:

In step one users rate themselves on standardized scales of interests, temperaments, abilities, physical activities, environmental conditions, education and training routes in order to produce a "personal qualifications" profile.

In step two users find occupations that fit their qualification profiles. This is done manually, mechanically, or through electronic search of a list of occupations drawn from the Canadian Classification and Dictionary of Occupations (CCDO). The CCDO, is coded so that each occupation is profiled in terms of the six characteristics specified in step one, i.e. interests, temperaments, abilities, physical activities, environmental conditions, and education and training.

In step three users narrow down their choices by selecting from the list of potential careers those occupations which they feel provide the besst fit for both their personal qualifications and specific job requirements.

Finally, in step four, users refer to a set of support documents that provide more information on such things as qualifications, job prospects, earnings for the occupation(s) that they have chosen.

The materials produced by the Department of Employment and Immigration exemplify a logic and a set of underlying assumptions which are built into the overwhelming majority of career development programs. Foremost among these is the principle of commodification, aimed at enhancing students' saleability by transforming them into marketable goods. This principle affirms that the "marketplace" metaphor is sufficient for understanding, and that labour "market mechanisms" are capable of resolving, the problem of youth unemployment. So the materials are designed to maximize exchange opportunities for students by packaging them – or helping them package themselves – in such a way that their "ingredients" enable them both to negotiate entry into the labour market and also participate in exchange relations. In turn, "salebility" provides the key rationale for the unemployed youth's understanding of himself or herself in relation to commodified forms and exchange relations.

"SALEABILITY" AND POSSESSIVE INDIVIDUALISM

The commodification of student labour presupposes other related characteristics to which students must conform. These are encapsulated in the concept of "possessive individualism" (MacPherson 1962; 247–74). For example, students are encouraged to construct commodified forms of identity based upon the possession of certain standardized – and, by implication, socially recognized and valued

– technical skills and personality traits. To enhance the saleability of themselves as commodities, students must either accumulate more "skills" or find a way of repackaging those they already possess. Second, as Offe and Ronge have said, students are expected to accept the legitimacy of "whatever material outcome emerges from their particular exchange relationships – this is especially true if this outcome is unfavorable to them. Such outcomes must, in other words, be attributed to either natural events or to the virtues and failures of the individual" (Offe and Ronge 1981, 84).

As a way of producing and organizing knowledge, talent matching is not a neutral process. Its categories and procedures express a particular structure of relevance and formulate a specific kind of "knowing" – a knowing that takes for granted abstract and categorical definitions of personal qualifications and job requirements. I will argue that the interest served by these materials is primarily, though not exclusively, an administrative interest in managing the labour force efficiently.

The process of allocating people to jobs is not new, but it becomes a special problem under certain economic circumstances: placing people with no prior work history into a wartime economy; reintegrating demobilized soldiers into a peacetime economy; or, as in this case, placing workers in a work force where skills have become redundant in the wake of technological change (Smith 1978). The concepts and procedures used in talent matching originate in the work of occupational analysts who, for most of this century, have been seeking to improve the efficiency of labour market mechanisms by accurately describing and classifying jobs and the "traits" that are required to do them. The very categories employed in the talent-matching procedures (interests, temperaments, abilities, etc.) are those which serve this administrative interest. They are not organized in ways relevant to those who seek knowledge of themselves and of the work world – ways which would enable them to make viable job-related decisions. Matching people and jobs requires an analytically compatible system of describing and classifying "workers" and "work." Standardized categories and descriptors are therefore essential for smooth and efficient operation. Of crucial importance is the identification of abstract and generalizable "worker functions" that can be reformulated as "qualifications" when describing workers, and as "requirements" when describing work. The standardized category scheme also provides commensurability between kinds of jobs in differing sectors of the economy. By creating relations of equivalence among and between occupations, the transferability of workers is enhanced and the problem of matching them to jobs is considerably reduced.

TECHNOCRATIC RATIONALITY AND THE CCDO

The form of rationality embedded in job descriptions derived from the CCDO is one intended to facilitate the efficient functioning of the labour market. It is one designed to produce what labour economists often term "elasticities of substitutions" among various occupations. The "facts of work" generated from within the job descriptions of the CCDO facilitate this process. In addition, career development materials which rely on these job descriptions provide a way of understanding the work world that supports processes of rationalization of production, job disaggregation, and the general de-skilling of labour in the service of flexibility and elasticity of substitution. By restricting what counts as "knowledge of work" to standardized job requirement profiles, these materials ignore fundamental worker concerns related to the terms and conditions of employment. They suppress the recognition that the workplace itself is a "contested terrain" (Edwards 1979) defined by human activity and struggle.

As a way of representing lived social relations, job descriptions such as those contained in the CCDO are woefully inadequate. The abstract categorizations that organize those descriptions are themselves products of ideological processes that sever the relation between such knowledge forms and the practical activities and lived social relations out of which they arise (Smith 1983). These categorizations, however, do more than determine how knowledge of the work world will be organized. They define the parameters and determine the procedures whereby self-knowledge will be produced. These materials are intended to help students produce profiles of personal qualifications that correspond to a set of abstract categories called "job requirements." The materials provide an interpretative frame, organized to serve an allocation process through which students come to know themselves, and to define themselves by appropriating to themselves characteristics that facilitate the matching procedure. They propose a fragmented version of self, unrelated to a social or material context except as a composite commodity.

The categories and procedures employed entail a reorganization from what students already know about themselves and the world into an objectified form of technical "knowledge." In the process, the social context which grounded the students' original self-knowledge is obliterated. All that was local, particular, and individual is lost as the student is reconstituted as an abstraction; as an object alien to him/herself. This reorganization is, in effect, disorganization, because it severs the relation between self-knowledge and the social-experiential world within which one is situated and on which one's knowledge is predicated. Rather than help students understand the social relations and institutions which are their social context, the concepts and procedures of these materials reproduce and legitimate the dominant metaphor of "self-as-commodity."

As a method of knowing, talent matching does more than propose a systematic way of describing the work world and discovering the marketable self. Its categories and procedures also serve to organize the way students think about the relation between themselves and the work world. If the work world is defined as a vast assortment of occupations each having fixed and specified requiremetns for adequate job performance, and if people are defined as either "having" or actually "being" a composite of certain fixed and specifiable characteristics which constitute their knowledge, skills, and experience, then the problem of choosing a career is simply a matter of "fitting in" and knowing how to "sell yourself."

So a technocratic form of rationality produces the objectified "facts of work" which an allegedly neutral matching procedure then transforms into allocations and placements. The methods used for such a transformation are patterned after those in the natural sciences. They produce a form of knowledge which is abstract and general and which ignores all that is not quantifiable and measurable. This knowledge is taken to be objective and neutral, although the very categories and concepts used serve the commodification rationale behind processes of allocation and placement.

In addition, "fitting in" legitimates a host of inequalities structured into contemporary Canadian society by presenting the work world "as it exists" as if somehow it is "as required." To "fit in" to an occupation, in other words, requires matching the profiles of job incumbents. For women seeking entry into non-traditional occupations, or ethnic groups trying to escape job ghettos, the implications are clear – to fit in, become who you aren't or try to package yourself as one of them! Selling yourself, as well, serves to reproduce possessive individualism as the taken-for-granted form of consciousness among students entering the labour force. As Apple has noted: "Hegemony operates in large part through the control of meaning, through the manipulation of the very categories and modes of thinking we commonsensically employ" (Apple 1979, 154). In this sense the technocratic rational is hegemonic, since it contributes to dominant modes of thinking about people and work, and also serves dominant interests in society. The efficient functioning of "labour market mechanisms" is facilitated when "elasticity of substitution" comes to be understood as a saleable personality trait – "flexibility." The legitimacy of using the CCDO and curricular materials based upon it clearly rests on the assumption that schools best serve the needs of students by making sure that students serve the "needs" of the economy.

CRITICAL PEDAGOGY

Work education materials designed to serve pedagogical interests based on critical forms of rationality articulate an orientation to work which contrasts sharply with the "fitting in" formulation embedded in talent-matching materials. First, the work world, though preexisting, is regarded as neither given nor neutral. Rather it is understood as structured sets of social relations, situated within specific historical and material conditions. A guiding assumption is that all work is organized in such a way that some people's interests are served, while other people's interests are ignored. The organization of processes of production, because they are designed and deliberate, cannot be taken as neutral, nor are they technologically determined. What is crucial to understand, therefore, is how work is organized and why it is organized as it is.

A second fundamental distinction is made with regard to how people are characterized and what things are taken to be relevant for developing an understanding of the relation between people and work. More than a composite of commodifiable use-values, people are understood as having human needs and requirements which productive labour is expected to satisfy. They enter into social relations of production with interests that extend beyond the terms of exchange relations. Employment and careers are not understood fundamentally as problems of "fitting in." Rather, because processes of production are designed and not given, deliberate but not determined, they can and should be organized in ways which serve human as well as economic interests.

The problem of reorganizing processes of production and democratizing the economic sphere must be considered in its practical aspect, not simply as an exercise in ideological critique. Nevertheless, ideological terms of reference structure the way we think about the relation between people and work. We need to develop a language of possibility which extends beyond the "self-making" of possessive individualism. And we need to redefine the nature of the link between education and the economy to counter claims that school effectiveness is best measured in terms of marketable use-values in students.

TOWARD CRITICALITY IN WORK EDUCATION: THE CASE OF COOPERATIVE EDUCATION

As I stated in the introduction to this article, we are interested, like Dewey, in contributing to a kind of work education which would enable students to participate effectively in the social relations of the economy and to effect those kinds of changes which would "alter the existing industrial regime and ultimately transform it" (Dewey 1977, 38). What we are interested in developing are curriculum materials which support the transformation of social relations and promote reciprocity in pedagogical practice. Such materials would enable students and teachers to explore the ambiguities, conflicts, and contradictions which are experienced in daily life at the workplace. They address those questions which remain unposed within the restricted discourse of conventional career education materials. To expand the scope of classroom inquiry it is important to abandon any generic, denatured conception of work and to start instead with the actual experiences of people working. For students, these experiences often will be vicarious, but coupled with their own work experiences, they can provide the counter-analyses and examples from which to sustain explorations into related themes and issues. This is why, in our view, coupled work/study programs offer a unique opportunity to redefine what it means to provide education for work.

In Ontario in recent years, politicians, business leaders, and the public at large have expressed growing concern over the nature and quality of work education in the province. There has been a virtual explosion in the numbers of cooperative education programs offered at the secondary school level. Students enrolled in such programs are usually required to spend two-thirds of the course credit "on the job," working in the community. The remaining course credit time is spent in school, in academic or technical studies related to work placement. By combining courses and coordinating timetables, it is possible for students to work full time for up to three months, or part time for a full school year. The range is from techical courses like hairdressing or auto mechanics to business courses like accounting or office practice; and from family studies like health care or early childhood education to academic courses like geography or social studies. Work placements might be in small businesses, large corporations, or government service agencies.

Over the past several years I have been involved with a group of academics, researchers, and high school co-op teachers in a joint research/curriculum development project. Part of the work of this project has been to develop resource materials for use in the in-school component of cooperative education programs. In addition to drawing upon observational and interview data that we have collected in the course of our own research, we have drawn material from a wide range of sources which includes:

a extracts from books and articles which propose explicit conceptual frameworks or theoretical positions;
b oral histories, autobiographies, and case studies which offer rich descriptions and first-hand accounts of people's working lives;
c literary, musical, and artistic works which give expression to some aspect of work in the world. (See also the Schools Council/Nuffield Humanities Project 1971.)

One of the strengths of such a compilation is the inclusion of multiple and sometimes contradictory discourses, each ideologically expressive. Items within the materials can be addressed from the standpoint of uncovering, or at least speculating about, the socio-historical grounds from which it was produced. An inquiry which aims to explore the production of knowledge about work must provide a framework for analysing the taken-for-granted understandings which the materials express. Such an inquiry should provide the occasion for students and teachers to make explicit the values and meanings, assumptions and definitions they hold with regard to work. The pedagogical challenge is to move beyond subjective meanings and to develop an understanding of how meanings are produced and grounded in social, historical, and material conditions. The pedagogical framework should serve also to support analysis of students' own work experiences.

The materials stand in another relation to student understanding as well. Within the materials are survey results, government reports, economic forecasts, and other authoritative, socially sanctioned versions of "knowledge" of the work world. While we are not particularly interested in the transmission of such knowledge, it is important to confront these authoritative forms if certain central questions posed by the materials – How is knowledge produced? Whose interests are served? – are to be taken seriously. All materials which eventually find their way into this curricular resource can be seen as making statements about the nature of work and the nature of knowledge simultaneously.

The claim we put forward is that through inquiry and discussion, dialogue and debate, students and teachers can come to an understanding of how knowledge in general, and knowledge of work in particular, is socially generated. Within the context of the classroom these materials provide a formal and structured opportunity for students and teachers to reexamine the grounds of their own sense-making practices. As well, they can explore contradictory claims as to which kinds of practices make sense. They give everyday reflection about the nature and meaning of work specific content and enhance the adoption of a more critical mode of thinking.

What follows is an explication of four imperatives which have served as theoretical guidelines in the organization and production of these materials. We believe they are consistent with a critical pedagogical interest.

1 *The materials and pedagogy must emphasize the constructed nature of the social world by making explicit how the production and reproduction of social practice is an outcome of human action and understanding.*

This is not to imply that people, within the contexts of their everyday lives, are consciously aware of their participation in processes of social structuration. On the contrary, the materials emphasize that while the production and reproduction of social practice is the result of what people do, it is never adequately understood in terms of what they intend. Such inquiry moves away from the static conceptualization of possessive individuals in career development materials and proposes instead active, dynamic human agents producing meaning.

Other taken-for-granted features need also to be called into question. How, for example, does "common sense" account for gender differentiation in the workplace? Does the notion of "choice," so prevalent in career development materials, provide an adequate explanation of difference?

2 *The materials and pedagogy must provide for an historically informed examination of experience; first, by demonstrating how sense-making practices are grounded in bio-history, and second, by presenting structures of socio-economic relations as resilient but not immutable.*

Working with the materials, students should be able to formulate plausible versions of how people's understandings are historically grounded and how their courses of action are historically circumscribed. Commonsense understandings and commonplace social relations do not emerge anew each day. Their enduring quality can only be recognized and understood through a process of historical inquiry.

Career development materials suggest that terms and conditions of employment are given or are technologically determined: in contrast, these materials seek to inquire into social relations which characterize occupations, economic sectors, and modes of production. Social relations and the constitution of experience are extended to include an examination of how ways of thinking support or suppress conditions for social and economic change.

3 *The materials and pedagogy must explicate the political dimension of all social relations by showing how power is mediated in social practice.*

If structures of social relations are constituted through human actions, then individuals are, in a sense, implicated in the production and reproduction of dominant forms of social life. What is more, institutionalized structures of social relations and practices – especially those which legitimate the differential distribution of power – are likewise implicated in the reproduction of a stratified social order. This pedagogy requires that judgments be made, therefore, with regard to the morality manifest in existing structures.

The intention is to provide a conceptual language and theoretical framework which would enable users of the materials to investigate the connections and contradictions between the so-called "separate spheres" of the social, the economic, and the ethical. Recognition of that connection enables users to explore the question of how social practices which they take for granted serve to support, and to suppress, their own life interests and the interests of others.

The importance of this dimension cannot be overstated. Because the experience of injustice and exploitation is not uniformly distributed throughout the population, questions of power and privilege tend to be well understood by some and difficult to grasp for others. Effaced and obscured in the abstract language of "market forces" and "choices" is the reality of domination, exploitation, harassment, and exclusion. To assess the uses and abuses of power both in the workplace and in the structure of the economy more generally, fundamental differences in the experiences of young, middle-aged, and older workers, of dominant and oppressed racial and ethnic groups, of men and women, of well- and under-educated, of mentally and physically advantaged and challenged and of the economically privileged and marginalized must all be recognized not merely as "different experiences" but as differences produced in structures of social relations and practices where inequalities of power and privilege prevail.

4 *The materials and pedagogy must show how contemporary structures of social relations are continually mediated through human agents.*

What must be developed, in other words, is a language which transcends the dichotomies of determinism and free will, reproduction and resistance. It is only through an analysis emphasizing human agency that the possibility of practical, transformative action becomes possible. This praxis is the aim of critical pedagogy.

Taken together, the materials and pedagogy propose a way of understanding how social and economic relations based on age, ethnicity, gender, and class impinge on the individual and collective desires of most people in modern industrial society. While such an understanding is not sufficient, it is a necessary prerequisite for initiating processes of social transformation.

FROM CONCEPT TO CLASSROOM

I have already suggested that social transformation is not an objective one would expect to find in curriculum guidelines or lesson plan books. Yet work with teachers using our materials tells us quite clearly that while social transformation is not their explicit aim, a deep-seated concern with providing "good education" provides for the development of a more critical approach to work education. Teachers we have talked to have a genuine interest in working with students to produce "really useful" knowledges, skills, and abilities. Still, in classroom after classroom we observed teachers and students reenacting variations of career development and employability themes. It is not so much that teachers are particularly committed to the ideas these materials espouse, but rather that they tend to use those materials which are widely available and used by other co-op teachers. In fact, these materials are becoming even more available as programs are devised to increase business influence on education. The growing popularity of Adopt-A-School Programs is a manifestation of this "new" business-education partnership.

Yet, most of the teachers we have worked with see themselves first and foremost as educators, and are ill at ease with the idea that their primary job is to prepare students to meet the demands of employers. Even among those teachers who accept this latter line of reasoning, there is an underlying suspicion that this is not the most appropriate way to meet the long-term employment needs of the students with whom they work.

Our challenge, then, has been to provide a credible analysis of co-op teaching practice which would not be dismissed out of hand as coming from "outsiders" (hence not relevant to everyday teaching concerns). In other words, we have tried to engage teachers through our work in a process of critical reflection and reevaluation of their own teaching practices. Finally, in this process, we have tried to demonstrate how the interests of students are better served through an alternative formulation of course content and classroom practice in the in-school component of co-op programs. The materials we have produced and the pedagogy we advocate begin with the notion of teacher-as-educator and expand on ideas about how to work in students' interests beyond the problem of getting a job and keeping it.

Our reformulations have direct implications for actual teaching practice. They challenge prevailing wisdom among co-op teachers that "Experience is the best teacher." All too often this way of thinking has led to a separation between what goes on at work and what happens in school. Work experience itself is taken for granted as complete or self-contained. As such, it has often been ignored in the classroom in favour of taking up employment skills, like résumé writing, or guidance and career development exercises.

The shift in focus towards student experience required corresponding changes in the structure of classroom social relations. Knowledge and expertise are legitimately claimed by students when their experiences are taken up in the classroom. This makes students more responsible for the form and content of the course, but it also places a different responsibility on the teacher. To give shape and focus to classroom discussion, teachers had to learn when and how to introduce terms, concepts, analysis, theory, and history at appropriate times. They had to learn how to hear, then appreciate, other points of view while at the same time insisting on the importance of evaluation of knowledge claims. What emerged from this field test were the outlines of a pedagogy for work education which was critically oriented, experience-based, and knowledge-focused.

During that year of field testing more and more teachers expressed an interest in what we were doing. We were invited by co-op teachers to come into their classrooms and demonstrate how our materials might be used. We were asked to conduct professional development workshops for co-op teachers in various boards of education in southern Ontario. This indicated to us a widespread sense of dissatisfaction among teachers, not only with the curriculum materials that were available, but more importantly with the limited range of ideas regarding the purpose of the in-school component. Our materials reformulated the central problem from "choosing a career" to learning about work. This more clearly served their interests as educators.

Members of the research/curriculum development team have been invited several times to make presentations at the annual meetings of the Ontario Co-operative Education Association (OCEA). At a time when "meeting the needs of employers" is becoming increasingly prevalent (employers' suggestions about how to restructure education are always the topic of at least one conference presentation), our invitation to present demonstrates the willingness of co-op teachers to raise questions about fundamental issues.

Several of us are regularly asked to be guest lecturers at Ministry of Education Co-op Certification Courses. The topics we most frequently address are reflective learning in the in-school component and using work experiences in the classroom. We try to use these opportunities to set out an approach consistent with the critical perspective on work education our resource materials are intended to serve.

What has become increasingly clear to us is that for advocacy to be effective there must be an expanded sense of commitment on the part of researchers to collaboration in the research process. This goes well beyond the collection of data and/or verification of analysis. It requires researchers to engage the communities in which they work as a central and ongoing feature of their own research practice. Here we claim a measure of success in our endeavours. We can attribute this success to several factors, among them the credibility we have established over time within the community of co-op teachers, the commitment we have demonstrated to teachers' concerns and everyday teaching problems, and the emphasis in our curriculum work on the development of a practical classroom pedagogy consistent with teachers' interests in working for and on behalf of students.

In all these activities our intention has been both critical and pedagogical; critical in the sense of raising questions about the assumptions which underlie teaching practice, and pedagogical in the sense of working with teachers to develop an alternative version of education for work. The degree to which teachers have shown an interest in our materials suggests that many are questioning assumptions and reformulating classroom practices. Our task now is to continue to advocate and provide support for the development of a critically oriented, experientially based program of work education.

CONCLUSION: PRAXIS AND ADVOCACY

The materials we have organized are intended as a resource for a systematic and indepth exploration of work and work-related issues. This pedagogy takes as its central concern the social and political organization of knowledge. Knowledge claims are evaluated, first, by seeking to re-embed those claims in the material conditions and social relations of their production; second, by attempting to uncover the interests which those claims articulate; and third, by explicating the social processes by which knowledge claims are legitimated. The emphasis is on the production of experience and the kinds of knowledge which experience provides. The pedagogical challenge is not merely to legitimate and/or authenticate students' social histories, but also to provide the languages, conceptual tools, and analytic frameworks with which students can interrogate their own experiences in a critical and theoretically salient manner.

The materials and pedagogy invite students and teachers to become active participants in the production of knowledge about the work world, and about themselves. By collaborating in this effort, students and teachers enhance their analytical skills and critical judgment. Finally, unlike talent matching, which goes to great length to transform social issues into individual problems, these materials show that many problems are, in fact, manifestations of large social issues contested every day in the workplace. Such an understanding is the foundation of a praxis aimed at the transformation of society. "By such means," writes C. Wright Mills, "the personal uneasiness of individuals is focused upon explicit troubles and the indifference of publics is transformed into involvement with public issues" (Mills 1959, 5).

REFERENCES

Anyon, Jean. 1979. "Ideology and United States History Textbooks." *Harvard Educational Review* no. 3:361–86.

Apple, Michael W. 1979. *Ideology and Curriculum.* Boston: Routledge and Kegan Paul.

– 1982. "Curricular Form and the Logic of Technical Control: Building the Possessive Individual." In Michael Apple, ed., *Cultural and Economic Reproduction in Education: Essays on Class, Ideology and the State.* Boston: Routledge and Kegan Paul.

Braverman, Harry. 1974. *Labour and Monopoly Capital: The Degradation of Work in the Twentieth Century.* New York and London: Monthly Review Press.

Browne, Ken. 1981. "Schooling, Capitalism and the Mental/Manual Division of Labour." *Sociological Review* 29, no. 3:445–73.

Canada. 1979. *Index to Canadian Occupations: Counsellors' Guide.* Department of Employment and Immigration, Advanced Development Division, Occupational and Career Analysis and Development Branch. Ottawa: Ministry of Supply and Services.

Dewey, John. 1966. *Democracy and Education.* New York: Free Press (first published 1916).

— 1977. "Education vs. Trade Training: Dr. Dewey's Reply." *Curriculum Inquiry* 7, no. 1:37–9.

Edwards, Richard C. 1979. *Contested Terrain: The Transformation of the Workplace in the Twentieth Century*. New York: Basic Books.

Gintis, Herbert, and Samuel Bowles. 1981. "Contradiction and Reproduction in Educational Theory." In Roger Dale et. al., eds., *Schooling and the National Interest*. Vol. 1. Sussex: Falmer Press and Open University Press.

Giroux, Henry A. 1981. *Ideology, Culture and the Process of Schooling*. Philadelphia: Temple University Press.

Gorz, André. 1972. "Domestic Contradiction of Advanced Capitalism." In Richard Edwards et. al., eds., *The Captialist System*. Englewood Cliffs, New Jersey: Prentice Hall.

MacPherson, C.B. 1962. *The Political Theory of Possessive Individualism*. New York: Oxford University Press.

Mills, C. Wright. 1959. *The Sociological Imagination*. London: Oxford University Press.

Offe, Claus, and Volker Ronge. 1981. "Thesis on the Theory of the State." In Roger Dale et. al., eds., *Schooling and the National Interest*. Vol. 1. Sussex: Falmer Press and Open University Press.

Osbourne, Ken. 1980. *Hardworking, Temperate and Peaceable: The Portrayal of Workers in Canadian History Textbooks*. Winnipeg: University of Manitoba, Educational Monograph no. 4.

The Schools Council/Nuffield Humanities Project. 1971. *People and Work: Teacher's Box*. London: Heinemann.

Simon, Roger. 1983. "But Who Will Let You Do It: Counter-hegemonic Approaches to Work Education." *Journal of Education* 165, no. 3:235–56.

Simon, Roger, and Don Dippo. 1987. "What Schools Can Do: Designing Programs for Work Education That Challenge the Wisdom of Experience." *Journal of Education* 169, no. 3:101–16.

Simon, Roger, Don Dippo, and Arleen Schenke. Forthcoming. *Learning Work: A Critical Pedagogy of Work Education*. Amherst, MA: Bergin and Garvey.

Smith, Dorothy. 1983. "No One Commits Suicide: Textual Analysis of Ideological Practices." *Human Studies* 6:309–59.

Smith, George. 1978. "Occupational Analysis." Thesis presented to Department of Sociology in Education, University of Toronto (OISE). Unpublished.

Taxel, Joel. 1979. "Justice and Cultural Conflict: Racism, Sexism and Instructional Materials." *Interchange* 9, no. 1:56–84.

Waugh, Colin. 1982. "Really Useful Knowledge?" *Schooling and Culture* 12:5–7.

PART THREE: FROM ADVOCACY TO SOCIAL MOVEMENTS

From Advocacy to Social Movements

A social movement is primarily an agency of contestation. The features which distinguish it from lobbying or small-scale empowerment/advocacy have to do with the social movement's desire to overturn the *social domination* of the group or class to which it is opposed. A social movement not only seeks to change society but, in addition, seeks to control how that change is implemented. The sources of protest in social movements are deep and they bring structural conflict to the fore. Even if a social movement appears to be muddleheaded in its diverse array of members and forms of dissent, structural conflict provides underlying coherence. In classical social movements, structural conflict centred on social class. In the "new" social movements, such as the ecology movement, the women's movement, and the anti-nuclear movement, issues of social class may still emerge, but these movements' formation was not a manifestation of class action. [1]

The introduction to this book reported the views of Touraine and other sociologists on this point. It is Touraine's belief that the organization of the new social movements lie somewhere between an expression of future cultural forms and the existing dialectic of power. Social movements may define strategy through confrontation with political authority, but it is a cultural vision which orients their activity. They test the capacity of society to act upon itself, by defining alternate social purposes from those of dominant élites and interest groups. The conflicts in which social movements engage have no other basis than "the struggle of social forces for the control of historicity" (Touraine 1977, 446ff.).

Modern society has developed an increasing ability to act upon itself, Touraine argues. By this he means that society is undergoing a rapid decline in the inherited pattern of social reproduction. Social transformations have been so many and varied that tradition itself is no longer positively valued throughout society and the persistence of traditional social forms are themselves part of collective conflict (Touraine 1981, 6ff.) Conflicts which social movements engender are in many ways related to society's own conception of historical purpose ("historicity").

In the language of the environmental movement, the struggle is one for the survival of the planet against ecological destruction caused by industrial economy; in the language of the peace movement, the struggle is for human survival against prevailing conceptions that nuclear war is possible; and in the language of the women's movement, the struggle is against the continued domination of patriarchy.

A social movement, by definition, is not an agent of political management. Nevertheless, the peace movement faces an ideological system which inhibits the development of national or global solutions. As for the women's movement, Frank has this comment to make about why it remains a "project," rather than becoming an institutionalized political party:

The incompatibility between social movement and state power is perhaps most intuitively obvious for the women's movement(s) ... The most numerous – because individually small-scale – social movements, which are community based, of course cannot seek state power. However, similarly to the women's movement, the very notion of state or even political party power for them would negate most of their grass-roots aims and essence. These community movements mobilise and organise their members in pursuit of material and non-material ends, which they often regard unjustly denied to them by the state and its institutions, including political parties. Among the non-material aims and methods of many local community movements is more grass-roots participatory democracy and bottom-up self-determination. (Frank and Fuentes 1988, 36)

In effect, "new" social movements are reflexive, but their reflexiveness creates a capacity to act by linking the possibilities of present social action to an alternative epistemology.

Cleveland and Leah have different verdicts on the success so far of the women's movement as "reflexive project." Both seem to agree that if women cannot manage to sustain political activity against male domination in *all* national institutions, they can proceed to advance by winning the support of *some* organizations dominated by men. Cleveland's paper raises additional questions about forms of conflict which incapacitate new social movements. Why don't all women belong to the women's movement? The greatest success of the women's movement has been to turn issues that previously seemed to belong to the personal domain into questions of female inequality and subordination in society, and a vision of a different social order. Yet the women's movement seems to have stopped at this point because of internal dissensions.

Cleveland and Leah show how the study of reflexiveness places special constraints on its researchers and observers. Researchers have to interpret both detailed proceedings and the broad social framework from which the social movement emerges. The first is full of details, singularities, individual actors and specific outcomes. The second relates these to the global concerns and future vision which give the social movement validity. Thus studies of local events "overflow" the framework in which they appear. Actors and events become "stakeholders" in a much larger conflict.

Supporting Touraine, Leah shows how empirical investigation of a new social movement always produces greater complexity than initial conceptual elaboration permits. At the same time Leah is against any researcher's attempting direct intervention in the social movement. Leah supports Marshall: while academics may provide certain knowledgeable and "objective" insights, they cannot determine the goals of a social movement from outside. They lack the credentials for the leadership. Touraine advocates interventionist research, but Leah argues that academic researchers should respect the autonomy of social movements and refrain from converting research insights into either prophecy or personal engagement (see also Spencer below).

Finally, Cleveland raises some important observations about the relationship between advocacy and the liberal democratic state. Liberalism conceptualizes equality of opportunity for abstract individuals but not equality of condition for concrete individuals. It ignores the fact that the opportunities of concrete individuals are also defined by social relations in collectivities. As a matter of political principle or ideology, liberalism cannot accept State intervention in order to secure the interests of a specific social group, especially if it hurts the interests of another group. This creates a fundamental dilemma for feminists when it comes to implementation of their key demands. Adelman made a similar statement above with regard to the respective position of refugees and immigrants to Canada. It would seem that reforms which ought to be achieved by State intervention in liberal democracies can often be achieved only through the aggressive struggles of non-governmental organizations.

NOTES

1 By contrast, structural conflict in countries like Chile – where the ruling class has total political and social control – produces *rupture conduct*. Rupture conduct is collective action directed towards the *political overthrow* of the ruling class. Social movements are likely to become a populist opposition which transforms "illegal activity," dissent, and exclusion into a revolutionary movement opposing élite political domination.

REFERENCES

Frank, André Gunder, and Marta Fuentes. 1988. "Nine Theses on Social Movements." *IFDA Dossier* 63:27–44.

Touraine, Alain. 1977. *The Self-Production of Society*. Chicago: University of Chicago Press.

– 1981. *The Voice and the Eye: An Analysis of Social Movements*. Cambridge: Cambridge University Press and Paris: Editions de la Maison des Sciences de l'Homme.

RONNIE LEAH

Day Care, Trade Unions, and the Women's Movement: Trade Union Women Organize for Change

This case study of union women organizing for day care in Ontario analyses the emergence of a women's movement within labour. It provides a social history of women's organizing efforts in the Ontario labour movement, tracing political mobilization of support for universally accessible, publicly funded child care. In addition, day care sheds light on recent developments in two Canadian social movements: the labour movement and the women's movement.[1] Developments in each of these areas have facilitated gains made by both. The active campaign of trade union women for women's equality in the unions has been integrally connected to the contemporary women's movement. While the growth of feminism established a foundation for the struggles of working-class women in unions around gender issues such as day care, a growing number of working women joined unions in the last decade to organize against the domination of the labour movement by men.

In conjunction with the community-based day care issue, union women mobilized support for day care within the Ontario Federation of Labour (OFL). Day care became the focal point for women's trade-union organizing in the OFL from 1975 to 1980, leading to a major OFL resolution on day care in November 1980. This event was pivotal for union women – day care was the first major gender issue to gain the support of labour. Labour support for this key women's demand can be seen as indicative of changing gender relations in the labour movement. As trade union women successfully mobilized labour support for day care, labour contributed materially to the growth of the day care movement; the day care issue was transformed from a gender issue to a working-class demand. This development of labour support for day care has facilitated the emergence of a national day care movement, one with a high public profile and a broad base of support. National support is reflected in recent debate about federal day care policy.[2]

The OFL Women's Committee (WC) was the primary union formation through which women organized for day care. Its credibility as an organizational base for trade union women was confirmed by the passage of the OFL Statement on Day Care at the 1980 annual convention. Through their organizing efforts for day care, union women extended the aims of the women's movement within labour, building a base for women's equality in the unions.

Effects of these developments have been evident in both the women's movement and the labour movement. The emergence of a trade union women's movement points to the need for a more class-conscious women's movement. At the same time, the continuing transformation of trade union gender relations highlights the potential for a more progressive, united labour movement which represents women as well as men in class struggle.

RESEARCH ON WOMEN AND LABOUR

My research is presented from the perspective of women and labour, advocating the struggles of trade union women for equality. This approach combines the "vantage point of women" (Smith 1980a) and the "labour point of view" (Marshall 1984 and above). The perspective takes into account the everyday experiences of working-class women in Canadian society. Such a position of advocacy in order to provide information and analysis useful to trade union women has achieved growing recognition in academic research.

Research consisted mainly of in-depth interviews with trade union women, utilizing the method of oral history (Langlois 1976). Personal accounts based on direct involvement in the union process enabled me to reconstruct the process of struggle, as women joined together to mobilize support for day care. I conducted interviews with union staff members, elected officials, and rank and file activists from the OFL as well as from several industrial and public sector unions. Examination of union documents such as publications, convention proceedings, resolutions, policy statements, correspondence, and minutes of labour bodies supplemented personal accounts. Together they provided a comprehensive overview of the complex process of women organizing.[3]

My study provides concrete evidence of how social relations of class and gender intersect in the lives of working-class women. While both women and men share common exploitation as workers, an exploitation based on capitalist class relations, working-class women also experience an additional level of oppression, based on gender relations.[4] The sexual division of labour and its accompanying subordination of women – integral to capitalist social relations – create divisions within classes based on gender.[5]

The example of trade union women organizing for day care provides a good understanding of women's labour history, one "which locate(s) women in relation to class" (Armstrong and Armstrong 1983b, 29). As advocacy, the research is "linked concretely to the struggle for women's equality" (Smith 1980b, 131). It documents effective means of organizing by trade union women, and assesses their changing status in the labour movement.

DAY CARE AND WOMEN'S ORGANIZING

Organizing for day care is rooted in the experiences of both the day care community and the women's movement. Labour women took the day care issue, as it was being highlighted in the community, and brought it within the framework of trade unionism. Moreover, their mode of organizing for day care grew out of women's efforts to organize in the OFL. Such organizing was a key lesson of the women's movement.

Day care had emerged as a basic issue for women active in unions by the late 1970s. The question of day care was becoming ever more urgent with the rapid growth in number of working mothers in Ontario. The changing material conditions of working-class family life were reflected in the growing number of married women active in the labour force – with the most profound changes in the traditional childbearing and childrearing years – and the growing number of sole-support mothers.[6] Thus by 1981, more than half the mothers of pre-school children in Ontario were working outside the home.

In spite of the growing need, working women did not have access to quality, affordable day care. Any expansion in day care facilities in Canada in the 1960s and early 1970s had been halted in 1975, as a result of cutbacks in government funding (Leah 1981). Combined with the growing labour force activity of mothers with young children, such cutbacks precipitated a serious crisis in day care; these factors contributed to both community and labour activism.[7] In response to government cutbacks, Action Day Care had undertaken organizing efforts in the Toronto community. The actions of the community day care movement served to highlight the day care issue as an important focus for trade union women's organizing.[8]

Trade union women perceived the issue of day care to be critical for their equality in the labour force, as well as in the union movement itself. Since most working-class women continued to have the primary responsibility for child care in their households, union women felt that day care was necessary in order to participate in the labour force on an equal basis with men; they also hoped that the provision of child care services at union meetings would encourage women to become more involved in union activity. In more general terms, the provision of day care was linked to the question of women's equality in society. Members of the OFL Women's Committee identified day care as the issue "most problematic ... for women," Chris explained.[9] Without day care women were unable to "either get a job in the first place, keep their jobs or become active in the labour movement."

Many union women related their activity around the day care issue to their experiences as working mothers. For example, Ann, a member of the Canadian Union of Public Employees (CUPE), became active when she was faced with the need for child care for her two young children; her personal experience "made the link between seeing the problem and suddenly being stuck in it." Donna, active in the Steelworkers Union, got "drawn into" the day care issue as a result of experiencing the problems caused by lack of child care with her own son; she "didn't want to see other women go through the struggles" that she went through. The lack of day care has had a negative effect on the representation of working women in the labour movement, Chris explained:[10] "To get women involved in unions means that you really have to have good day care ... [it was] critical in women's push to be equal members of their unions."

Not only was the issue of day care a priority for union women, but it was also strategically important for women's organizing in the labour movement. Although women's concerns had often been seen as divisive by the male union leadership, day care was one issue that could "bring people together," according to Diane. The day care issue had been raised when women were "pushing hard for the establishment of women's committees [in their unions] and the Federation Women's Committee." In Diane's union, the Ontario Public Service Employees Union (OPSEU), women had encountered "a lot of very negative backlash ... everything was presented as very divisive." Since men could also begin to understand the need for day care from their experience as parents, Diane felt that men did not feel threatened by day care as was the case in other gender issues. Nancy pointed out that the provision of child care at union functions also encouraged men to see it as a legitimate "concern of the whole union."

ORIGINS OF TRADE UNION WOMEN'S ORGANIZING

Union women's day care organizing grew out of women's efforts in the 1970s to establish an organizational base in the Ontario labour movement. These efforts arose out of four related developments, including the growing number of women in the labour movement and the growing influence of the women's movement on labour. As I have already noted, developments in each area gave mutual support to all.

First, growing numbers of working women turned to unionization as the best means of improving their low pay and poor working conditions. In the last two decades, "women have dominated union membership growth... almost doubling their share of organized workers" (Armstrong and Armstrong 1983a, 108). Women in Ontario more than doubled their representation in unions between 1965 and 1975; by 1981, close to one third of all union members in Ontario were women.[11] Their growing numbers increased the visibility of women in unions; it also facilitated their organizing activities, particularly in unions such as OPSEU where women constituted a high proportion of the membership.

Second, changing gender relations in Canadian society established a foundation for the struggles of working-class women in unions. By 1975, union women had recognized the need to organize collectively in order to challenge male domination of the labour movement.[12] For example, union women had begun organizing in special formations such as Organized Working Women (OWW), formed in March 1976 "to bring more women trade unionists into union activity" (*Union Woman* 1980). Women also began organizing within a number of unions, most notably OPSEU; with women comprising 50 per cent of OPSEU's membership by 1979, this union was one of the first to focus on equal opportunity for women. Another example of success came when union women won support for a day care resolution at the Ontario Federation of Labour annual convention in 1980. This development would not have been likely ten years earlier, but by 1980 the labour movement was becoming more receptive to women's demands for their rights, owing to developing awareness of the oppression of women.[13]

Third, growing consciousness concerning women's equality can be traced to the rise of the contemporary women's movement, which challenged male domination in all aspects of Canadian society. While working-class support for the women's movement is a recent development (Mackie 1983, 293), there is evidence of growing gender consciousness among trade union women. The women's movement has provided strong impetus for the organizing efforts of union women in the last decade.[14] Chris explained that the women's movement has had a positive effect on labour and particularly on women trade unionists, in "building up consciousness and the recognition that these issues are critical."

The ideological and political impact of the women's movement on unions has been complemented by personal ties between union women and the women's movement. It is a "very important" connection, according to Nancy. While many trade union women developed as feminists "through their work as unionists," other union women were "first politicized in the women's movement" (Egan and Yanz 1983, 363). For example, several activists in the OFL Women's Committee had been members of the International Women's Day Committee (IWDC), a socialist-feminist collective in Toronto. Through a number of working women's struggles, these personal ties developed into organizational links between labour and women's groups. Strike support by women's groups for the 1978 Fleck strike was especially significant in building this alliance.[15] Nancy remarked that the women's solidarity picket at Fleck marked "the first time ... there was a direct alliance between the women's movement and the trade union movement." Women's strikes, such as the one waged by the United Auto Workers Union (UAW) women at Fleck, also created pressure on the Ontario labour leadership to recognize union women's concerns.

Fourth, the women's movement has had a direct impact on the Ontario labour movement, which facilitated trade union women's organizing. The "hiring of women into union staff positions by the OFL and its affiliates" has accelerated the "process of feminization" in the Ontario labour movement (see Cleveland below). Women staffers were to play an active role in agitating for greater participation by women in Ontario unions. These union women also played a key role in the formation of the OFL Women's Committee, which enabled them to incorporate women's concerns into the formal structures of the OFL.

STRATEGY AND TACTICS OF DAY CARE ORGANIZING

The Women's Committee successfully mobilized support for a day care resolution at the 1979 OFL Convention, which provided official labour endorsement and an OFL Conference on Day Care.[16] Diane recalled how this gave the WC an "opening" in making day care organizing "their major work in the next year."

The Conference on Day Care was an integral part of the WC's strategy for day care organizing: "to develop a comprehensive policy, publicize the issue, educate unionists and plan strategies for change" (WC Letters, 27 June 1980). Nancy explained this process: "The logical thing is to hold a conference and invite people who, by their attendance at the conference, have already shown they'll support the issue. And that will bring people together." The WC accomplished their goal of having a major recommendation come forward from the conference, which served to strengthen the OFL's commitment to a day care campaign. The "Discussion Paper on Day Care," formulated by the WC "after several lengthy meetings and consultations with [day care] activists in the field" (WC Documents, 1980b, 4), served as the basis for discussion at the conference strategy sessions. This discussion paper, plus the recommendations for a comprehensive child care plan which came forward from the conference, formed the basis of the official OFL policy paper on day care passed by the 1980 OFL Convention. The WC had also won the agreement of the OFL executive to present a policy paper on day care to the annual convention.

There were definite benefits for the Women's Committee in being able to utilize official trade union networks in building support for day care. The Conference on Day care was advertised through OFL channels of communication (WC Letters, 3 June 1980 and 26 August 1980). Publicity during the conference served to increase public awareness about labour support for day care. For example, the then OFL president, Cliff Pilkey, pledged during a press conference that "the OFL has committed itself to making universal, publicly-funded daycare a major labour issue" (*Ontario Labour*, Nov.-Dec. 1980).

While the delegates to the day care conference were "primarily women," according to Chris, there was participation from men "both in the community and the labour movement itself." In her estimation, about 10 per cent of the conference delegates were men. One hundred and forty-five union delegates attended the conference, most of them from unions represented on the Women's Committee, thereby demonstrating their commitment to the issue of daycare (OFL 1980b, 1). Trade unionists were further educated about this issue through their participation in debate and discussion at the conference.

Events at the OFL Conference on Day Care reflected the state of flux in trade union gender relations at that time. Despite the support of trade union men for the day care issue, there was an indication of conflict over the priority to be accorded women's issues in the OFL. Even as the OFL leadership publicly committed itself to making day care a priority for labour, it scheduled a major OFL demonstration against plant closures for the same weekend as the day care conference. Members of the WC perceived this to be a lack of concern for women's issues. According to Nancy, they "were furious about the scheduling conflict" and consequently had to compress the agenda into an unsatisfactory period of time (OFL 1980b, 4). Making an accommodation to the OFL leadership, organizers of the day care conference publicly endorsed the OFL rally against layoffs. Despite this one conflict, the Women's Committee judged the conference to be an overall success in terms of building support for a major trade union campaign on day care.

Strong support for an OFL day care resolution was evident at the 1980 OFL convention. The Women's Committee won most of its demands around the day care issue, as delegates endorsed the Statement on Day Care. In one minor setback, Chris recalled how the demand for an OFL day care coordinator was lost, even though WC members had fought for this demand.[17] In her view, the OFL leadership responded to the pressure for day care by demonstrating its "willingness to put on any staff needed to carry it [the day care campaign] out effectively."[18]

In effect, the day care campaign was a vital factor contributing to the growth of a women's movement within the OFL and affiliated unions. Through organizing labour support for the day care issue, members of the Women's Committee gained crucial experience in working within the Ontario labour movement. The day care organizing also helped to establish the credibility of the WC as an integral part of trade unionism. Diane noted how the OFL resolution on daycare was "politically important in terms of establishing the credibility for the Women's Committee. And not just the actual body, but what the women's trade union movement embodies through the women's committees and the OFL Women's Committee." Other members also agreed that the WC "came of age" through this political process of building trade union support for the daycare campaign (Acheson and Macleod 1982, 1). As Gwen remarked, adoption of the 1980 day care resolution was "a turning point for women" in the unions. She considered it the "most important thing that's happened ... in terms of women's issues."

THE DEVELOPMENT OF A TRADE UNION
WOMEN'S MOVEMENT

The *Statement on Day Care*, the 1980 OFL policy paper, proposed an active campaign in order to achieve a "system of universal, comprehensive child care." It outlined a plan of action, including proposals for internal union action and a political action campaign for legislative change. Internal union action focused on the provision of child care services at union functions, union education programs on day care, and collective bargaining for day care subsidies and workplace day care. The internal provision of child care at union meetings was of practical importance for union women, encouraging them to participate directly in the labour movement. Day care has been provided at OFL conferences and conventions since 1979.[19] Other unions such as OPSEU and the UAW (CAW) have also adopted internal policies for child care at union meetings.[20] Collective bargaining for workplace day care and day care subsidies became part of negotiations in public sector unions, as well as in some industrial unions.[21] Collective bargaining for day care was linked to negotiations for other parental rights and benefits in the OFL Women's Committee's bargaining guide for unions, *Parental Rights and Daycare* (Acheson and Macleod 1982).

As the evidence suggests, the 1980 policy statement by the OFL made a significant contribution both to the labour movement and the women's movement, and in this section I am going to consider how the success of the day care issue facilitated gains in each of these movements.

The OFL *Statement on Day Care* focused on the political nature of labour's role for building a broad social and political movement of support for universal, publicly funded day care. According to Acheson, the adoption of this plan of action by the OFL constituted "a critical event ... [as] the day care movement won a major new ally – the union movement" (Acheson 1982, 2). Certainly labour took specific steps towards this goal. Together with the Labour Council of Metropolitan Toronto, the OFL established a task force on day care in Toronto. Labour organized a series of community forums on day care throughout the province, and built a province-wide day care coalition in Ontario. Labour support for day care was obviously essential if the issue of day care was to develop into a broadly based political and social movement. According to John, who was involved in union organizing for day care in Toronto, the labour movement "provided the organizational expertise, they provided the money, they provided the time."

The Women's Committee proceeded to implement the OFL policy, working through the Federation structure. The WC proposed OFL sponsorship of eight community forums both to raise public awareness and as an organizational base for further community action (WC Letters, 9 Feb. 1981). The OFL also promoted day care organizing at the local level through district labour councils; such support at the local level was "crucial to the success of the [day care] campaign," as labour councils played a key role in co-sponsoring the community day care forums and promoting the participation of local community organizations in the sessions (WC Letters, 29 Jan. 1981).

Labour's endorsement of the day care issue not only brought union resources and expertise to bear but also served to broaden support for a provincial – and subsequently national – day care campaign. Prior to this support, in Ann's assessment, supporters of day care had been "fighting through a community base which was very limited, very frustrating." John felt that day care groups alone would not have had "the ability or the clout to pull together a province-wide organization." Jean stated that the OFL support for day care contributed to government recognition of day care "as a very serious issue ... Queen's Park had to listen." Chris explained: "Day care became an issue once the labour movement made it an issue ... [The unions] put a force behind it that hadn't been there." As the *Globe and Mail* reported on 20 May 1986, labour support raised day care "from obscure conferences and position papers to one of the top positions on the agenda of public debate" in Canada.

In turn, the day care issue motivated women in their union struggles. As they were "building their confidence and their courage" on the day care issue, women also got involved in many other issues that affected them. Donna pointed to "The women's committees that were formed in and around that time, because the drive was on. And the Steelworkers' Women's Policy Paper was passed in [19]'81, which calls for all kinds of affirmative action programs." Donna also asserted that positive developments for union women, in particular, "have come out of the [Ontario] Federation Women's Committee, the day care issue and just the general way it's moving in the labour movement." But she concluded that the growing strength of union women, while related to the day care issue, had also developed as part of a general trend in the labour movement. Labour support for the day care issue was indicative of developmentss taking place in trade union gender relations in the 1970s and early 1980s, as women organized within the labour movement and raised their demands.

Chris, too, explained that the OFL support for day care reflected a situation in which women were becoming more aware of their power, demanding recognition as trade unionists, on an equal footing with men. These developments "showed the strength of women who felt that now they could push this ... [because] they had reached a point where there was a much greater increase of women's participation within unions." Other activist women have described the growing support for women's demands and the increasing respect accorded women in unions. Their joint experience illustrates the ongoing transformation of trade union gender relations as union women struggle for equality.

One small but significant example is the change visible at OFL conventions. Women's concerns are now recognized as serious issues. Chris explained: "They're not laughed at or snickered at, people don't leave the hall, [although] that kind of thing ... used to be the case." Donna said that as increasing numbers of women participate at conventions as delegates and speakers, women have gained more and more respect. From her experience, women are now speaking up on a broad spectrum of trade union issues and "the men are respecting and listening to what they have to say." While she feels that union women are now getting the support of men, she recognized that "this process has taken years to develop." Chris added that the changes have taken place in response to militancy as well as to growing participation of women in the unions, with women's militancy no longer seen as "quite such a threatening thing as it once was."

The changing responses of union men reflect women's growing confidence in themselves, Donna explained. They have decided, "This is enough of being put down – I'm a person." Donna contrasted her early experience in a Steel local, where "women were intimidated ... and wouldn't talk back to [management]," to the present situation where women are becoming stewards and "fighting for their rights along with their brothers' rights." In Donna's estimation, women themselves have changed as they demanded equal recognition from men, "because women were not going to sit back and take it, like they had for so many years." She thinks "men are realizing that they're dealing with a whole different type of woman." As a result of these changes, a growing interchange has developed between women and men in the labour movement which was "never there before."

The OFL resolution on day care also had the effect of being a turning point in relations between feminists and the labour movement. Diane explained that it helped to establish "credibility for the work that union women do within the union movement" with outside groups. In her estimation, the gains union women made on day care "politicized people outside the trade union movement ... particularly feminists ... who had always been very critical of how the union movement has not addressed women's issues."

At the same time that union women like Diane wanted to "reach out and link up with the traditional women's movement," they were also engaged in redefining that movement. As activist union women organized for day care within the union structures, they contributed new insights to feminism, based on their class outlook, their personal experience as working women, and their practical knowledge of trade union organizing.[22] While activist union women in the OFL were fully committed to the struggle for women's rights, they saw themselves primarily as trade unionists. Chris explained: "Many of us had more of a commitment to the labour movement than to the women's movement."[23] From this perspective, women in the OFL organized for day care as a working-class demand, concentrating on winning the support of the entire labour movement for this demand. With the class organization – the trade union movement – the primary focus of their organizing, activist union women were committed to building support for women's issues within the framework of trade unionism. This was an important factor in their ability to win labour support for the day care issue, transforming day care from a gender to a class issue.

The new relationship had reciprocal effects; the labour movement has provided the women's movement with certain advantages in organizing support for women's struggles. For example, women activists now have a definite constituency of working women, Nancy explained. During the organizing campaign for day care, they had access to "trade union women organized in certain local unions with telephone numbers and addresses"; this helped to focus the work of organizing. Nancy concluded that the union constituency provided a "real advantage to the women's movement in general." By organizing within unions, feminist women hope to do more than improve the status of women in unions; they have joined the process of building a stronger, revitalized movement for women's equality in Canadian society.

In the past, working-class women have not joined women's groups in large numbers, a point made by Cleveland in this book. Informants like Donna, who addressed this problem, saw an urgent need for the women's movement to make working-class "bread and butter" issues a priority in order to reach more of these women. Chris hopes that issues important to working-class women will be taken up more often in the future by the women's movement as a whole. She feels that it is more likely to happen as women in the labour movement "become more conscious and fight harder on those issues and they [the women's movement] recognize that the issues of unemployment and equal pay and day care are as critical for the overall women's movement as they are for trade union women."

Women's labour activism has helped create the basis for a class-conscious women's movement. Both the women's movement and the labour movement have been enriched through the interaction of women and unions, as women's concerns have become incorporated within the framework of trade unionism.

BUILDING A REVITALIZED LABOUR MOVEMENT: THE ROLE OF RESEARCH

The evidence presented here shows that women's trade union organizing not only strengthens the movement for women's equality but also contributes to the development of a stronger, united labour movement, serving as a force for progressive change in the unions.[24] In general, women's demands for greater representation in the unions have helped to democratize labour structures and open up access to decision making. The specific day care campaign has been instrumental in building working-class unity around demands for women's equality. Women active in unions have identified their goal of building a women's movement within the unions, concluding that it is "the place to get things done in the trade union movement." This is a response to feminist criticism that labour is male-dominated and therefore does not fight on behalf of women. Chris argued that the feminist approach fails to take account of what has recently been accomplished by trade union women; such criticism "does an injustice to the women who are already fighting hard to change that."

Women activists in the OFL who chose to organize within the formal labour movement struggled to build an official Women's Committee, mobilized labour support for day care – producing this women's issue as a class issue – and established a base for women organizing within the unions. These developments have enabled union women to mobilize labour support for affirmative action and other demands as they have continued the struggle for women's equality.[25] Through this process, union activists like Diane have identified the unions as vehicles of change for women. Donna explains how they are hopeful that male domination is changing and is giving way to a labour movement based on equality.

Through their double struggle against male resistance and class exploitation, women have moved to strengthen their own representation in the labour movement. They believe they have also contributed to the long-term process by which the working class is producing its unity across divisions of gender. When activist union women like Ann address the future development of Canadian labour, which stands at a "really critical time in its history," she concludes: "Women have the potential to come forward now and be part of that, and help in building the trade union movement, and help it survive. If they can do that, it will never be the same."

The goal of this research is to contribute to this process of revitalization. I believe that the knowledge gained from this contemporary social history of union women will contribute to more effective organizing by women in unions. In this research, I adopted the method of oral history in order to explore two key questions for union women: how can women effectively organize within the union movement (Fitzgerald 1981, 19) and what can be accomplished by women within the mainstream trade unions? (J. White 1980, 116).

This method of oral history provides a particular orientation to academic research on labour, one which can be contrasted with Touraine's approach on sociological intervention. Advocacy research through oral history can provide critical analysis of labour issues, generating ideas and information for trade unionists which enables them to understand their struggles in a broader context. Thus the social history of labour struggles can "contribute to workers' awareness of their own biographies and their continuing struggles" (Marshall 1984, 17). The union women interviewed for this research demonstrated a good understanding of this process. Chris voiced her interest in the study of day care organizing when she commented: "I always thought that this should be written up because it is important ... you learn so much from it [the history] in terms of organizing yourself." Ann also felt that the day care campaign should be documented as an important struggle of union women and as an example of how women can organize effectively in the unions.

A number of feminist researchers have undertaken research on working-class women, proceeding from a similar concern for advocacy.[26] Their research methods have emphasized sympathy for the struggles of women rather than the mechanical collection of data (Oakley 1981, 63). Recording the personal histories of union women enables researchers to place the "specific experiences of individual women in a larger social and economic framework" (Luxton 1980, 13).

I undertook ten in-depth interviews, primarily with women actively engaged in trade union organizing around the day care issue. Utilizing methods developed by oral historians, I conducted the interviews in a cooperative and interactive manner.[27] Close rapport developed between me and the people interviewed, given our common experiences as trade unionists, feminists, and working mothers. As part of this research process, the results of the case study have been made available to the union activists I interviewed.[28] Union women's knowledge and understanding of their own social history, gained through such research, can have an empowering effect, contributing both to consciousness raising and to further action around women's demands. This "collective critical reconstitution of the meaning of women's social experience, as women live through it," has been identified as a key aspect of feminist research methods.[29]

In addition, the documentation of union women's organizing experiences around the day care issue can provide further insight into women's methods of organizing in the unions, while also providing union women with a model for organizing efforts around other issues such as affirmative action. In this way, the research enters into the practical process of building a trade union movement which is fully committed to women's equality.

This approach bears some similarity to Touraine's sociological intervention (Touraine 1981, 14), which also seeks to provide insight into the particular struggles of activists, placing these struggles in the broader context of social movements. However, I do not accept Touraine's recommendation that the researcher actively participate in a group's self-analysis through intervention. This is beyond the scope of appropriate advocacy research. While academics may provide certain objective insights into trade unionism based on their analysis of the labour movement, academic researchers cannot determine the goals of labour from outside the labour movement. Academics lack credentials for the leadership of labour and have little first-hand knowledge of trade union realities. Marshall has put this argument elsewhere in this book.

Certainly it is important for academics and researchers to utilize their skills in supporting the struggles of union women. Such personal commitment to and sympathy for women's concerns are also important aspects of feminist research. Nevertheless, this crucial support can be distinguished from that of direct intervention, as described by Touraine. As noted earlier, the different strategies developed by activist union women, on the one hand, and feminists located primarily in the autonomous women's movement, on the other, reflect in large part their different experiences in these formations. By the same token, academics – even those supportive of working-class struggles – cannot claim to be leaders and strategists for the working class.

I feel that my primary contribution can be made through documentation of union women's organizing for day care, and that this research may empower supporters of the day care issue, the women's movement, and the labour movement.

NOTES

1 This study forms part of a larger research project undertaken for a doctoral dissertation (Leah 1986).

2 Toronto *Globe and Mail*, 20 May 1986.

3 A total of ten people (nine of them women) were interviewed in May and June, 1983. The trade unionists referred to in this study include members and staff of the Canadian Union of Public Employees (CUPE), Ontario Federation of Labour (OFL), Ontario Public Service Employees Union (OPSEU), International Union of Electrical Workers (IUE), United Steelworkers of America (USWA), and United Auto Workers, Canada (UAW), now called the Canadian auto workers (CAW). Several women were member of the OFL Women's Committee and a number of people were active in day care coalitions.

4 Under capitalism, women and men are "oppressed by a social order that separates them from the means necessary to produce their own subsistence, from the products of their labour and from each other in their daily work lives" (Fox 1980, 12). Our analysis of class relations is based on the Marxist conception of class, which "differentiates classes on the basis of a differing relation to the means of production" (Smith 1980b, 8). Gender relations are defined as "the social relations between men and women" (Game and Pringle 1983, 15).

5 The sexual division of labour entails the "allocation of work on the basis of sex, within both the home and the work place, as well as that division between home and work place which has been characteristic of capitalism" (Game and Pringle 1983, 14). Fox (1980) and Smith (1980b) have argued that class relations, the division between the classes, also shape relations between the sexes in the working class. This creates a division within classes, based on gender (see also Armstrong and Armstrong 1983b).

6 In the last two decades, there have been profound changes in the labour force participation rates for married women, and women in the twenty-five to forty-four year age group (Armstrong and Armstrong 1978; Ontario Ministry of Labour 1982; Yanz and Smith 1983). While only a minority of married women in Ontario 31.6 per cent) worked outside the home in 1966, by 1983 substantially more than half (56 per cent) of all married women were working or seeking work. The increase in labour force activity has been most pronounced for women in the twenty-five to forty-four year age group (the traditional childbearing and childrearing years), rising from less than a third (30.5 per cent) in 1956 to more than two thirds (73 per cent) in 1983 (Ontario Statistics 1984, tables 5.11, 6.5, 6.7). See also Ontario Ministry of Labour 1982.

7 The day care crisis was documented by a number of studies; for example, a Social Planning Council report concluded that "the levels of access to

a daycare in Metro [Toronto] are frighteningly inadequate" (SPC 1980, 193).

8 Similar trends in the rest of Canada have given rise to a national day care movement. Growing demands for day care have led to the formation of the Canadian Day Care Advocacy Association (CDCAA). With active labour support, the CDCAA has coordinated lobbying efforts in the last few years for a federally funded system of child care.

9 Pseudonyms are used in this article. Comments from interviewees have been transcribed from interview tapes and are cited in the text as comments from Ann, Chris, Diane, Donna, Jean, John, Nancy, and Gwen.

10 The OFL *Statement on Day Care* addressed these concerns; it called for the provision of child care services "at union meetings, conferences and conventions" (OFL 1980d).

11 While women constituted only 15.3 per cent of total union membership in Ontario in 1965, their proportions had risen to 22.9 per cent in 1975. In 1981, 29.5 per cent of all union members in Ontario were women (Ontario Ministry of Labour 1982). At the same time, women constituted 42.2 per cent of the Ontario work force and thus continued to be underrepresented in unions (Ontario Statistics 1984, tables 5.11, 5.26). For a general discussion of women's unionization, see Armstrong and Armstrong 1983a; Briskin 1983a; J. White 1980.

12 For a discussion of the connection between changing gender relations and women's activity in unions, see Briskin 1983a; Colley 1981; Egan and Yanz 1983; Leah 1986. A number of studies have documented the history of the discrimination against working women in the Canadian labour movement, including Frager 1983; Sangster 1981; J. White 1980.

13 OPSEU hired a full-time Equal Opportunity Coordinator in 1978 in order to implement the union's Equal Opportunity Program; its first women's caucus had been organized in Region 5 (Toronto) as early as 1976 (*Women's Rights Bulletin,* May 1980). Debbie Field was OPSEU's first equal opportunity coordinator (Field 1981 discusses this period). Labour's developing awareness of women's rights is addressed by Colley 1981, 31 and 1983, 315; and Acheson 1981, 5.

14 The importance of the women's movement for union women's organizing is noted by Briskin 1983a; Egan and Yanz 1983; Field 1981; Gallagher 1982; McCune 1981.

15 For details on the impact of the Fleck strike, see Cuthbertson 1978–79; Egan and Yanz 1983; J. White 1980.

16 The day care campaign is outlined in the *Statement on Day Care* (OFL 1980d). See resolution no. 183, "concurrence as amended" (OFL 1979b).

17 The OFL leadership maintained that the executive board – not delegates to annual conventions – reserves the right to hire staff (OFL Proceedings 1980, 10, 45–6).

18 For example, André Foucault, OFL Programs Director, was assigned to

work on the day care campaign. He coordinated activities in early 1981, including the organization of regional community forums on day care and the formation of a provincial day care coalition.

19 A 1978 OFL resolution called for "an examination of the feasibility of providing childcare services at future functions" (resolution no. 52, OFL Proceedings 1978, 34). Following a pilot project at the first OFL Women's Conference in April 1979 – which accommodated sixteen children of conference participants – the 1979 OFL Convention approved the provision of day care at all future OFL conventions and conferences (resolution no. 202, OFL Proceedings 1979, 40).

20 OPSEU voted to provide child care facilities at conventions and educational conferences at its 1978 convention. According to Diane, in 1980 a more comprehensive policy was adopted, providing for an expense claim for the child care costs, as well as the continuing child care services. According to Nancy, the UAW provides for child care at union meetings, including the Canadian Council, its highest decision-making body in Canada.

21 For example, the Women's Committee of CUPE, Local 1000, played an active role in the four-year process of setting up workplace day care at Ontario Hydro. This centre opened in September 1985. Workplace day care was raised as a final demand by OPSEU in the 1981–82 negotiations with the Ontario government. According to Diane, while the union did not win the day care issue during negotiations, the government has set up four pilot projects with on-site day care since that time. In its December 1983 contract, UAW Local 1325 successfully negotiated for employer contributions to an employee day care fund (*Solidarity*, Winter 1983, 11). This contract for Canadian Fab workers in Stratford, Ontario, was seen as a milestone in collective bargaining for child care.

22 In contrast to the working-class composition of unions, the women's movement has been characterized as largely middle class in its composition, including many professional women, students, and intellectuals (Ambert 1976, 179–80; Mackie 1983, 293).

23 Members of the autonomous women's movement – even those engaged in strike support activities – have tended to identify primarily with the women's movement (Egan and Yanz 1983).

24 A distrust of male-dominated unions has led some feminists to reject the mainstream labour movement, by turning to women-only unions, such as the Service, Office and Retail Workers Union of Canada (SORWUC). A discussion of this is contained in Ainsworth et al. 1982; Marchak 1973; McFarland 1979.

25 Nancy and Diane recalled how the political strategy used in the day care organizing was repeated with their campaign for affirmative action. In November 1982, OFL delegates endorsed the *Statement on Women and*

Affirmative Action. This called for mandatory affirmative action at work and equal representation of women in the unions.

26 Armstrong and Armstrong 1983a; Luxton 1980; and Oakley 1981.

27 These methods are also used by Langlois 1976; Laslett and Rapaport 1975.

28 The final version of my Ph.D. dissertation has been provided to the OFL Women's Committee; another copy is being circulated to several of the union activists involved in this study. Articles based on the research have also been made available to trade union women. It is hoped that a revised version of the thesis will be published in the near future, and so provide more general access to this social history.

29 Maher 1985, 35.

REFERENCES

Acheson, Shelley. 1982. "Daycare in the 80's: the Experience of the OFL." Remarks to the Equality Forum, CLC Convention, May.

Acheson, Shelley and Catherine Macleod. 1982. *Parental Rights and Daycare: A Bargaining Guide for Unions.* Toronto: Ontario Federation of Labour.

Adams, Jane, and Julie Griffin. 1983. "Bargaining for Equality." In Briskin and Yanz 1983.

Ainsworth, Jackie, et al. 1982. "Getting Organized ... in the Feminist Unions." In Fitzgerald et al. 1982.

Ambert, Anne-Marie. 1976. *Sex Structure.* Toronto: Longman.

Armstrong, Pat. 1984. *Labour Pains: Women's Work in Crisis.* Toronto: Women's Educational Press.

Armstrong, Pat, and Hugh Armstrong. 1978. *The Double Ghetto.* Toronto: McClelland and Stewart.

– 1983a. *A Working Majority: What Women Must Do for Pay.* Ottawa: CACSW.

– 1983b. "Towards Feminist Marxism." *Studies in Political Economy* Winter: 7–44.

Attenborough, Susan. 1982. *Bargaining for Equality.* Ottawa: National Union of Provincial Government Employees (NUPGE).

Bank Book Collective. 1979. *An Account to Settle.* Vancouver: Press Gang.

Beale, Jenny. 1982. *Getting it Together: Women as Trade Unionists.* London: Pluto Press.

Bickerton, Geoff. 1984. "The Role of Industrial Relations Research." *Labour Files* 1, no. 1.

Briskin, Linda. 1983a. "Women's Challenge to Organized Labour." In Briskin and Yanz 1983.

– 1983b. "Women and Unions: A Statistical Overview." In Briskin and Yanz 1983.

Briskin, Linda, and Lynda Yanz, eds. 1983. *Union Sisters*. Toronto: Women's Press.

CLC (Canadian Labour Congress). 1976. *Equality of Opportunity and Treatment for Women Workers*. Policy Statement, 11th CLC Constitutional Convention, 1976. Ottawa: CLC.

— 1979. Women's Bureau. *Equal Partners for Change: Women and the Unions*. Ottawa: CLC.

Cleveland, John. n.d. "The Mainstreaming of Feminist Issues: The Toronto Women's Movement, 1966–1984." Unpublished.

Colley, Sue. 1981. "Day Care and the Trade Union Movement in Ontario." Resources for Feminist Research 10, no. 2, part 2: 29–31.

— 1983. "Free Universal Day Care: The OFL Takes a Stand." In Briskin and Yanz 1983.

CUPE (Canadian Union of Public Employees). 1981. Local 1000 (Ontario Hydro Employees' Union), Women's Committee. "Submission to OFL Sharing the Caring Public Forum on Day Care," prepared by Margaret Smith, Day Care Subcommittee, 11 April. Unpublished.

CUPW (Canadian Union of Postal Workers). 1981. *Negotiations Backgrounder No. 3: Parental Rights*. Ottawa: CUPW.

Cuthbertson, Wendy. 1978–79. "Fleck – the Unionization of Women." *Canadian Women's Studies* 1, no. 2.

Day Care Research Group. 1982. *The Daycare Kit*. Toronto: Day Care Research Group.

Egan, Carolyn, and Lynda Yanz. 1983. "Building Links: Labour and the Women's Movement. In Briskin and Yanz 1983.

Field, Debbie. 1981. "Women's Committees in Unions." *Resources for Feminist Research* 10, no. 2, part 2: 8–11.

Fitzgerald, Maureen. 1981. "Whither the Feminist Unions?" *Resources for Feminist Research* 10, no. 2, part 2: 19–21.

Fitzgerald, Maureen, et. al., eds. 1982. *Still Ain't Satisfied: Canadian Feminism Today*. Toronto: Women's Press.

Fox, Bonnie. 1980. Introduction to Bonnie Fox, ed., *Hidden in the Household*. Toronto: Women's Press.

Frager, Ruth. 1983. "Women Workers and the Canadian Labour Movement, 1879–1940." In Briskin and Yanz 1983.

Gallagher, Deirdre. 1982. "Getting Organized ... in the CLC." In Fitzgerald 1982.

Game, Ann, and R. Pringle. 1983. *Gender at Work*. London: George Allen & Unwin, 1986.

Globe and Mail. 1986. "Daycare does from Marginal to Big Social Issue for Ottawa," by Murray Campbell, 20 May 1986: 1, 15.

Hartman, Grace. 1976. "Women and the Unions." In G. Matheson, ed., *Women in the Canadian Mosaic*. Toronto: Peter Martin Associates.

Hunt, Judith. 1982. "A Women's Place is in her Union." In Jackie West, ed., *Work, Women and the Labour Market*. London: Routledge & Kegan Paul.

Lane, Arja. 1983. "Wives Supporting the Strike." In Briskin and Yanz 1983.

Langan, Joy. 1976. "Trade Union Women's Committees." *Canadian Labour* 21, no. 3.

Langlois, W.J., ed. 1976. *A Guide to Aural History Research*. Victoria: Aural History, Provincial Archives of British Columbia.

Laslett, Barbara, and Rhona Rapaport. 1975. "Collaborative Interviewing and Interactive Research." *Journal of Marriage and the Family* Nov.

Leah, Ronnie. 1981. "Women's Labour Force Participation and Day Care Cutbacks in Ontario." *Atlantis* 7, no. 1.

– 1986. "The Day Care Issue and the Development of a Trade Union Women's Movement." Doctoral Dissertation, Department of Education, University of Toronto.

– 1987. "Organizing for Daycare." In Robert Argue, ed., *Working People and Hard Times*. Toronto: Garamond Press.

Luxton, Meg. 1980. *More than a Labour of Love*. Toronto: Women's Press.

Mackie, Marlene. 1983. *Exploring Gender Relations*. Toronto: Butterworths.

Maher, Frances. 1973. "Classroom Pedagogy and the New Scholarship on Women." In M. Culley and C. Portuges, eds., *Gendered Subjects: the Dynamics of Feminist Teaching*. London: Routledge and Kegan Paul.

Marchak, Patricia. 1973. "Women Workers and White Collar Unions." *Canadian Review of Sociology and Anthropology* 10, no. 2:134–47.

Marshall, Stan. 1984. "Trade Unionists and Academics: Overcoming Tension?" Paper presented at OASA meetings, Toronto. Unpublished.

McCune, Micki. 1981. "Fighting for our Rights." *Resources for Feminist Research* 10, no. 2:11–12.

McFarland, Joan. 1979. "Women and Unions: Help or Hindrance?" *Atlantis* 4, no. 2:48–66.

Oakley, Ann. 1981. "Interviewing Women: A Contradiction in Terms." In Helen Roberts, ed., *Doing Feminist Research*. London: Routledge and Kegan Paul.

OASA (Ontario Association of Sociology and Anthropology). 1985. *Newsletter* 7, no. 1.

OFL (Documents of the Ontario Federation of Labour, Toronto)

1975. *Statement on Women*, Resolution of OFL Convention.

1978. *A Woman's Place is in her Union*. Resolution of OFL Convention.

1979a. *Report of the First OFL Women's conference: Bargaining for Equality*, April.

1979b. "Resolutions," 23rd Annual OFL convention, Nov.

1979c. "Convention 1979: Disposition of Resolutions," Nov.

1980a. Agenda, OFL Conference on Day Care, Oct.

1980b. *Report of the OFL Conference on Day Care: Sharing the Caring*, Oct.

1980c. OFL Information, "OFL Day Care Conference a First for Labour," 6 Oct.

1980d. *Statement on Day Care*, Resolution of OFL Convention, Nov.

1981. *Daycare: Deadline 1990*, Brief to Government of Ontario.

1982a. *Statement on Women and Affirmative Action*, Resolution of OFL Convention, Nov.

1982b. *Policies.*

OFL Proceedings. 1975 to 1980. *Report of Proceedings of the Annual Convention of the Ontario Federation of Labour*. Toronto: OFL.

Ontario Labour. 1978 to 1981. Bi-monthly publication of the Ontario Federation of Labour. Toronto: OFL.

Ontario Ministry of Labour, Women's Bureau. 1982. "Basic Facts." *Women in the Labour Force Factsheets*. Toronto: Ministry of Labour.

Ontario Statistics. 1984. *Ontario Statistics, 1984*. Toronto: Ontario Ministry of Treasury and Economics.

OPSEU (Ontario Public Service Employees Union). n.d. Resolutions on Day Care. Toronto: OPSEU, Office of the Equal Opportunities Coordinator. Unpublished.

– 1982. President's Report, *Women in OPSEU – A Statistical Analysis of Participation in Union Affairs by Women*. Toronto: OPSEU.

Pilkey, Cliff. 1980. "Speaker's Notes." Address to OFL Conference on Day Care, Ontario Federation of Labour, 17 Oct. Unpublished.

Phillips, Paul, and Erin Phillips. 1983. *Women and Work: Inequality in the Labour Market*. Toronto: James Lorimer.

Public Archives Canada. 1983. *Archival Citations*. Ottawa: Ministry of Supply and Services Canada.

Resources for Feminist Research (RFR). 1981. Special Issue on Women and Trade Unions. 10, no. 2, part 2.

Ritchie, Laurell. 1983. "Why are So Many Women Unorganized?" In Briskin and Yanz 1983.

Sangster, Joan. 1981. "Women and Unions: A Review of Historical Research." *Resources for Feminist Research* 10, no. 2: 2–6.

Smith, Dorothy. 1980a. "Concluding Address: CRIAW in the 1980's." *Resources for Feminist Research*, Special Publication 8.

– 1980b. "Women, Class and Family." Paper prepared for SSHRC Workshop on Women and the Canadian Labour Force. UBC. Unpublished.

– 1981. "Women and Trade Unions: The U.S. and British Experience." *Resources for Feminist Research* 10, no. 2, part 2: 53–60.

Solidarity Sept. 1980 to Winter 1983. Publication of the United Auto Workers. Toronto: UAW (CAW).

SPC (Social Planning Council of Metro Toronto). 1980. *Metro's Suburbs in Transition: Part II*, Toronto: SPC.

Touraine, Alain. 1981. *The Voice and the Eye: An Analysis of Social Movements.* Cambridge: Cambridge University Press.

UAW (United Auto Workers). 1981. "A Women's Committee Can Make Your Union Work for You." Toronto: UAW (CAW).

Union Woman. 1980. Publication of Organized Working Women (OWW) 4, no. 1.

USWA (United Steelworkers). 1983. *Women of Steel – Equality in the Economy, on the Job and in the Union.* Research Paper. Toronto: USWA.

WC (Documents and Letters of the OFL Women's Committee, Toronto) Documents:

    1980a. "Day Care – Outline for Discussion."

    1980b. "Sharing the Caring": OFL Discussion Paper on Day Care, prepared for OFL Conference on Day Care, Oct.

    1982. "Our Fair Share," OFL Discussion Paper on Women and Affirmative Action, May.

Letters:

    3 June 1980. Terry Meagher to OFL Affiliates.

    27 June 1980. OFL Women's Committee to Action Day Care.

    26 August 1980. T. Meagher to OFL Affiliates.

    18 Sept. 1980. OFL WC to WC Members.

    26 Jan. 1981. Cliff Pilkey to (organizations interested in daycare),

    29 Jan. 1981. Andre Foucault to OFL Executive Council.

    4 Feb. 1981. Shelley Acheson to delegates to the OFL Conference on Day Care.

    9 Feb. 1981. T. Meagher to OFL Affiliates, "Preliminary Call: OFL Public Forums on Daycare."

Minutes (Meetings of the OFL (Women's Committee), 1978 to 1980.

White, Julie. 1980. *Women and Unions.* Prepared for CACSW. Ottawa: Ministry of Supply and Services Canada.

White, Robert. 1979. *Report to the UAW Canadian Collective Bargaining Conference.* Toronto: UAW (CAW).

– 1982. *Report to the Canadian UAW Collective Bargaining and Legislative Conference.* Toronto: UAW (CAW).

Women's Rights Bulletin. 1980 to 1981. Publication of the OFL Women's Committee.

Yanz, Lynda, and David Smith. 1983. "Women at Work in Canada." In Briskin and Yanz 1983.

JOHN CLEVELAND

Why Is the Feminist Movement Still Politically Marginal?

In the 1960s, there was a revival of the feminist movement around the world, particularly in industrialized countries like Canada. This revival or "second wave" was driven by tangible social contradictions: conflicting pressures on most women to be simultaneously independent and dependent, both equal and subordinate to men. Women felt these contradictory pressures in family and work roles, as well as in conflicts between family and work.

The feminist movement has succeeded in changing the way women look at themselves and their place in the social world, especially on a cultural and interpersonal level. The new consciousness among women and the greater recognition of the social contradictions which gave rise to it have legitimized some feminist cultural norms. It has obliged the men who control the major institutions of Canadian society to take feminist-defined issues seriously.[1]

Despite this, the feminist movement remains politically marginal. Government and business deal with their representatives as lobbyists for one interest group among many, or as marginal protesters, not as members of a movement seeking power for women in State and other institutions. At best, politicians are particularly careful to be seen as non-antagonistic to feminism because over half the voters are women. In a world where men still set the rules, women have the right to vote for the men of their choice or to be deputies who help the men run things. Some feminist-defined issues are now on the political agenda; the right of women to run things is not.

Why is the feminist movement still politically marginal when its impact on cultural norms continues to grow? My answers to this question are based on research into the Toronto women's movement since the mid-1960s. This has involved reading movement files and publications stored in the Women's Movement Archives and interviewing fifty-five movement activists. Put simply, there are two main reasons: the men who control societal institutions continue to resist, and the feminist movement is not yet oriented towards achieving feminist political power in State or other institutions. Hence feminist activism focuses on changing cultural norms.

MEN CONTINUE TO RESIST FEMALE POWER AND AUTHORITY

Women, let alone feminist women, have never exercised significant power in the Canadian political system. After the First World War, the "first wave" of organized feminism won the right of women to vote, to control their own wages and property, and to have access to higher education. A decision of the Privy Council in Britain in 1929 enabled Canadian women to be declared legal "persons" and become eligible for appointment to the federal Senate. In recent years this lack of political power has slowly begun to change, with the appointment of a few female Cabinet ministers and deputy ministers on both the provincial and federal levels. It is too early to tell whether such change will be more than cosmetic.

A traditional explanation by (mostly male) academics for the absence of females from political posts is that women are not interested in politics. Political scientists cite statistics that show a lower voter turnout by women before the Second World War or a pattern of wives voting the same way as their husbands. Another traditional explanation is that women have not acquired the necessary skills to get elected, although polls show that the electorate is prepared to vote for women candidates. Feminist academics have countered these arguments – which at best amount to blaming the powerless for showing some of the symptoms of their powerlessness – by arguing that the men who control political parties and State bureaucracies have systematically excluded women from posts of power and authority. They contend that the exclusion is increasingly complete at higher levels (Bashevkin 1985).

Patterns of exclusion have begun to break down in both extra-parliamentary and parliamentary political organizations as women members have organized for change. In the first case, struggles over sexism within New Left campus groups in the late 1960s, and in Marxist and other left extra-parliamentary groups in the late 1970s, led to efforts at radical changes. Yet changes made were too late to keep most of the female activists from leaving.[2]

The challenges raised within the parliamentary parties have been more modest but more successful in keeping women members as members. One example is a women's caucus organized at the initiative of women from the radical Waffle caucus in the Ontario New Democratic Party (ONDP) in 1972. After the Waffle was purged in 1974, many of the younger activist women left and the caucus became quiet. But from 1977 on, a number of ONDP women active at the constituency level joined women trade unionists from the Ontario Federation of Labour Women's Committee. They participated jointly in the annual March 8 celebrations and in the regular strike support activities organized by the socialist feminist International Women's Day Committee. These same women began to demand changes within their party, pointing out that men controlled key executive posts and that the party ran men in most of the winnable seats.

The party establishment was impressed by surveys showing that the ONDP was suffering electorally from a "gender gap" – far fewer union wives and women union members voted NDP than did union men.[3] The ONDP leadership responded by accepting a decidedly more feminist policy platform in 1981 and thereafter. The federal NDP followed suit in the 1984 election. It adopted affirmative action measures to encourage equal representation of women on party executives and committees.

Since the First World War, the federal Liberal and Conservative parties have encouraged women to join the party women's auxiliary rather than the party itself. Women gradually entered party ranks in the 1950s and 1960s. The Liberal party established a standing national Women's Commission in 1973 to encourage direct female participation. A National PC Women's Caucus, affiliated to the National Action Committee on the Status of Women, was founded in 1981 within the federal Conservative party. There has been a major increase in the number of women delegates at the conventions of both the Liberal and Progressive Conservative parties at provincial and federal levels the last several years.

Progress in getting posts of power and authority in business and the professions has also been slow. There is a still tiny but growing female middle class. Its numbers will likely expand more quickly in Ontario as a consequence of the new law on family property. Enrolment of women is up markedly in professional and business schools. The percentage of managers who are female increased from 18.7 to 25.2 per cent in Canada between 1975 and 1980, albeit mainly in female job ghettos, where they exert authority over other women (Armstrong and Armstrong 1983, 252).

An increase in upward mobility prospects for some women has affected the aspirations of others. There is still only room for a minority to "make it." Those who do are expected to conform to male standards and role models on the job while remaining "feminine" in personal interactions and when they go home. Women continue to carry the extra burden of primary responsibility for planning and doing most of the housework and child care. While a husband may help his working wife with "her" responsibilities, in most cases this is only a matter of a few minutes more per day, even when the couple have pre-school children (Berk 1985, Robinson 1977, Michelson 1985 and Meissner et al. 1975). Governments have yet to offset this resistance to change by husbands through measures such as funding a universal day care system and requiring companies to introduce flextime and extended parental leaves for either parent.

The formal barriers to the participation of women in the political system are coming down, but several important obstacles remain. The reluctance of men to equalize responsibility in the home, and the insistence by the men who run the political parties and State bureaucracies that women conform to a male behaviour model, are chief among these. Men simply presume that the system will always be controlled by men.

THE FEMINIST MOVEMENT IS NOT ORIENTED TO POLITICAL POWER

The other main reason why the feminist movement is still politically marginal is that the movement has yet to orient itself to the achievement of political power.

One example drawn from my Toronto research symbolizes the feminist movement's stand on the issue of seeking political power. This is the outcome of a six-month-long effort in 1984 to achieve agreement on the creation of a permanent Toronto area women's council, roughly similar to the union movement's local labour council. The hope was that a permanent coalition of women's groups would be able to represent the grass-roots movement to the media, organize regular campaigns, and mobilize the solidarity of all groups for the battle of any one of them. At one point or another groups from virtually every section of the Toronto movement were involved in the discussions. They ended in failure.

On the surface the reason for the impasse seemed clear enough. Political differences such as dealing with pornography gave way to arguments about political process. In various ways small groups expressed nervousness about the creation of representative institutions, even though these would be composed exclusively of women and would operate on a local (city-wide) level. De facto centralization of decision making would undermine the autonomy of the small groups. It would reinforce the idea of a movement which is made up of formal groups rather than the spirit of an informal network of individual "sisters." Formalization of leadership in an élite decision-making body would lead permanent spokespeople to be given star treatment in the media. The need to take political stands would aggravate the possibility of splits among women and "dirty linen" washed in public. There was danger of getting sidetracked onto partisan and/or left politics rather than continuing to focus on feminist consciousness raising around issues the small groups were then working on.[4]

As some activists put it, the central problem was whether to maintain feminist politics as participatory democracy, an atmosphere of mutual emotional support and concern for personal growth, and a task-based division of responsibilities, or be integrated into the male-controlled political system. I shall argue later that radical rhetoric of this sort conceals a conservative political practice. Both the socialist feminist caution about cooption into the bourgeois State and the radical feminist warning that the feminist movement must be kept autonomous provide rationales for not seeking power in national political institutions. A number of feminist groups seek change *from* the current political system, through a combination of lobbying and media-oriented protest tactics, but very few seek political power in or through it.

REASONS FOR A FOCUS ON CULTURAL NORMS

Most feminist groups are oriented instead to consciousness raising, and to challenging and changing cultural norms. There are both solid historical and structural reasons for this.

Female exclusion from political power has been embedded in cultural rules and practices of human societies for centuries. Anthropologists and historians have documented many exceptions, particularly instances where the importance of class outweighs gender considerations, permitting upper-class women to accede to the positions of deceased fathers or husbands. They have described the intricate ways in which women exercise real power – informally, separately, or invisibly, despite norms of male authority and authoritativeness (Friedl 1975, Reiter 1975, Rosaldo and Lamphere 1974). The fact remains that cultural prescriptions and proscriptions about kinship, sexuality, marriage and divorce, the division of labour in the household and economy, political authority, and property rights sanction the power of some men and the powerlessness of most women.

Bourgeois political revolutions and the replacement of feudalism by capitalism have had a double impact on the status of women. The historical position of women was in many ways degraded. Under feudalism and early capitalism, women's status was specified by their status in the family, and in their independent contribution to domestically organized agricultural and home production. Industrialization destroyed the family-based economy and the statuses rooted in it. Families and women became dependent on male wages. On the other hand, increased social mobility and the ideology of the rights of the individual regardless of "estate" removed much of the justification for maintaining different and unequal rights for women. Mary Wollestonecraft argued this point in *Vindication of the Rights of Women* in 1792 and John Stuart Mill repeated it in *The Subjection of Women* in 1869.

The "first wave" of the women's movement addressed itself to both the devaluation of the woman's family role and the denial of full citizenship status, and hence equal rights, to women.

The forward thrust of the first wave movement came from the struggle for a new status to replace the lost family-based one, the struggle for women to be accorded the full rights of legal individuals or citizens. The immediate target was not so much political power for women, or even more limited political rights such as the vote, as civil rights in marriage and property, and the removal of barriers to education and employment.

The battle to establish women as the potential legal, social, and economic equals of men had to be won first.[5] This limitation of scope was accepted by the socialist women's movement too. Marxists saw the ending of legal discrimination, and the entry of women into wage labour, as critical. They did not feel that working-class women could get any real political power until after a socialist revolution.

By the mid-1960s, after winning the vote and formal access to the political system, women continued to have reasons to be sceptical about participation in politics. As I have noted, women were by and large excluded from a significant role in the political parties and government. The extra-parliamentary New Left was more open to female participation, but feminist issues were downgraded as "merely personal" and "secondary" to the pursuit of political power by national minorities and the working class. A focus on political power did not seem to lead to the empowerment of women.

The "second wave" of feminism arises in a period where women have many more rights as legal individuals. The main contradiction is between rights women enjoy in so far as they are treated as individuals, and the lack of both equality and autonomy in so far as they are treated as female. This contradiction is exacerbated by conflicting pressures on women to be both "individual" and female."

On the one hand, women have greater economic and reproductive independence than at any other time in history. Married women with pre-school children work to maintain the economic viability of the heterosexual nuclear family household and thus most women have a major attachment to the labour force. In industrial urban societies, demographic pressures for a low birth rate require planning and spacing of births. Women spend less of their lives as mothers and, with some control over reproduction, have greater leverage in negotiating terms of personal relationships. On the other hand, there are still female job ghettos and unequal pay. The primary responsibility for childrearing and housework continues to be assigned to females. Female sexuality is objectified in the arts and media, and women are the main victims of personal assaults in the family and on the street.

The "second wave" has targeted as the key obstacle to women's liberation those cultural processes which construct girls as "female" and boys as "male" and reinforce adult women and men in gender-appropriate roles. Referred to variously as the practices of "institutionalized sexism" or "patriarchy," there is still little theoretical accord on how these cultural processes operate. Nor is there much agreement as to how they vary between cultures and historical periods, or how they interact with other factors – such as capitalist class relations or institutionalized racism – to oppress women. But there is widespread consensus on what they produce. A society in which the notion of "male" as active, superior, and dominant and "female" as passive, inferior, and subordinate is built into the normative structure of most institutions. As a result, men, and ideologies rooted mainly in male experience, dominate.

CULTURAL CONTESTATION:
THEORETICAL ISSUES FOR ADVOCATES

Gender, and hence gender-based roles in specific institutions, are typically presented as "natural" or biologically based. The "natural" quality of gender differences is accepted by women as well as men as part of "common sense" and gender is seen as the property of the individual's personality rather than the property of social relationships. Challenging institutionalized gender relations requires argument that what appears natural is to a large extent culturally created, and that what appears as gender-neutral "common sense" is in fact an ideology based mostly on male interests. An advocate must argue that "merely personal" difficulties of individual women are also problems of being female in a socially constructed collectivity. Advocacy is effected by a broad range of cultural contestation, from the writing of women's history to a critiquing of scientific, artistic, and political discourses in order to uncover their male perspective, to encouraging self-esteem and solidarity among individual women through consciousness raising. Advocacy requires building a female counter-culture where women can have their own space. It requires an exposure of how institutions discriminate against the female, and a demand for remedial measures such as affirmative action. Advocates must insist that power and inequality in personal life – from freedom of sexual expression, to division of labour in the household, to domestic violence – be treated as issues of the same weight as government or the economy.

Many analysts have observed that concern with establishing an autonomous cultural identity, which is explicit in the women's movement's challenge to institutionalized gender relations, is common to all of the "new social movements" which have become prominent in the 1970s and 1980s. Most analysts, especially Touraine, explain the concern for autonomous cultural identity in terms of the increased ability of society to "produce itself." That is to say, society can now consciously set cultural orientations and proceed to implement or institutionalize them in the economy, civil society, and State. This, in turn, is said to be the consequence of two other factors. First, the success of welfare state capitalism in providing for basic material needs enables people to concern themselves more closely with their "higher" moral and cultural needs. Second, advances in technology have put power into the hands of technocrats who are driven by a desire to control human nature through the manipulation of symbolic systems. As Touraine has observed: "In our time we feel that our capacity for self-production, self-transformation and self-destruction is boundless. [Society today] produces not only means but ends of production, demands and representations. It is already able to transform our body, our sexuality, our mental life" (Touraine 1985, 778).[6]

This has evident implications for women. The maintenance of adults and the socialization and maintenance of children have long been the responsibility of women and the family or kinship group. At the same time, biological and social reproduction activities have been the object of concern and action by the State, Church, and other institutions. Under industrial capitalism the responsibility of women and family for their own reproduction is more private than in previous social systems; compare for example the degree to which the lord of the estate took final responsibility for the maintenance of peasant subjects in most feudal societies. But capitalism must continually expand in order to maintain itself, and capitalist societies have sought to increase control over the conditions of production. This includes the conditions of "production" of personalities, group identities, values, beliefs, and skills. Touraine and others point out that this trend reaches its zenith in post-industrial society, where the qualitative characteristics of "mental labour" are an increasingly important variable in production.

The logic of a private-ownership-based society requires that the socially recognized individual "own," i.e. take ultimate responsibility for and have final authority over, his or her means of reproduction. Thus increasing concern with "ownership" of social reproduction is a new dimension of social conflict. Previously responsibility for social reproduction of children has been in the hands of parents and other kin, and women have played a particular role in meeting the maintenance needs of adult men. In industrializing capitalism the "individual" which owned was the individual family and rights were accorded first and foremost to the male family head. This has broken down over time as women have been drawn into wage labour, and have had social reproduction activities either supplemented or replaced by the school, public health facilities, and marketplace. In the process they have achieved more rights as individuals.

The two imperatives – the State and economic élites' control of the production of people and capitalism's need to preserve individual ownership and responsibility – give rise to contradictions. The first contradiction lies between the family as a social individual and the individual rights of women and children within it. The second lies between "society" and both family and individuals. The abstract solution is to supplant the family as social individual by individual men, women, and children responsible for their own social reproduction, and to strengthen individual rights vis-à-vis society. But the abstract solution glosses over a host of concrete problems.

Far-reaching measures may be necessary to offset the impact of biological differences between women and men or maturity differences between adults and children in order to make them equal individuals. Will test-tube babies be needed to equalize biological reproductive capacity? Will children be brought up in public institutions instead of private families from birth? Will either of these changes actually guarantee that one sex or age group will not exercise arbitrary control over the reproduction process of the other?

Overcoming both sex and age difference in reality rather than abstractly would mean questioning the very idea of distinct genders and consequently everything now organized on the basis of gender, from sexuality to aspects of the social division of labour. Will bisexuality replace heterosexual monogamy? Will repression of childhood sexuality give way to child-child and adult-child sex? Will masculine and feminine gender dissolve into a single androgynous human gender identity? Will gender disappear as a criterion for the division of labour? How will the desire of people for both individual autonomy and community, including intimate communal bonds, be met at the same time? How will individuals meet their need for both economic and emotional support and stability if the family as we know it disappears? Finally, how will men be reconciled to the loss of power and privilege which are necessary for the empowerment of women?

It is easy to understand why advocates devote so much attention to articulating cultural alternatives and promoting "workable solutions" to these rhetorical questions. Yet to laud cultural contestation as the birth of a "new politics" is to abandon struggle for the restructuring of the economy or the State in favour of a singular focus on cultural identity and autonomy (Cohen 1985, 663–716).[7] Very few of the demands of the women's movement can be realized without making parallel decisions about such restructuring. It is virtually impossible to conceptualize a society in which cultural norms designate the female as equal and autonomous but where women do not play an equal role in the economy or in political decision making.

A practice of cultural contestation is indispensable. Advocacy confined to culture is problematic. This is becoming increasingly evident as the feminist movement in Canada faces strong attacks from a well-financed, well-connected, and organized political counter-movement spearheaded by the "pro-family" REAL Women and the anti-abortion Right to Life movement.[8]

THE FAILURE TO REORIENT
THE WOMEN'S MOVEMENT

There have been several attempts to orient the women's movement towards achievement of political power. Both liberal and socialist feminist groups have tried. Their failure demonstrates the limitations of their respective epistemologies as guides for feminist political struggle.

The second wave of the English-Canadian feminist movement emanated from two distinct sources. One source was the women within the New Left of the 1960s. They eventually set up the decentralized extra-parliamentary "autonomous women's movement," which continues to be led mainly by socialist and radical feminists.

The other source was professional women from women's organizations. These women, generally a bit older than the New Left students, organized the National Action Committee on the Status of Women (NAC) in 1972 to pressure the federal government to implement the recommendations of the Royal Commission on the Status of Women. NAC, which has evolved into a permanent federal lobby dependent on Ottawa for 70 per cent of its funds, remains the most important organization led by liberal feminists. An increasing number of socialist feminists and some radical feminists are working within it; at the moment it is the only country-wide women's structure.

Liberal feminist groups like NAC have focused their energies on achieving equal legal rights and in getting governments to appoint women to posts. They have supported other organizations in successful challenges over the application of equal rights laws. NAC includes 290 affiliates. Crucial to NAC's credibility as representatives of the women's movement was the battle over equal rights clauses in the 1981 constitution. NAC leaders acted through an *ad hoc* committee rather than NAC itself in that campaign, but in 1984, the three federal political parties conferred further legitimacy on NAC by accepting it as the organizer of the federal leaders' television debate on "women's issues." Despite these successes, NAC has not become the focus for the building of a mass political women's movement.

Women for Political Action was formed in Toronto and three women ran as independents in one federal election. WPA never really got off the ground and continued merely as a monthly luncheon speakers' club. In 1979, some of the WPA women joined with radical feminists from Women Against Violence Against Women to form the Feminist Party of Canada. The latter also failed to grow, in part because it could never resolve whether to be an electoral party – and therefore open to men – or to become a consciousness-raising and political-education-oriented women-only feminist group.

Like WPA, NAC has shown ambivalence about building a women's movement which is in competition with the existing political parties. NAC sees its role as a non-partisan interest group acting as an intermediary between women's groups and the parliamentary political parties. Up until 1986 it had never waged a public campaign against any government party. A brief campaign over proposed changes to family allowances marked the emergence of a trend within NAC to advocacy politics to supplement its quiet lobbying approach. NAC has also joined coalitions led by other groups, notably the affirmative action and day care coalitions initiated by the Ontario Federation of Labour (Leah above), and it has endorsed several women's strikes. But it has not yet reached the point of proposing its own campaigns.

In general liberal feminists in NAC have been just as unwilling to challenge the power structure in the economy and the State as they have been to challenge the political party system. One exception, already noted, has been the support shown for strikes and campaigns led by trade union women. On issues such as racism, sexual politics, and the right of Quebec and Native peoples to self-determination, NAC has been silent. Most Canadian women, if asked, would not likely protest that NAC has failed to take broad political stands. In contrast, each subgroup of women is much more radical when it comes to their own issue – trade union women on union issues, immigrant women on super-exploitation in Canada or liberation movements in former home countries. The same applies to Quebecois women on nationalist issues, women of colour on racism, Native women on self-government and land claims, lesbian and young women on sexual politics, and so on. By ignoring such issues, NAC reinforces its image as an organization of self-promoting white middle-class career women. This has helped keep each of the subgroups listed above unenthusiastic about NAC as a vehicle for their interests. Of particular note is NAC's reluctance to be perceived as "radical feminist" or "anti-family." Until recently it had avoided most issues of sexual politics altogether and had no lesbian organizations in its membership.[9] This ambivalence on the part of NAC is precisely the terrain on which antifeminists have chosen to launch their political countermovement.

LIMITS OF THE LIBERAL APPROACH TO FEMINISM

Groups like NAC are trying to complete the struggle of "first wave" feminists by winning rights for women as abstract individuals,[10] but in practice are unable to do anything about subordination based on gender, except to say that everyone should be treated as if they did not have a gender (Bem 1974, 155–62, Bem and Lenney 1976, 48–54, Silvern and Ryan 1979, 739–63).

The failure of liberal feminist efforts to mobilize women politically reflects the limits of the liberal framework. Liberalism conceptualizes equality of opportunity for abstract individuals but not equality of condition for concrete individuals, whose opportunities are defined by their membership in a collective category – or, more precisely, by the social relations which tie their group to other groups. Liberalism cannot accept State intervention in order to secure the interest of a specific social group, especially if it hurts the interests of another group.[11] This creates dilemmas for liberal feminists when it comes to the practial implementation of many key feminist demands. Experience shows that affirmative action, equal pay for work of equal value, and universal day care will not be implemented voluntarily by the private sector (Leah above; Barrett and McIntosh 1983).[12] Reforms will only be achieved by aggressive State intervention from above in favour of a specific social group (women), complemented by struggles from below. Feminist groups and unions are necessary to get women's special rights written into contracts and to ensure compliance.

In an era when liberalism is returning to its eighteenth-century pre-welfare-State roots, liberal feminists will eventually have to choose between their liberalism and their feminism.[13] Most liberal feminists seem to be choosing feminism and the extension of the welfare State in support of women's interests. They pay a political price for this. Since many male liberals in the political parties, business, and State are not making the same choice, organizations like NAC may find some of their funding cut back in future, while organizations like REAL Women may continue to gain ground. In addition, measures like universal day care appear to hurt women caught in the exclusive housewife and mother role, by "State-izing" some of their functions. The full-time homemaker's status is devalued, while those women who seek greater access to the labour force are helped. Groups like REAL Women play directly to the fears of those women who think that they will be devalued, or unable to compete successfully, and they do so with liberal rhetoric, claiming that they are the "real" liberals.[14]

THE LIMITS OF MARXISM AND SOCIALIST FEMINISM

Socialist feminists do not share the same ambivalences about interfering in the market economy or developing a radical opposition to existing political parties or State. Their ambivalence, as we shall see, is about their Marxism. Socialist feminists have done more than anyone else to promote political mobilization at the grass-roots level. However, they too have failed to build a mass movement oriented to securing political power.

The main socialist feminist grouping in Toronto is the International Women's Day Committee (IWDC). Founded in 1978, its short-term objectives were twofold. First, it brought women from different nationalities, classes, and sexual orientations together in various coalition actions. Its most important vehicle for letting women learn about, and express support for, one another's demands was the annual week of public meetings and demonstrations around March 8. The March 8 events were an important force for unity in a movement of particularistic identities and concerns. One notable success was integrating the issue of lesbianism within sexual politics as a valid and positive sexual choice. Second, IWDC sought to promote an alliance between the women's movement and the labour movement by promoting feminism in the unions, and unionism among feminists. Here again IWDC contributed indirectly, but in a significant way, to feminist reforms in the Ontario Federation of Labour (OFL) and its member unions. This in turn facilitated changes within the Ontario NDP.

The battle for reform in the unions was led by union women, initially by Organized Working Women and subsequently by union women's committees, particularly the province-wide OFL Women's Committee. The Women's Committee was appointed by the OFL executive in response to agitation by women unionists and to a series of women-led first contract strikes (Fleck, Radio Shack, Blue Cross). The IWDC mobilized women from the feminist movement into support pickets for strikes of women workers. This helped to improve the image of feminism among trade unionists. It also helped raise the feminist consciousness of many union women activists by drawing them into its coalition work, particularly the annual March 8 events.

As Leah shows in another chapter of this book, the Ontario Federation of Labour launched in 1982 a province-wide coalition to press for government-legislated mandatory affirmative action and equal pay for women in traditionally female jobs. It also voted to apply affirmative action to itself. For example, it changed the composition of the OFL executive board. It added five female vice-presidents in order to bring the number of women on the board up to the percentage they represent in the OFL membership. Other changes made by OFL-affiliated unions included the formation of provincial women's committees and regular women's conferences, adoption of a full range of feminist policies on issues from sexual orientation to equal pay and maternity leave and day care provisions in union contracts. In addition, Ontario unions have participated in an OFL-led provincial coalition for public day care, supported the Dr Henry Morgentaler clinics, which provide greater access to abortion than is available from the hospitals alone, and established internal skill-training and educational programs to increase participation of women in union affairs.

Adoption of many feminist policies and structures to help open up former male preserves in the work force, and in the unions themselves, has not yet resulted in an alliance between labour and the feminist groups as two coequal movements, each seeking political power for its constituency. Instead there are feminist amendments to labour's political program, and union-led (and therefore NDP-controlled) coalitions on some feminist-defined issues.

While many union women have joined other women in campaigns led by socialist feminists, very few have been won over to Marxist feminism, or tried to join socialist feminist groups like IWDC. One reason for this is the discrediting of socialism as a political goal. The discrediting is due to the blatant failure of "socialist" States established by Marxist-led movements to perform better than capitalist regimes in either raising living standards or increasing the democratic power of the lower classes.

The failures of socialist countries extend to their inability to bring about effective change in the status of women. It is undeniable that women's lot has improved in most socialist countries, mainly in provisions for extended maternity leave, child care, and so on. Indeed, more has been done than in many capitalist countries to enable women to work full time and still meet domestic obligations. Yet women face the same basic conflicting pressures in socialist countries as already noted in capitalist countries like Canada (Molyneaux 1981).[15] Contrary to Marxist theory, State control in socialist countries has not brought about socialization of the means of production or of domestic labour. It has eliminated neither the arbitrary power of a dominant class in production nor the arbitrary power of a dominant sex in the private household. It has not desegregated the economy or put women into positions of political power on a par with men in State institutions.

Socialist feminists have also failed to win women to continued use of Marxist tactics in relation to existing practices of the liberal democratic State. Marxism views liberal democracy as a "sham" which covers up the reality of a class dictatorship. Marxist-Leninists participate in the political system to expose this reality, and to organize an extra-parliamentary movement aimed at the overthrow of the liberal-democratic State. Socialist feminists, like other New Left radicals who took up Marxism in the 1960s and 1970s, have abandoned a strict Leninist approach. While they are not preparing strategy for the political overthrow of the capitalist state, a Leninist type of tactical orientation remains.

Hence socialist feminists continue to go back and forth between building a movement outside the existing political system and manoeuvring to get concessions from it. They try to build an extra-parliamentary movement centred on the unions in order to engage in radical protest politics. At the same time they lobby existing parties, or in some cases seek feminist amendments to the political program of basically non-feminist parties like the NDP. An alternative tactic is to advance the full feminist program as part of an explicitly feminist coalition by running at least 50 per cent women candidates, with at least 50 per cent female leadership, and respecting the autonomy and political status of the grass-roots women's movement. Alternatives to the Marxist approach, such as that evolved by the West German Greens, lead extra-parliamentary movements into getting direct representation and leverage in the political system. This starts from the assumption that liberal democracy is a concession won from capitalism, a concession which needs to be defended through building ever more direct and extensive forms of democracy.

THE LIMITS OF RADICAL FEMINISM

Radical feminists have tried to develop a new approach to politics which escapes the problems associated with the old "male-defined" political models. They have had even less success than feminists deploying socialist and liberal strategies.

Radical feminist analysis starts from the notion that society is patriarchal: it is structured to give men systemic powers and privileges over women. In particular, radical feminists stress unmediated control by individual men over women's bodies. Male control over female sexuality and fertility is sanctioned by the norms of male authority in the family and household. It is legitimated by the fact that male experience and production activities are the basis of the normative in culture, not female biological and social reproduction activities. Radical feminism has produced insights into the nature of male violence and "sexual politics" which have challenged and changed public opinion. Nevertheless, attempts to build a new politics exclusively around the articulation of women's common interests in eliminating patriarchy have run into major difficulties.

Women share an interest in opposing patriarchy but they are divided by sexual orientation, social class, nation State, ethnicity, religion, politics, kin role (e.g. mother vs. daughter), and so on. For example, Black lesbian feminist writer Audre Lorde has criticized Mary Daly, author of *Gyn/Ecology*, for falling into racism through assuming that shared values of the counter-culture among White heterosexual Amerian women create a universal female culture (Lorde 1984).

Another reason why building politics around an exclusive anti-patriarchal focus has not worked is that it leads towards withdrawal into a counter-culture rather than to outreach. It leads away from building long-term alliances with other social forces on the basis of mutual support for one another's fundamental issues. For example, in 1978, radical feminists in Toronto challenged socialist feminists on the issue of how to mobilize for International Women's Day. They disagreed with the overly "political" approach of linking of patriarchal issues with issues of concern to unionists, immigrant communities, and so on. Ignoring the tactics of coalition, radical feminists tried to organize a separate demonstration making an appeal to existing women's community, to express their solidarity as a community. The socialist feminists drew over two thousand to their march; the radical feminists mustered barely two hundred. "Outreach" and "coalition with other movements" approaches have prevailed in Toronto ever since.

The radical feminists' failure to mobilize for March 8 symbolizes the general problem of their approach to political power. In effect, radical feminism has a utopian anarchist vision of supplanting the power structure in the economy, civil society, and the State by building a voluntaristic community that is marginal but exemplary. While the development of a counter-culture and consciousness raising are important to any strategy for empowering women, this anarchist abstentionist approach is not likely to work any better for women than it has for other groups in the past.

CONCLUSION

The feminist movement in Toronto, as elsewhere, is politically marginal. The men who control society's institutions are taking various feminist-defined issues seriously, but the notion of feminist political power in the State and other social institutions – including the household – is not on their agenda. The women's movement itself has not yet posed concrete issues of empowerment. Neither liberalism nor Marxism offers adequate conceptions of feminist empowerment and therefore neither is able to provide models for restructuring the family, economy, or State.

The feminist movement's focus on challenging personal and institutionalized norms is not enough to overcome its political marginalization. The challenge before the women's movement is to integrate that focus into a new politics that will.

NOTES

1 The change in official attitudes on some issues has been quite dramatic. In 1982, NDP MP Margaret Mitchell provoked catcalls and a titter of

laughter from male MPs when she raised a question in the House of Commons about funding for shelters for battered women. Now, no politician would dream about making light of this issue.

2 This was what happened for example to the SDS-style student activist groups at universities like Simon Fraser, University of Toronto, and Waterloo in 1969–70. Women challenged sexism within 1970s Marxist groups like the Revolutionary Workers' League, In Struggle, and the Workers' Communist Party, and led the exodus from their ranks in 1980–82.

3 The results of the surveys were reported in an Ontario NDP convention document in 1981.

4 Several of the activists that I interviewed pointed out that very few of the small groups which make up the bulk of the feminist movement in Toronto could function in a body like the women's council without changing their own internal organization and priorities. Most groups do not have an explicit basis of political unity nor do they spend much time developing policies and stands on current issues.

5 Lovenduski gives an indication of just how far women had to go even to attain those rights as of the end of the nineteenth century in Europe: "Politically they had no right to vote or to hold public office. In parts of Eastern and Central Europe, women were forbidden to join political organizations or to attend political meetings. Economic restrictions were severe. Women were barred from owning property, their inherited wealth was transferred to their husbands upon marriage, and they were prevented from engaging in a trade, running a business or joining a profession. Legally, women were not persons in most countries" (Lovenduski 1986, 14).

6 The new social movements do not just seek individual autonomy but also the autonomy of a *voluntary community* from the bureaucratic, technocratic, and commercial imperatives of the economy and the State. This is reflected in the way these movements are structured internally around the principle of community rather than organization: minimal vertical differentiation between leader and member, minimal horizontal differentiation between member and non-member, decision making by consensus to avoid imposing ends on others, a concern for the personal growth of individual members, etc.

7 Cohen celebrates the fact that "Contemporary collective actors consciously struggle over the power to socially construct new identities, to create democratic spaces for autonomous social action, and to reinterpret norms and reshape institutions" (Cohen 1985, 690). The result is what Cohen refers to favourably as "self-limiting radicalism," which seeks to transform "civil society" rather than the economy or the State."

8 REAL Women was originally created in 1983. It first came to prominence

when it campaigned in favour of the right of women to choose to be housewives and mothers in response to federal government proposals to do away with family allowance cheques. There is considerable overlap of members and resources with the Right to Life movement, which continues to campaign to make abortion illegal. Feminist groups fear that federal recognition and funding of REAL Women as legitimate spokespersons will permit politicians to play feminists off against antifeminists and thereby justify inaction on feminist issues.

9 This is not to say that liberal feminists have been inactive on issues related to the family, only that organizations like NAC have generally taken the heterosexual monogamous family as given rather than developing its policy proposals in relation to alternate family structures and sexual choices.

10 Bem's theory of psychological androgyny starts with the assumption that both men and women with healthy adaptive and flexible personalities can express the full range of sex-typed "masculine" and "feminine" traits and behaviours. Being sex-typed is therefore an artificial limitation of the expression of one's full genderless individuality. (Bem 1974; Bem and Lenney 1976).

11 Liberalism sees social collectivities as either normatively based institutionalizations of behaviour by individuals or as abstract functional imperatives of the social system as a whole. Liberal analysis does not start from the real existence of collectivities with shared material conditions, social relations with other groups and interests. This has evident implications for any attempt to theorize the specific oppression of women as females.

12 The very fact that the women's movement is raising demands for things like public day care is an indication that even a radical change in the cultural attitudes and behaviour of individual women and men on the level of "civil society" will not be enough to free and empower women. As Barrett and McIntosh (1983) point out, society will have to create the necessary material economic and social conditions as well.

13 I do not wish to be misunderstood as saying that liberalism is philosophically antithetical to women's liberation. Winning rights as individuals is an important part of the feminist struggle. Eisenstein (1981) makes the same political prediction for the U.S. as I have for Canada, when she predicts that feminists will have to choose between those liberals (called conservatives in American political jargon) who back away from equality of opportunity in the name of liberty and those liberals who continue to support State measures to guarantee equal rights.

14 The former president of REAL Women, Grace Petrasek, argued in a letter to the *Globe and Mail* (1 July 1986) that her group simply sought

government policies which gave women genuine freedom of choice between the roles of housewife and career woman.

15 Molyneux (1981) provides a balanced and insightful summary of the achievements and failures of socialist countries in making feminist reforms prior to the 1980s.

REFERENCES

Armstrong, P., and Hugh Armstrong. 1983. *A Working Majority*. Ottawa: Canadian Advisory Council on the Status of Women. (See table 5, p. 252).

Barrett, Michele and Mary McIntosh. 1983. *The Anti-Social Family*. London: Tavistock Press.

Bashevkin, Sylvia B. 1985. *Toeing the Lines: Women and Party Politics in Canada*. Toronto: University of Toronto Press. (See chs. 2, 3, and 4 for discussion of these issues.)

Bem, Sandra J. 1974. "The Measurement of Psychological Androgyny." *Journal of Consulting and Clinical Psychology* 42: 155–162.

Bem, Sandra J., and Ellen Lenney. 1976. "Sex Typing and the Avoidance of Cross-Sex Behaviour." *Journal of Personality and Social Psychology* 33, no. 1: 48–54.

Berk, Sarah F. 1985. *The Gender Factory*. New York: Plenum Press.

Cohen, Jean L. 1985. "Strategy or Identity: New Theoretical Paradigms and Contemporary Social Movements." *Social Research* 52, no. 4: 663–716.

Eisenstein, Zillah. 1981. *The Radical Future of Liberal Feminism*. New York: Longman.

Friedl, Ernestine. 1975. *Women and Men*. New York: Holt, Rinehart and Winston.

Lorde, Audre. 1984. "An Open Letter to Mary Daly." In *Sister Outsider: Essays and Speeches*. Trumansburg, N.Y.: Crossing Press.

Lovenduski, Joni. 1986. *Women and European Politics*. Amherst: University of Massachusetts Press.

Meissner, Martin, "No Exit for Wives: Sexual Division of Labour and the Cumulation of Household Demands." *Canadian Review of Sociology and Anthropology* 12, no. 4: 424–39.

Michelson, William. 1985. *From Sun to Sun*. Totowa: Rowman and Allanheld.

Molyneux, Maxine. 1981. "Socialist Societies Old and New: Progress Towards Women's Emancipation." *Feminist Review* no. 8: 00–00.

Reiter, Rayna. 1975. *Toward an Anthropology of Women*. New York: Monthly Review Press.

Rosaldo, Michelle and Louise Lamphere. 1974. *Women, Culture and Society*. Stanford: Stanford University Press.

Robinson, John P. 1977. *How Americans Use Time*. New York: Praeger.

Silvern, Louis E. and Victor L. Ryan. 1979. "Self Rated Adjustment and Sex-Typing on the Bem Sex-Role Inventory: Is Masculinity the Primary Predictor of Adjustment?" *Sex Roles* 5, no. 6: 739–63.

Touraine, Alain. 1985. "An Introduction to the Study of Social Movements." *Social Research*.

PART FOUR: THE OBSERVERS AND THE OBSERVED — ADVOCACY AND METHOD

The Observers and the Observed –
Advocacy and Method

The validity of conventional social research relies to a large extent on its correct correspondence with scientific method. The first step in this method is to make all descriptive data as self-evident as possible. A second step is to match the data to some model of events, or to some larger theoretical scheme. In quantitative terms the model will be validated by conventions of mathematical probability. In qualitative terms it will be validated by the terms and propositions of a theoretical argument.

Though social research uses both quantitative and qualitative models, its claim to status as science rests on its success in explaining how social data fit quantitative models of statistical probability. The more a social act can be transformed into a likeness of mechanical activity, the more the rules of probability can be used in order to examine and explain its dimensions. One well-known set of examples lies in the field of scientific management. Here division of labour, primarily a social activity, is redefined by strict criteria of optimal performance. Scientific management measures optimal performance through matching a specific mechanical rate – typically, the motion of an assembly line – to human effort.

The analogue of scientific management in social research is to be found wherever ideas, beliefs, and opinions become treated as if they were instrumental acts of message channelling. In a technocratic vision, research becomes a matter of feeding longitudinal data bases, and fitting survey information into data banks. Under these circumstances, the relationship of researcher to researched, observer to observed, can only be manipulative – oriented towards capturing social data for use as a commmodity. In short, scientific management extends the Administrative Point of View (see Marshall above) to the whole of research in social science.[1]

Nevertheless, it is apparent that there is crisis over the "utility" and "effectiveness" of sociology and anthropology in Canada and the United States which in part arises from inflexibilities in the time taken to produce results. The "science" of the scientific method is, apparently, not quick or "useful" in a managerial sense for those who hold the public purse in Canada.[2] For example, government is supposedly a major client for social research, yet senior people in government deliberately neglect its results. According to a recent report on the apparent stagnation in social research, senior civil servants in the federal government consult anyone but academic researchers. Bureaucrats consult the media, business leaders, provincial government officials, and friends – in that order. Then they consult political leaders, opinion polls, and citizens' groups. Only a small proportion, 15 per cent of senior bureaucrats, ever consulted academics, but even senior bureaucrats regarded academic advice as unreliable. The most reliable consultants, from the senior bureaucrats' point of view, are business leaders and provincial government officials. (Science Council of Canada 1985, 171). The situation seems to have arisen in which academic researchers are writing for themselves.

The prospects for evoking a counter-practice to conventional method in social sciences could not come at a more appropriate time. The contributions which follow take up the question of how advocacy can reconceptualize method in social sciences. Advocacy promotes "interested knowledge"; that is, knowledge arising from the close relationship between observer and observed. Nineteenth-century Marxism dubbed this relationship "praxis." Marx insisted that the objectivity of the objective world was not external to the speaker in the sense of being cut off and separate. Rather, it is in the "working over" of the objective world that people first affirm themselves as species-beings (Bauman 1973, 171). The articles in this part take up the thrust of Marx's argument but do not limit their observations to social class as examples of praxis. The thesis here is that advocacy in social science embraces both equity and social equality, both distributive aspects of justice and the inequalities of class.

Spencer's contribution shows how conventional social science has disempowered social advocacy. Social scientists could contribute to social movements, but the rhetoric of academic discourse calls for cool disinterest and commitment to basic research. Spencer argues that cool disinterest is a general malaise in sociology, for standing aside from societal issues is never a good way to test the power of one's own thought. Crysdale disagrees. While he supports advocacy, he takes a longer-term view from the standpoint of the sociology of knowledge. The distinctions between basic research and advocacy embedded in policy research should be conceived as mere constructs. Historically, policy research in Canada has yielded impressive results, though its contribution has been evident only in times of social crisis, he states.

Morgan supports Spencer: research should be judged on the appropriateness of the stance taken by the observer. Advocacy is not, as is often assumed, unreflective, untutored, and unrigorous. The task is to find ways and means that will ensure both that reflective inquiry becomes embedded in practice and that critical reframing of the problem becomes the means through which solutions emerge.

For Spencer and Morgan, a science of advocacy must in turn be advocated within the universities. As Heyworth points out above, universities do not value the range of skills required for advocacy research. Second, the lack of practitioners in social sciences inhibits natural progression from the university to disparate social fields. Advocacy training and action-research projects in universities are minimal, and the literature correspondingly absent.

In effect, advocates must advocate for counter-practice. Morgan states: "knowledge is pluralistic rather than unitary, relativistic rather than absolute, and a set of potentialities waiting to be realized rather than a concrete, objective artifact." Far from conceiving knowledge as a form of authoritative "truth," the method of advocacy must examine the process of how "truths" are socially constructed. The advocates' method must be matched to the advocates' task: making knowledge count. Advocates must uncover selective processes through which dominant forms of knowledge have come into being, reframe them, and propose epistemological alternatives. Such a method might be called "reflection in action" – combining as it does the twin processes of critical reflection and action-learning.

The method of advocacy for both Spencer and Morgan can be summed up as that of a conversation with the researched – but a conversation employing the criteria of systematic doubt. Spencer stresses the need for researchers to monitor themselves but always to commit their activity to the service of human liberation. Morgan stresses that the principle of systematic doubt can contribute to a different kind of generalizability from that produced by the scientist. Both assume advocacy can empower and that the five-step process of social empowerment discussed in part two of this book can be used to make the advocacy process much more rigorous. Empowerment leads to an increased quality of understanding and of the process of decision making generally.

NOTES

1 As an example, the United States has a Panel Study on Income Dynamics and a National Longitudinal Survey which run indefinitely. In Canada, there is already an established view that "high quality" information is data which can be fitted into an information base that can be used across separate studies. The Administrative Point of View in Canada is represented by the argument that most current social research is useless for large data bases, even misleading. Only by radically improving data bases can government hope to make any progress on unemployment, education-labour interactions, and the issues of equal pay and affirmative action. Science Council of Canada 1985, 214.

2 In recent years the government of Canada has attempted to skew the distribution of research money to project its labels "strategic funding." This has produced mixed results. Streaming research towards areas which the government approves can enhance the political visibility of the government in power as much as create socially relevant research.

REFERENCES

Bauman, Zygmunt. 1973. *Culture as Praxis*. London: Routledge and Kegan Paul.

Science Council of Canada. 1985. *Social Science Research in Canada: Stagnation or Regeneration?* Ottawa: Ministry of Supply and Services.

Touraine, Alain. 1981. *The Voice and the Eye: An Analysis of Social Movements*. Cambridge: Cambridge University Press and Paris: Edition de la Maison des Sciences de l'Homme.

METTA SPENCER

Advocating Peace

As civilized human beings, we are the inheritors ... of a conversation, begun in the primeval forests and extended and made more articulate in the course of centuries. It is a conversation which goes on both in public and within each of ourselves ... Education, properly speaking, is an initiation into the skill and partnership of this conversation in which we ... acquire the intellectual and moral habits appropriate to conversation ... [T]he final measure of intellectual achievement is in terms of its contribution to the conversation in which all universes of discourse meet. (Oakeshott 1962, 199)

Society is most aptly described as a *conversation* – a conversation carried on in print, on computer screens, by television, in concert halls, in university lecture halls, and by bullhorn in protest demonstrations. The paramount human responsibility is to forward this living discourse, which is at once our legacy and humankind's future. This paper will appraise the self-imposed limits on the conversations of social scientists and of social activists.

THE CHALLENGE

Universities are in a period of unusual calm, precisely while our biosphere is undergoing the gravest social problems in history – problems which may already be beyond solution. Among these challenges are the nuclear arms race, the increase of militarization around the globe, the increasing gap between the world's rich and the poor, the ecological and health effects of nuclear power, the militarization of space, the poisoning of air, land, and seas, the depletion of the ozone, the indebtedness of Third World countries, the daily extinction of living species, the division of the world into rival nation states, the loss from the tropical rain forest of vegetation by which the planet's oxygen system is replenished, unparalleled hunger, the desertification of Africa, and the depletion of non-renewable energy sources. None of these problems are "acts of God." All result from the collective actions of human beings.

Flawed collective actions result from ignorance of facts or the belief in false theories. To dispel popular and consequential myths is the responsibility of the intellectuals of every society. While many journalists, popular writers, and talk show hosts do try to examine these myths, they are not backed up by a strong community of scholars who generate the primary research that make their conversations useful. The strange disjuncture between the forms of academic discourse and the urgent policy deliberations of the wider society calls for an explanation.

Social scientists – academics – are paid to combine research with other intellectual work, notably teaching. Alternatively, they *may* serve by identifying social problems, calling attention to them in public forums, promoting inquiries into their solutions, and publicizing the proposals that seem most promising. Actually, not enough choose this path. Crysdale's account of policy research in Canada (below) represents only a small portion of ongoing activity in social science; and policy research usually avoids concern with intervention strategy.

According to the principle of academic freedom, university professors are entitled to select the topic of their study. The liberty granted by this arrangement is partially offset by collegial accountability, as when candidates are selected for their specializations; also, research funds are allocated by professional reviewers. While funds are mainly derived from government sources – taxpayers – academics are shielded from any direct demand that they show the social value of their work by proving the usefulness of the knowledge they generate. This principle of academic freedom has favourable consequences, allowing for work on abstract ideas that could never be defended on pragmatic grounds. It also has some unfavourable consequences.

Scanning articles in four recent issues of the two most prestigious sociological journals, I counted the sentences that offer a judgment on an issue of public policy. They are as follows:

1 A statement that nothing can be done to impede the flow of migrants from Mexico to the United States.

2 Another comment by the same author in a different journal to the same effect.

3 An observation that reduction in government employment is es-

pecially detrimental to Black Americans. (This is not phrased as a direct recommendation, but can be loosely construed as advocacy.)
4 A remark that, since use of the index of economic productivity is fraught with methodological problems, social scientists should "proceed in this area with great caution." (This may amount only to methodological advocacy, but I will throw it in to prove the inclusiveness of my counting procedure.)
5 A comment that, if they can do so, protest groups will be better off mobilizing their own social movements instead of relying on professional organizers paid by outsiders.[1]

I found five comments – none of them exactly radical. From this, I conclude that advocacy is taboo in the pages of mainstream academic sociology.

This does not mean that sociology can contribute nothing to the solution of social problems. Many of the articles dealt with topics that are regarded as social problems – e.g., social inequality of women and minorities, worldwide urbanization trends, and the effect of labelling people as mental patients. None of those articles, however, proposed intervention strategies to ameliorate the trouble. Moreover, the eight journals contained no articles on any of the urgent topics listed above.

There are five possibilities. Either (a) sociologists believe themselves incapable of addressing the world's pressing problems, or (b) they do not want to do so, or (c) they believe that others would disapprove of their doing so, or (d) they have done so but their comments have been edited out before publication, or (e) the idea never occurred to them.

PRISONERS OF THEORY

If the ills of the planet are at all susceptible to remedy, the project must involve analyses of existing arrangements and some vision of a better world. Such a vision must be informed both by theory and praxis – by action in the service of human liberation. A cramped, technical concept of one's profession is too limited to elicit mastery of our problems. If academics are to fulfil their responsibilities in dispelling crucial myths, they must liberate their self-images first.

Social movements depend on visionaries. If they are to succeed, they must coalesce as a comprehensive agenda, nurtured by scholarly research, and manifest themselves as campaigns of reform. Our problems arise from common causes, and can be resolved only when the linkages among them are recognized as global in scope. Yet the social sciences today lack any analyst with the breadth of vision and political engagement of, say, C. Wright Mills, whose insights into the causes of our present difficulties have been confirmed fully only during the past decade. What is impeding this intellectual process?

Several explanations are possible for the current reluctance of social scientists to tackle issues and advocate corrective policies. One explanation is purely material – that research funds and professional honour go to those who do not challenge the business interests and ideological beliefs of élites. This view portrays universities as the research arm of the military-industrial complex and researchers as too greedy to kill the goose that lays their golden eggs.

There is something to this view, but perhaps not much. True, scientific funding has become increasingly tied to military research, but nevertheless a substantial proportion of physical scientists have publicly vowed never to accept research contracts for Star Wars, and their professional associations have denounced militarization of space as an impractical and destabilizing project. Moreover, physicists and engineers have more actively opposed this militarization than have their colleagues in the humanities and social sciences – people who have fewer career interests at stake in the military-industrial complex. Thus it is going too far to claim that the universities feel the direct pressure of militarists and cannot extricate themselves from this control.

Instead of responding to the ideological demands of their "capitalist masters," as Marxian analysts might allege, academics seem to be monitoring *themselves* and obeying the umpires they have chosen. Oddly, in the 1980s, theoretical opposition to advocacy diminished with no corresponding increase in the *practice* of advocacy. Today advocacy is avoided – no doubt, for the ordinary reason, to preserve harmony and civility in the academic community – but so is policy-related work. Not much appreciation is accorded the production of knowledge for practical applications. And indeed, little social research has been generated since the 1960s in the context of political or moral campaigns of social reform.[2]

Far from being new, this avoidance of advocacy or public policy research on the part of sociologists involves traditional values in research. It is constrained, not by material interests, but by theoretic considerations. Three issues may be especially important in this regard: 1 The near-bankruptcy of the two models on which sociology grew up – functionalism and Marxism; 2 an unsettled view of the relationship between knowledge and interests; and 3 an inherited sociological assumption linking authority to violence. Just as lesser mortals, sociologists are prisoners of their own beliefs. And they, too, deserve liberation.

TWO LOST PARADIGMS

It was Gouldner, twenty years ago, who anticipated a crisis in which sociology would fail the social revolution that needed it, because it did not fully recognize its need. He wrote:

The profound transformation of society that many radicals seek cannot be accomplished by political means alone; it cannot be confined to a purely political embodiment. For the old society is not held together merely by force and violence, or expedience and prudence. The old society maintains itself also through theories and ideologies that establish its hegemony over the minds of men, who therefore do not merely bite their tongues but submit to it willingly. It will be impossible either to emancipate men from the old society or to build a humane new one, without beginning, here and now, the construction of a total counter-culture, including new social theories; and it is impossible to do this without a critique of the social theories dominant today. (Gouldner 1970, 5)

Gouldner's prophetic view of the coming crisis was not entirely accurate, but he foresaw our theoretical impoverishment. This, in his analysis, was to be expected from the inadequacy of functionalism (specifically "Parsonsianism") and Marxism, or the feeble version of it that was all American sociologists knew, to meet the demand to help guide a "Welfare-Warfare state."

He need not have worried about the American Welfare State; there is none of it left. The Warfare aspect is another matter.

Gouldner made a career of criticizing functionalism, particularly as promoted by Parsons. He depicted sociology as sharply divided into two blocs, functionalism and Marxism, which roughly corresponded to the capitalist and socialist worlds. Academic sociology, he said, was basically American sociology, and American sociology was basically "Parsonsian."

The inadequacies of Parson's model were becoming apparent even before Gouldner published his final, major attack in 1970. It had become apparent that the model offered reassurances that everything was all right instead of useful diagnoses of societal problems. By saying that all variables formed a system, the model did not highlight any of them as causal and hence offered no insights as to how to fix what was wrong.

Gouldner added an observation, however, not apparent to other sociologists: when pressed to account for social change, Parsons actually incorporated Marxist ideas into his scheme, creating from the synthesis an evolutionary model (Gouldner 1970, 354–62). That synthesis would not offer any useful guidelines for programmatic work, he noted. The result was the "entropy of functionalism and the rise of new theories," such as Goffman's dramaturgical model, ethnomethodology, and exchange theory (Gouldner 1970, 373–96). None of these would satisfy the New Left, which was then in its prime, and which was influenced by the unreconstructed version of Marxism that had prevailed in the u.s. but had been superseded in Europe by the emendations of theorists such as Lukács and Gramsci.

For its own part, the Eastern bloc had been influenced by Parsons too, according to Gouldner, and was developing its own synthesis of the two systems, with as little success as the Americans. There was evidently not much theoretical insight to gain from that quarter.

Gouldner did have good things to say about C. Wright Mills, who had died almost a decade before, and about critical sociologists, who were developing an activist, non-positivistic, post-Marxist approach to sociological work that took human liberation and social criticism seriously. That approach, like the New Left itself, has diminished in this era of political conservatism. Nevertheless, sociologists can still find in critical sociology the inspiration to pursue both theory and praxis in ways that count. In any case, if only as a moral boost towards broader sociological visioning, the writings of Habermas have been valuable. For example, he has attempted to straighten out the problem of the relationship between interests and knowledge.

INTERESTS AND KNOWLEDGE

Intellectuals' quest for "objectivity" used to be grounded on the ancient philosophical assumption that reality is not "constructed" but "essential" – i.e. independent of human judgment and apprehension. As Habermas described this view, "The only knowledge that [it considers] can truly orient action is knowledge that frees itself from mere human interests and is based on Ideas – in other words, knowledge that has taken a theoretical attitude" (Habermas 1968, 301). Yet when phenomenology overtook Greek metaphysics early in this century, the ivory towers did not topple; the academics' commitment to theoretical (as opposed to practical) work continued, though justified on a moral, not an ontological, basis. The separation of knowledge and interests was reemphasized, along with the admonition that the new reflexive sociologists should strive as hard as objective sociologists for scientific purity when analysing a problem, by bracketing their interests as phenomena for observation.

Habermas has thus described the attitude of modern social scientists:

In this field of inquiry, which is so close to [existing sociological] practice, the concept of value-freedom (or ethical neutrality) has simply reaffirmed the ethos that modern science owes to the beginnings of theoretical thought in Greek philosophy: psychologically an unnconditional commitment to theory, and epistemologically the severance of knowledge from interest. This is represented in logic by the distinction between descriptive and prescriptive statements, which makes grammatically obligatory the filtering out of merely emotive from cognitive contents. (Habermas 1968, 303)

To Habermas, this is a perversion of intellectual work. Far from being obliged to estrange themselves from their own interests, it is the highest task of social scientists to *uncover* them. Interests take their shape in the activities of work, of languaging, of interpretation – all of which require participation in the discourse of the broader society. Work on "pure theory" is unproductive delusion; what truly contributes is to participate unreservedly in humanity's unbroken conversation. "The unity of knowledge and interest proves itself in a dialectic that takes the historical traces of suppressed dialogue and reconstructs what has been suppressed" (Habermas 1968, 315).

Thus critical sociology promoted the combination of research with advocacy, but not, of course, by reducing research to inquiries at a technical level. Critical sociology never devalues the significance of the symbolic, communicative realm as the distinctively human domain (Habermas 1981), and no one influenced by the Frankfurt school is likely to devalue ideas, or become an ideological hack, turning out research to support some party line. There have been such possibilities for other Marxists and among them a good deal of attention has had to be paid to the restoration of the status of ideas in orienting human action. One of most frequently quoted of Marx's admonitions is, after all, a passage from *Theses on Feuerbach*: "the philosophers have only *interpreted* the world in various ways; the point however is to *change* it." This is usually understood as a prediction that philosophy will be replaced by revolutionary action, that there will be no room in the post-revolutionary world for mere speculation.

As a prediction it may still come true; as a moral admonition, however, it is too pat a slogan. It was Gramsci who sought to clarify again the relationship between praxis and abstraction, as indeed he claimed would have to be done again and again once for each generation. Gramsci, in addressing this issue, specifically denied that philosophy could ever be supplanted by political action. He gave historical materialism a new twist: While historical circumstances do create the necessary conditions for the emergence of new ideas, it cannot be taken for granted that any ideas will develop automatically simply because the time and circumstances are ripe. To Gramsci, this is the responsibility of intellectuals, and it matches precisely the requirements of the revolution – it is up to them to turn private thinking into historically effective mass beliefs and ethics. In describing this responsibility and putting forth a vision of how it would be achieved, the importance of struggling with ideas, of engaging in abstract discourse, was again recognized. Gramsci gave back to intellectuals the work of creating and sustaining culture – including post-revolutionary culture.

Of course, no one needs to read Habermas or Gramsci in order to conduct social research into programmatic concerns – except perhaps those social scientists who still worry about jeopardizing their intellectual status by such work. Unfortunately, they may be in the majority.

AUTHORITY AND VIOLENCE

A third theoretical myth may have some bearing on social scientists' diffidence about committing themselves to work on contemporary social problems. It is the prevailing definition of power.

People do not normally want to disempower their own societies – even when they perceive the root cause of the global world crisis as the aggression and imperialism of their societies. In the case of social scientists, the reluctance may be related to an inherited theory of power that equates it to dominance. Power, we learn in our first course in sociology, is the ability to impose one's will on others – to dominate. Coercion need not always be used, to be sure, especially when it is recognized as legitimate, in which case we are dealing with *authority*. Nevertheless, under authority lies power, and under power lies some an instrument of coercion – a whip, a bomb, a lock. Max Weber defined the state as "the rule of men over men based on the means of legitimate, that is allegedly legitimate, violence." Since authority is necessary to social order, any reduction in the state's stockpile of weapons would represent, by definition, a weakening of the polity. To propose such a policy might, by an extension of this logic, constitute treason. No wonder social scientists fail to challenge the legitimacy of participating in arms races!

This is not the place for an extended discussion of politial theory, but it *is* appropriate to point out that the equation between power and violence, while pervasive, is not universally shared by theorists. Thus Arendt denied that any government has ever existed that was based exclusively on violent means. "Power," she wrote, "is indeed of the essence of all government, but violence is not." She did not see power as the ability to command, but as the "human ability to act in concert. Power is never the property of an individual; it belongs to a group and remains in existence only so long as the group keeps together. When we say of somebody that he is 'in power' we actually refer to his being empowered by a certain number of people to act in their name" (Arendt 1969, 44). Strength, on the other hand, designates a property of individuals, "though the strength of even the strongest individual can always be overpowered by the many." Violence is not exactly either of the former, but is based on weaponry. "Phenomenologically, it is close to strength, since the implements of violence, like all other tools, are designed and used for the purpose of multiplying natural strength until, in the last stage of their development, they can substitute for it" (Arendt 1969, 46).

Commonly, violence is used not by the powerful, but by the powerless to compensate for their weakness. Social groups that *can* act in concert, that *can* attain their collective purposes, normally get on with the job and do so. Groups that *cannot* do so may try to force their will by violence. Arendt points out that, when small nations and terrorist groups get nuclear weapons, it will be clear that the least powerful groups may be capable of the greatest violence. At that moment, it may occur to some theorist to redefine power along lines that depart from Weber's.

The point is a small one, but it is true that our theoretical constructs limit our perceptions and shape our politics. It is time to root out of our sociological assumptions the belief that the effectiveness of polities depends upon the weaponry that they amass.

TOWARDS A NEW PRAXIS

If Marx's vision of a post-revolutionary utopia sounds archaic now, his suggested method of orienting one's intellectual work towards significant human projects – through praxis – remains contemporary and useful, at least when interpreted in the light of Gramsci's and Habermas's insights.

The eerie indifference of the academic community to these responsibilities was foreseen in 1970 by Gouldner. He recommended as a corrective what he called "Reflexive Sociology": "What is needed is a new praxis that transforms the person of the sociologist[s]," he wrote. "[As] their most immediate work environments – the universities themselves – become drawn into the coalescing military-industrial-welfare complex, it becomes unblinkingly evident that sociology has become dangerously dependent upon the very world it has pledged to study objectively ... There is no way of making a new sociology without undertaking a new praxis" (Gouldner 1970, 512). Of course, the same advice applies to other intellectual professions as well.

There are many degrees of political engagement, and no single praxis will suit all intellectuals. Perhaps the most extreme approach to this question can be seen in method by which the French sociologist Alain Touraine fuses scholarship with advocacy. Touraine's main work has been on the issue of nuclear power. He is interested in the most important type of social movement – a "value-oriented" one. He maintains that it is through the discourse of such social movements that society clarifies and revises its values. The activists in such movements do the work that one might properly expect social theorists and researchers to do – engage in public dialogue concerning important issues and seek the information that is crucial to such debates as they unfold. Touraine, therefore, studies movements by participating in the work of proselytizing for them.

His method is to engage in what he calls "intervention." Pairs of researchers, an "agitator" and a "secretary," engage in dialogue with a group in a deliberate effort to shape its aspirations and self-interpretation in a direction that will forward their social movement. This is a role that goes far beyond the practice of sociology, and Touraine does seem to be mindful of the possible excesses of his method. Thus Touraine suggests:

Confusion, doubt, and resistance must be dispelled so that one can come closer to the fire of society. The researcher realizes, humbly, that he is not an actor; but at the crucial moment of intervention he is a prophet. He does not call upon the group to move towards him but to go towards what he has proclaimed and yet does not possess – towards the movement, of which he will never be the guide. At this point, the relation between the group and the researcher is dramatic, and the researcher is drained by it. He is even in danger of becoming too personally engaged and of mixing his prophetic role with this personal situation and his reactions to the group. His co-researcher must therefore protect the group against over-intervention on his part and ensure that the group maintains control over its own self-analysis ... The researcher does not endeavor to please the group, but he feels himself to be responsible towards the movement, as constructed both by analysis and by the militants' ideology. (Touraine 1977, 194–5, 197)

Touraine is emulated methodologically by few North Americans. Of the possibility that his method may impair his objectivity, Touraine acknowledges: "No researcher, in fact, can maintain perfect balance between analysis and participation" (Touraine 1977, 197).

What is at issue is not Touraine's particular method, but a general stance that keeps intellectual work oriented towards issues that are significant for policy. It invariably happens that participation in the discourse of social movements forces one to grapple with the urgent questions of humankind. Participation in action-oriented conversations hones academic questions in a salutary way that cannot be expected of routine scholarly discussions.

Let me cite a couple of examples of heuristic usefulness of political debate for the sharpening of research questions. On one of her visits to Canada, Margaret Thatcher stated with supreme assurance to a political journalist that "history shows" militarily strong countries to be less likely to get into wars than under-armed countries. I have mentioned this claim to several military historians, none of whom challenged it. Not surprisingly, independent peace researchers have given the lie to this claim. Thus numerous studies show that over-armed countries are far more likely than under-armed ones to get into wars. Newcombe's research, for example, estimates the probability as thirty times as great.[3]

Other peace researchers have also established that military deterrence is rarely successful. A "deterred" adversary normally tries to match or exceed the threat from the other side,, so that the usual outcome is an arms race and finally war. Throughout history, about 70 per cent of the arms races have resulted in war (Singer 1980, 359). Contrary to Thatcher's supposition, nations that are armed heavily rarely attack "weak" ones; they fight each other instead. The reason for arming is not to prevent wars, but to *win* them. As a practical policy, while military preparedness has made war far more likely, it also has historically increased the likelihood of victory over a less heavily armed adversary. This provided a certain logical justification for militarization in times past; no longer, of course, since *no side* will win a nuclear war.

My second example is the relatively unchallenged public myth that military investment is good for the economy or even necessary for prosperity. Most adults have heard that the Great Depression was cured by World War II, and not by the half-hearted government programs of job creation that preceded it – predisposing belief that military spending *generally* benefits the economy. It does not. We need to know more about the effect of military expenditure as a mechanism for stabilizing the demand cycle for commodities and assure business a steady, predictable market for their products. Who benefits from this arrangement and who loses? How can the stabilizing effect be created in other ways?

The main justification offered for military spending is that it creates employment. Yet those few disarmament researchers who have studied the question have concluded that spending on military production is a poor way of creating jobs. Such production is capital-, not labour-intensive. Investing in almost any other sector – such as construction or education – would create many more jobs than would an equivalent expenditure on the military (Sivard 1981, 20; Tuomi and Vayrynen 1982).

Comparative studies of national productivity have shown that the more income an industrialized nation puts into the military, the less productive it becomes and the less able to compete on world markets (Sivard 1981, 19). If this is so, the fact needs far better publicity, for industrialists do not realize that military expenditure is bad for the economy, and social scientists should dispel the myth of armament as productive enterprise.

CONCLUSION

The urgent global problems of our day – economic, environmental, and military – are interrelated, arising from the capacity of élites to divert humanity's resources into expenditure on military destruction; that are elements of a reduced but continuing international struggle for hegemony; and the economic dominance by nations of the North over the South; through maintaining institutions of excessive, privatized consumerism, instead of global, sustainable economic development.

The catastrophic consequences of these distorted priorities loom large: famine, irreversible environmental destruction, local wars, and, potentially, nuclear annihilation – all resulting from endemic militarism and from the weakness of alternative systems of international conflict management, such as the World Court and the United Nations.

These social problems are held in place by prevailing myths that are unexamined – such beliefs as that keeping the peace requires enormous weaponry, and that military expenditures keep economies healthy.

Social scientists of the North enjoy sufficient academic freedom to work without fear in dispelling such myths. They also have access to media and suitable forums for dispelling these myths. Social movements exist outside of academia that need their research expertise for providing crucial information to address these global problems.

Despite all this, social scientists have not responded to the challenge. This is because norms of academic discourse have traditionally called for a rhetoric of cool disinterest and "value free" scholarship. However, much more than this is involved. I suggest that social scientists – like lesser mortals – are disempowered by their own faulty theories.

As Gouldner foresaw, neither functionalism nor Marxism has repaid sociologists with insights that help address our current global crisis. Social scientists of the socialist countries have done no better. More promising approaches – notably a critical sociology that would bring back praxis – dried up on the vine during the long conservative period of the 1970s and 1980s. It is worth reading Habermas on this question, if only to restore legitimacy to the concept of uncovering interests through participating in the discourse of the broader society.

New ideas will not automatically develop simply because they are needed. Social scientists have an opportunity to contribute to vital social movements; by doing so they will not jeopardize their analytical integrity but rather participate in the very dialogue that will best stimulate their intellectual work. Standing apart from societal issues is no way to test the power of one's thoughts. Conversations at universities will be better, not worse, for adopting the rhetoric and purposiveness of advocacy.

NOTES

1 The sources for this are Massey 1986, 683 and 1987, 1399; Pomer 1986, 657; Block and Burns 1986, 778; Jenkins and Eckert 1986, 827.

2 I am thinking of such U.S. projects as the Coleman Report, evaluation studies of Headstart, opportunity programs for minorities, and studies of economic development. In Canada, comparable examples of programmatic research of the same period were the Bilingualism and Biculturalism Report, the Gray Report on foreign ownership, and a number of studies of immigration policy.

3 The sources for this are numerous. They include: Michael D. Wallace, "Armaments and Escalation: Two Competing Hypotheses," paper, Canadian Peace Research and Education Association, University of Quebec at Montreal, 2 June 1980; "Arms Races and Escalation: Some New Evidence," *Journal of Conflict Resolution*, 23, no. 1, 1979, 1980; Alan Newcombe and James Wert, "An Inter-Nation Tensiometer for the Prediction of War," Peace Research Institute, Dundas, Ont. 1972, 326pp; Alan G. Newcombe, Nora S. Newcombe, and Gary A. Landrus, "The Development of an International Tensiometer," *International Interactions*,

1 (Jan. 1974): 3–18; Alan Newcombe and Frank Klaassen, "The Ten-siometer Prediction of Nations Likely to be Involved in International War in the Years 1977–1980," *Korean Institute of International Studies*, 10, no. 1 (1978–79): 1–43; Alan G. Newcombe, "The Prediction of War," Peace Research Institute, Dundas, Ont., p. 1, 1982.

REFERENCES

Arendt, Hannah. 1969. *On Violence*. New York: Harcourt, Brace and World.

Block, Fred, and Gene A. Burns. 1986. "Productivity as a Social Problem: The Uses and Misuses of Social Indicators." *American Sociological Review* 51, no. 6: 767–80.

Craig, Jenkins J., and C.M. Eckert. "Channeling Black Insurgency: Elite Patronage and Professional Social Movement Organizations in the Development of the Black Movement." *American Sociological Review* 51, no. 6: 812–29.

Gouldner, Alvin W. 1970. *The Coming Crisis of Western Sociology*. New York: Basic Books.

Habermas, Jurgen. 1968. *Knowledge and Human Interests*. Boston: Beacon Press.

— 1981. *The Theory of Communicative Action*. Volume 1: *Reason and the Rationalizaton of Society*. Boston: Beacon Press.

Massey, Douglas S. 1986. "The Settlement Process among Mexican Migrants to the United States." *American Sociological Review* 51. no. 5: 670–84.

— 1987. "Understanding Mexican Migration to the United States." *American Journal of Sociology* 92, no. 6: 372–1403.

Oakeshott, Michael. 1962. *Rationalism in Politics and Other Essays*. London: Methuen.

Pomer, Marshall. 1986. "Black Male Advancement." *American Sociological Review* 51, no. 5: 650–9.

Singer, David J. 1980. "Accounting for International War: The State of the Discipline." In *Annual Review of Sociology*. Palo Alto: Annual Reviews.

Sivard, Ruth Leger. 1981. *World Military and Social Expenditure*. Leesburg, Virginia: World Priorities.

Touraine, Alain. 1981. *The Voice and the Eye: An Analysis of Social Movements*. Cambridge: Cambridge University Press and Paris: Edition de la Maison des Sciences de l'Homme.

Tuomi, Helena, and Raimo Vayrynen. 1982. *Transnational Corporations, Armaments and Development*. Aldershot, England: Gower Press.

Advocacy as a Form of Social Science

Can advocacy count as a valid form of social research?

Is it possible to counter the criticism that advocacy is inevitably subjective and unscientific, and incapable of producing objective forms of understanding?

Is it possible to argue that advocacy has a rightful place in the tool-chest of science, and that it should play an important role in all institutions concerned with the generation of knowledge?

SCIENCE AND THE MYTH OF OBJECTIVITY

In this paper I wish to address some of the issues underlying these questions, and argue that advocacy can be made as scientific as any other form of research, and has a rightful place among social science methodologies of the present day. I take my point of departure from an argument developed at greater length in *Beyond Method* (Morgan 1983): that research is basically a process of conversing with the object or phenomenon being researched, and that in research, as in conversation, we ultimately meet ourselves, a point also put by Spencer above.

This view of the research process stands against that underpinning many discussions about the nature of science and scientific knowledge. For example, science is often presented as a means for gaining objective knowledge about the world around us. It is often presented as a means of gaining a "true" understanding of the way things are.

This view of science propagates a myth: it ignores how scientific researchers are locked into a circle of relations with the object being researched. The idea that science produces "objective" knowledge attempts to break this circle by assuming that the scientist is independent of the world being studied. But this is not credible. For, as

Kuhn (1971) and many others have shown (e.g. Burrell and Morgan 1979; Mitroff 1973), what a scientist sees and discovers is inevitably linked with the world views and patterns of assumption that are brought to the investigation. The scientist never sees and understands the phenomenon studied in an objective way. He or she merely "engages" the phenomenon in a partial, socially constructed way.

It is in this sense that we can say that science is a process of conversation, engaging and probing the qualities of a situation through interaction with that situation. Science is circular rather than linear or detached. And it can only claim any kind of objectivity by *assuming* otherwise. The assumption that there is an independent external world that can be observed by the scientist *creates* the guise of objectivity. But when we recognize the circular pattern of relations linking observer and observed, we have to recognize that objectivity is as much a part of the observer as of the object observed, and is vitally influenced by the perspectives, values, and general assumptions that shape investigation.

This view leads us to see that there can be many different kinds of objectivity, since we can adopt many different standpoints and values in attempting to understand a phenomenon. And we also see that any object or phenomenon being studied is thus full of many potential knowledges, different objectivities, just as the researcher can adopt many different perspectives as agent in the realization of knowledge. Once the notion of an independent external world is broken, we recognize that knowledge is pluralistic rather than unitary, relativistic rather than absolute, and a set of potentialities waiting to be realized rather than a concrete, objective artifact. The realization of knowledge is a socially constructed process that ultimately depends on the stance adopted by the researcher. An understanding of the nature of knowledge must thus grasp the whole circle of relations that link the researcher with the researched.

What then falls within the bounds of scientific inquiry? If science is not characterized by the production of objective knowledge, what are the characteristics which set it apart form other modes of inquiry?

SCIENCE, DOUBT, AND GENERALIZATION

Two characteristics seem particularly crucial. First, science is distinguished from other systems of knowledge and belief such as religion, magic, mysticism, intuition, and other forms of personal knowledge in that it is supposed to bring *systematic doubt* to bear on what is known. Consider, for example, the process of hypothesis testing.

The whole purpose in developing and testing hypotheses is to create a situation where one's theory can, in principle, be disproved. Rather than cling to cherished hunches, ideas, and beliefs, science is supposed to subject them to criticisms and stern tests that will allow the scientist to reject those theories and ideas that fail to command sufficient support (Popper 1958).

Of course, though crucial in distinguishing science from other kinds of belief, this view of scientific practice is rather an idealized one. Scientists are frequently passionate in their commitments to their theories and hypotheses (Mitroff 1973), and often are more concerned to prove them correct than to refute them. For example, they often apply relatively weak tests, and often alter experimental methods to produce supportive results, rather than bring the level of doubt that Popper's (1958) work on the logic of scientific discovery suggests is necessary. As a result, much of what passes as science is patently unscientific. Its stance, like that of other systems of belief, is affirmatory rather than refutational in nature. However, the idea that science does subject knowledge to scientific doubt is crucial to the enterprise, and is a key attribute of what is formally recognized as scientific knowledge. Indeed, it is this characteristic of scientific knowledge that is often misunderstood as a sign of its objectivity.

The second all-important characteristic of science rests in its quest for *generalizability*. Science, as opposed to many other forms of knowing, is concerned to generate understandings of one situation that apply to other situations. Thus, the so-called "positivist" approach in both the natural and social sciences places emphasis on discovering regularities, laws, and relationships that apply to whole populations of phenomena. The quest is to find quasi-universal patterns of knowledge that will allow one to draw conclusions that go well beyond the individual cases studied. This view of knowledge as a kind of "generalizable fact," "generalizable law," or "generalizable pattern of relation" is a very powerful one. And as a principle, it is probably much more consistently applied than the idea of doubt and refutation.

ADVOCACY AS A FORM OF SOCIAL SCIENCE

It is against this backdrop that we must examine the claims of advocacy research as a valid approach to social science. Our discussion already serves to dispel the criticism that advocacy is unscientific because it is inevitably subjective and incapable of producing objective forms of understanding. For no science is truly objective and value free. All approaches to inquiry are bounded within some kind of subjectivity, even though the scientists concerned may not be explicitly aware of this. In so far as one chooses to defend advocacy in terms of its objectivity, one is drawn onto the ground of those who believe that the scientist is separate from the world he or she is studying. As we have noted, this is an erroneous premise, and it is the scientist holding this view who should really be held to account.

The issues of systematic doubt and generalizability have more substance. For, given that we accept science as a distinctive means of generating knowledge, despite all its warts and wrinkles, any claim that advocacy can be a form of social science must pay attention to its distinguishing features. In other words, the scientific merits of advocacy as a style of research can only be defended to the extent that advocacy researchers bring a measure of systematic doubt to bear on their work and seek a generalizability in the knowledge that they produce.

However, this does not mean to say that advocacy must be made to fit the canons of scientific method in a rigid way. Rather, it means that advocacy researchers must adopt the basic principles guiding science for their own ends. And in so doing, I believe that they can enrich and refine many aspects of advocacy research. For there is much in the scientific process that can sharpen the skills and insights of the advocate.

ADVOCACY AND SYSTEMATIC DOUBT

The use of doubt can act as a defence against dogmatism; it can create insight in place of blindness; and it can provide the basis for an evolving, learning-oriented platform for the advocate's interactions with the problems to be addressed. For example, any advocacy activity is based on some kind of view or definition of the situation or problems at hand. In adopting the kind of scientific attitude which encourages us to identify *both* facts and counter-facts, arguments and counter-arguments, it is possible to build a rich and changing picture of the problems at hand, and to guard against the traps that often accompany the advocate's strong value-orientation. It is possible to find means of framing old issues in new ways that may create new opportunities for action. And to the extent that this process of critical framing and reframing becomes a central aspect of the way advocates develop and change their positions, it has much to commend it as a quasi-scientific form of activity. Much of traditional science is concerned with this process of framing and reframing, which is usually called paradigm change. Paradigm change is concerned with the progression of knowledge in a rigorous way, with experiments, surveys, hypothesis testing, and stern tests relating to the validity of concepts and ideas serving as a means towards this end. In recognizing how the use of systematic doubt can enrich and change personal and collective understandings of a given issue, and develop alternative action strategies, advocacy indeed shares much with science. The kind of knowledge that it generates is likely to be very different because the mode of engagement is different (Morgan 1983). But that does not mean that it is unscientific.

Advocates deserve to have a voice on many issues where the voice of science is now paramount, and an awareness of its possible links with science may do much to strengthen its right to be heard. Very often advocacy is viewed and practised as a kind of missionary activity characterized by all kinds of inflexible and dogmatic commitments. And to this extent it is rightly labelled as anti-science. But to the extent that it incorporates the kind of self-reflection and capacity for self-criticism which underpins the philosophy of systematic doubt, it embraces the basic philosophy of science, if not its methods.

Thus to take a practical illustration, consider how advocacy research can contribute to activities such as the peace movement. One approach might be to place emphasis on the critical scrutiny of facts and other data to produce arguments, counter-arguments, and positions that embrace one's opponents' criticisms. The approach here can be highly "scientific," using systematic methods in the development of "facts," "evidence," and new frames of interpretation that have been subjected to stern tests of criticism and doubt. In addition to producing new interpretations and new action strategies, the method can be used to challenge the most fundamental premises of those on opposite sides in an advocacy debate, as well as to debunk much of the rhetoric used in developing arguments.

Another approach (illustrated by Harries-Jones in this volume) might place more emphasis on analysing and challenging the premises that shape the context of communication and argument, rather than on marshalling facts and counter-facts. Systematic doubt can play an important role here in allowing the advocate to question whether the issue being discussed is the "best" issue. For example, is the prospect of nuclear war best framed in terms of an arms race where one party is in the leading position, or in terms of a war where there are going to be winners and losers? Or is it best framed in terms of a "nuclear winter hypothesis," which allows us to understand the consequences of the arms race in terms of irreversible damage to our planet and the creation of a situation where no one can win? Or is the arms race best framed as a socio-political problem where the real trade-off is between social progress and military expenditure? By challenging the basic definition of the problem at hand, it is possible to redefine the context of communication and begin to reshape the outcomes that are likely to result. The process of re-framing can be conducted in a clear and systematic manner, one scenario being set against another in a way that allows new modes of thinking, issues, and alternatives to emerge.

In these ways, the principle of systematic doubt can be used to make the advocacy process much more rigorous. It can make the scientific attitude work to the advantage of the advocate, in a way that is likely to improve the quality of understanding, and of the decision-making process generally.

ADVOCACY AND GENERALIZABILITY

The key to understanding how a quest for generalizability can help develop advocacy research rests in understanding that advocacy can generate a different kind of generalizability from that produced by the scientist. As has been noted, the assumption of an independent external world leads the positivist scientist approach to search for generalizable facts, laws, and relations through "objective" compar-isons. Clearly, this is not a viable aim for the advocate, because he or she usually becomes a fundamental and active part of the problem being researched, and becomes so immersed in that problem that it is not usually possible to take a similar point of view. It is possible to reflect on, and write reports about, one's practice and what one has learned, but these usually stand as accounts of single case studies. While experience through involvement in different projects at dif-ferent times, or knowledge of other people's experiences and results, may provide the basis for generalizing beyond the immediate situ-ation, by and large it is difficult to counter the scientist's charge that "you're only involved in one or two situations, and therefore have no basis for generalizing beyond those situations."

This criticism has merit if one presumes that generalization can only result from systematic comparisons. But in actuality there are many different ways that generalization can emerge. For example, an advocate writing a report on a single case may produce a docu-ment that is read by and resonates with the experience of someone else. The insights presented give rise to an "aha" feeling in the other: "That makes sense." This is a form of generalizability and has good credentials in certain approaches to social research. Consider, for example, the position of the ethnographer-anthropologist who spends his or her time studying the culture of a group of people. The research produces numerous ideas and insights, which, when communicated, resonate with what is found elsewhere in different studies. This provides the basis for an important form of generalizability that contributes to a quasi-scientific understanding of the phenomenon we call culture. It gives rise to a shared system of knowledge among a group of people interested in a particular issue or set of problems. And this, of course, is what science and scientific knowledge is all about; it is a community-specific and methodologically bound mode of understanding.

Clearly, if advocacy researchers can find ways of generalizing their findings and learning so that they resonate with people who work in other situations or who share a general interest in the problems being investigated, their work has a good claim to quasi-scientific status. And in doing so, as in the case of using systematic doubt, they have another means of improving their practice. All too often the results of advocacy research are seen as situation-specific in that they are never written up in a systematic and comprehensive way, and much of the learning and knowledge generated by a given project is lost. At a minimum, an awareness of the importance of generalizability can encourage advocacy researchers to produce more systematic and self-reflective reports on their work that will improve the knowledge and practice of fellow practitioners, or those who wish to learn more about the details of the projects they have conducted.

In addition, there are other ways in which generalizability can arise. For example, it can be claimed that advocates are in the business of developing action methodologies or prototypes for tackling particular sets of problems. As in much action research, it can be argued that the purpose of research is to clarify or resolve certain problems, and to use the insights and methods developed in tackling similar problems elsewhere. Here generalizability rests in the capacity for diffusing relevant insights in a practical way, so that experience in situation x creates a knowledge which is then used in situation y. Advocacy researchers know that they owe much of their knowledge to this kind of learning – e.g., by using skills and methods developed in the civil rights and anti-war movements in the 1960s and 1970s to mobilize people around issues such as the nuclear problem in the 1980s and toxic pollution in the 1990s. This involves a generalization of knowledge that is every bit as important as the kind of generalization that occurs in science.

Again, advocates can argue that the kinds of generalizability that stem from their work have more to do with practical problems relating to the empowerment of people than with the production of formal kinds of knowledge. Many advocacy projects make interventions that will allow others to take action for themselves, and the insights that emerge from this have much to contribute to a generalized understanding of what it takes to make passive citizens "come alive" in relation to problematic issues, and so on. This empowering dimension of advocacy research is often crucial in determining whether an advocacy project is a success, and hinges on the generalization of patterns of awareness that underpin the general idea of empowerment. In many cases advocacy can be understood as a research technique where the aim is to empower people to research situations for themselves rather than to rely on others (see, for example, the concept of action learning discussed by Morgan and Ramirez 1984). Empowerment involves a generalization of local and personal knowledge and capacities that parallels the kind of "expert," "universal knowledge" generated and generalized through science.

CONCLUDING REMARKS

I thus believe that there are considerable grounds for arguing that advocacy can and should attempt to be more scientific, while avoiding being drawn into the grounds of traditional science. Advocacy researchers can enrich their practice by being aware of the benefits to be derived from the use of systematic doubt and the quest for generalizability. They can use the great insights of science, if not the precise methods, to create more robust forms of advocacy. The challenge facing advocacy researchers is to develop a science of advocacy rather than to make advocacy scientific in a strict sense, and to learn how to develop and defend their position within the social science establishment by being aware of the circle of relations that always links the researcher and researched. To do this they must learn to go beyond the specific methods that define their craft, and ground their practice in an understanding of the processes and assumptions that guide social science generally.

REFERENCES

Burrell, Gibson, and Gareth Morgan. 1979. *Sociological Paradigms and Organizational Analysis*. London and Exeter, NH: Heinemann.

Kuhn, Thomas. 1971. *The Structure of Scientific Revolutions*. 2nd ed., Chicago: University of Chicago Press.

Mitroff, Ian. 1973. *The Subjective Side of Science*. New York: Elsevier.

Morgan, Gareth. 1983. *Beyond Method: Strategies for Social Research*. Beverley Hills: Sage.

Morgan, Gareth, and Rafael Ramirez. 1984. "Action Learning: A Holographic Metaphor for Guiding Social Change." *Human Relations* 37: 1–28.

Popper, Karl. 1958. *The Logic of Scientific Discovery*. London: Hutchinson.

STEWART CRYSDALE

Policy Research, Advocacy, and Human Rights in Canada

The concern of social scientists in Canada with human rights, and with advocacy stemming from human rights legislation, is the latest step in a long history of research oriented towards social policy. During relatively stable times social scientists tend to work at improving methods and building better theories, but when crises arise many specialists deal with them directly and specifically. The erosion of human rights during and after the Second World War drew social scientists into the advocacy of changes in government policies and legislation to win for powerless people the protection of law and approved practice.

The blending of policy and basic research is a hallmark of the Canadian approach and has roots in the earliest sociological studies in this country. Most of these were sponsored by churches and governments. Their chief purpose was programmatic – to learn more about the conditions of people uprooted by advancing urbanization and industrialization. Their findings exposed widespread exploitation of workers and minority groups by powerful élites. The latter built often their wealth directly on the violation of basic human rights. This early research linked social science with religious and political organizations and legitimated the advocacy of policy changes.

In 1915, for example, three young men were appointed by the Presbyterian and Methodist churches to conduct surveys of new urban communities. These were to serve as a basis for building programs and organizations to help masses of newcomers cope with high unemployment, poor housing, little education, and hazards to health and safety. One of these investigators was Dr W.A. Riddell, an active Protestant layman who later became the first deputy minister of labour for Ontario. Another was Bryce M. Stewart, who was later appointed deputy minister of labour for Canada. The third was J.S. Woodsworth, a Methodist minister who was to found the Cooperative Commonwealth Federation (later the New Democratic Party) based on socialist principles. Their pioneering activist careers grew out of religious commitment and early experience as social researchers (Crysdale 1961, ch. 2).

In the opening decades of the twentieth century, Canadians faced tempestuous changes which accompanied industrial take-off, expanding trade, world war, and catastrophic depression. The work of pioneers in sociology, such as Carl Dawson at McGill University, R.M. McIver and E.J. Urwick at Toronto, and Leon Gerin and Father G.H. Lévesque in Quebec, laid foundations for both basic and policy research, with emphasis on the latter (Hiller 1980; Falardeau 1974; Rocher 1970). Further, as Canada attempted to free itself from dependency on Britain, France, and the United States, in culture as well as economics and politics, indigenous social sciences emerged.

The 1940s and 1950s were marked by vast organizational changes, and during this period economists and political scientists dominated policy research. Most of them tended to react against the swelling tide of Marxism that was dividing social thought and political action in Europe. Similarly, most sociologists and anthropologists, still few in number and lacking traditional support, turned their backs on social criticism. There was a trend away from advocacy and towards basic research, preoccupation with social facts, following Durkheim, and a quest for recognition as a respectable science. The dominant American model was structural functionalism in which all the parts of a social system, even deviance and protest, were thought to conform in the long run to the total system. This accorded well with a broad fusion of liberal and conservative thought, which was fostered by trust in knowledge and belief in progress.

In this general euphoria, however, cracks began to appear. By the 1960s, disenchantment among youth followed disclosure of corruption in high places, deception and frustration in the conduct of the Vietnam war, and distrust of science as a panacea, particularly with its creation of nuclear weaponry and disregard for the environment. The conviction spread that "value-free" social science was at worst a sham to justify or conceal vast inequalities in power or at best a misguided and unattainable ideal. Rather, an increasing number of social scientists said, the honest inquirer should declare his or her values and then proceed to apply scientific objectivity in analysing data methodically gathered from random, representative samples. Social structures and relations have come to be seen as too complex for analysis by the narrow concepts which had guided dominant traditional theorists. Issues that accompany metropolitanization, increasing technology, regionalism, ethnic pluralism, and class stratification are too complex for simplistic prognosis. With recognition of the dehumanization that often accompanies application of outmoded solutions, growing numbers of social scientists and knowledgeable lay people have been coming to approve a remarriage of social science with concern for justice.

A strong case exists for the argument that sound theory must be tested by application. When this has been done in the past, enduring accumulations of knowledge have been accomplished in social science, as in medical and natural sciences. Studies in social history, such as those by Harold Innes, dealing with the development of resources, and by C.W. Topping, on deviant behaviour and the criminal justice system, are notable examples. The historical sociology of S.D. Clark in Anglo-Canada and Jean-Charles Falardeau in Franco-Canada provides further evidence of a concern for social justice. In this perspective the preoccupation of social scientists in North America in the 1950s with form and order, or structuralism, may be regarded as an aberration.

Human rights emerged as a focal issue during the 1960s, and became widely recognized through the inquiries conducted by social scientists for the Royal Commission on Bilingualism and Biculturalism. Language and cultural variation has always been at the heart of a Canadian approach to human rights; in this case it became a central question for extensive research on what was happening in Canadian society. Also, the federal government created the Canada Council and provided it with a budget to support social science and humanities research, as well as subsidizing the arts. Social science resumed one of its historic roles in providing a factual basis for the development of social policy. A signal event in this return to the mainstream was the publication in 1965 of Porter's study of the Canadian mosaic, portraying the historic tendency in Canada to perpetuate inequalities in stratification and power.

By the 1970s the post-war boom had faltered, inflation had gathered momentum, and the cost and effectiveness of the vast welfare apparatus had become problematic. North American society was confronted with the crisis in values and beliefs that had challenged Europe after the First World War. Heralded by youth's protest against militarism and imperialism, the belief crisis was reinforced and crystallized as social movements formed around civil rights for Blacks and equal rights for women.

In the 1980s there was widespread doubt as to the efficacy of a political-economic order that not only tolerates high unemployment and persistent poverty alongside affluence, but actually generates them. Neo-Marxists laid the blame on the capitalist system, which fattens large and small bourgeoisie at the expense of the workers. Liberal reformers strove to modify systems by reducing inequality of opportunity. Socialists faltered as old panaceas failed to win new supporters. The churches thundered against greed in high places but left to others social prognosis, prescription, and treatment. An example was the statement condemning unemployment by the Canadian Conference of Catholic Bishops in 1983. Today, hanging over the scene – an ominous cloud – are the grim possibilities of nuclear war and progressive ecological destruction of the planet.

Social scientists have few qualifications for solving deeply entrenched problems directly. But they do have two major aids for problem solving: they can help others understand the linkages between structures, events, and situations, and they can trace the distribution and operation of power in decision making. They also have accumulated an understanding of the relation of social theory to social policy formation. They insist that the clamour for justice by groups with minority status and power – human rights issues – be understood and dealt with in this light.

Preoccupied for two decades with problems of expansion in the universities to accommodate the baby boom of the late 1940s and early 1950s, sociology and anthropology, for example, were unprepared at first for direct engagement with changes on so massive a scale. Moreover, the 1960s and 1970s were arid times for the development of theory. Positivism had never won the dominance among social scientists in Canada that it had in Europe and the United States, and structural functionalism had run its course. But alternative scenarios were lacking. In this gap, critical analysis, whether in neo-Marxist or reformist form, has made headway. It is congenial for the times and serves as a broad base for a resurgence in policy analysis.

There is also a decisive turn away from the preoccupation with individualistic indicators that characterized North American social science over several decades. And there is a recognition that past sociological models of society were far too static. They fostered simplistic analysis and led to over-confidence in the ability of social science to predict outcomes in the study of structures and behaviour. The ascendant view is well stated by Smelser. He argues that it is the power positions of contending groups that account for persistence or change, and not functional concepts of homeostasis and adaptation (Smelser 1984).

The new sophistication of social science lies in its ability to provide for contingencies in the planning process. It is aware that it is not possible to control all the conditions which bear on social processes, especially when interaction among multiple forces is taken into account. Smelser, like many others, is critical of a reliance on research models that are based on contingency predictions of one factor leading to one outcome, under specified or controlled conditions. Moreover, when a policy is implemented it may generate unanticipated side-effects, some favouring but others countering desired outcomes. Smelser adds that faith factors must be also taken into account – the assumptions, values, and beliefs that affect the choice of priorities and goals.

These considerations draw attention to another essential factor. Sorokin's famous statement that researchers stand on the shoulders of intellectual giants is only part of the story. Researchers also stand on the backs of the ordinary people who constitute their subject matter. Research is based only partly on sociological abstractions; the other reality is more immediate – actors' everyday experiences and the interpretations *they* themselves place on them. Sociology and anthropology have steadily come to realize that the validity of observers' understanding of social reality depends on how accurately and sensitively the observers read actors' views of the world. The durability of pioneers' theories grew out of a correct understanding of the central concerns of the people they studied, rather than out of formal, general theories. Durkheim sought new foundations for social cohesion when old ones crumbled. Weber probed the energizing force of ideals grounded in the struggle for freedom in a bureaucratized world. Marx's central interest was justice for masses unprotected from exploitation. Early social anthropologists sought to establish the basis of cultural legitimacy in a complex multicultural world. In every case, sound theories implied correct reading of the actors' values and interpretations of reality.

It is evident, therefore, that from the standpoint of the sociology of knowledge, distinctions between basic research and policy research are theoretical constructs. Whether a project is deemed to be one or the other is largely a matter of focus. Controversy on the question is inherent in social science because values, relations, and behaviour are always subject to historical change. And, as in other disciplines or institutions, change generates friction between conservative social scientists who defend established ways and reformers or radicals who think that new conditions call for new approaches and solutions.

Advocacy can be an integral part of the research process. In advocacy, researchers take the roles of actors for the purposes of understanding their standpoint and of indicating possible courses of action. Advocacy does not mean that the researcher should abandon objectivity or assume the role of lobbyist. The latter's tasks are quite distinct from those of the skilled observer-as-advisor, and normally the two roles are performed by different persons.

POLICY AND ADVOCACY RESEARCH TODAY

The rise of policy research, then, has esteemed precedents. Today, as before, it promises substantial additions to knowledge, not just of the times, but of the persistent human condition. Examples of current policy research in Canada abound, but space permits references to only a few. They are commonly oriented around the quest for human rights, in the context of complex social organization.

The most prominent studies deal with social stratification or segmentation in general. The recurrent theme is the obduracy of the system – its resistance to reform in the direction of more equal opportunity. Notable among sociologists with this concern is Porter (1965, 1979), whose classic, *The Vertical Mosaic*, describes Canadian society as one where basic economic and political institutions are dominated by a relatively small élite. This consists of White Anglo-Saxon Protestant men, many of whom have inherited their wealth and power and whose sons are raised in exclusive circles designed to perpetuate privilege. Others who critically develop related themes include Clement (1975), Forcese (1975), Tepperman (1975), and Pineo and Looker (1983), Crysdale (1991).

The struggle for justice by Native peoples is the subject of research by a number of anthropologists, including Salisbury (1972, 1976), Brody (1975, 1981), and Balikci (1967, 1971, 1972). In advocating Native rights, social scientists collaborate with environmentalists and major churches. The latter have worked together with Native groups in Project North. These coalitions oppose mega-projects for the development of energy in the north by corporate consortiums which have little regard for the environment or the rights of Native peoples. Their submissions to the Thomas Berger Commission led to the report in 1977 which had the effect of delaying permission for building the Mackenzie Valley Pipeline until Native land claims are settled and Native people have time to develop stronger institutions and a more stable economy. While social scientists contributed special knowledge as a basis for recommendations, it was the churches which acted as effective lobbyers and activists (Hutchinson 1984; Bregha 1981; Berger 1977).

Unfortunately, this recess in northern exploitation is passing without much being done by governments to aid Native peoples either in achieving settlement of their land claims or in building institutions to stabilize their future place in northern society. But an exceptional sociologist, Alexander Lockhart (1982, 1985), helps both Native peoples and Whites understand ways by which northern communities may become more self-reliant rather than dependant on external commercial interests and public bureaucracies.

Other social scientists trace the negative social effects of some industrial enterprises. Anthropologist Elliott Leyton (1975) took up the cause of asbestos miners who contracted lung disease in his study *Dying Hard*. Ralph Matthews (1976) writes about the loss of jobs, community, and identity among Newfoundland fisher people in books such as *There's No Better Place Than Here*.

Anthropologists in Newfoundland, Canada's newest province, provide almost a classic example of involvement by social scientists in the daily life of residents and in the large institutions, political and economic, that govern this life. Advocacy has followed Newfoundland's profound social upheaval associated with union to Canada, technological change in the fishing industry, and, most recently, the intrusion of the petroleum industry in the sea. A central figure has been Gordon Inglis, director of the Centre for Development of Community Initiatives at Memorial University. Articles in numerous journals chronicle his work on development policies, community services, unemployment, and unionization. The impact of offshore oil development has been analysed in recent writing. Among the work of others which has important policy implications is that by Peter Sinclair on the reciprocal relations between new technologies and social organization in fisheries.

Women's rights is another major field for policy and advocacy research. Prominent work has been done by Smith (1977, 1985), Luxton (1980), O'Brien (1981), Marchak (1976), Armstrong and Armstrong (1978, 1983), Wilson (1982), McCormack (1981), Mackie (1983), Eichler (1983), and Meissner (1977, 1980). Their studies elaborate the subordination of women to men in family life, education, employment, politics, and religion. Advocacy varies from attacks on capitalism as the root cause of inequality to reform proposals aimed at achieving justice for women in every area of life. Using in-depth interviews, the Armstrongs' (1983) study indicates that segmentation by gender is greater than shown by census analysis. Job titles, composition, authority, and pay all favour men to a larger extent than had been disclosed earlier. Women suffer more through underemployment and unemployment partly because they are relegated to fields which are low-paid, part-time, and not unionized. As governments make low family income a condition for welfare and other benefits, many women are forced into illegal forms of work, furthering exploitation.

Recent studies on racism, prejudice, and discrimination, aimed particularly against visible minorities, are strongly advocative. Henry (1978), in a survey conducted in Toronto, found that 16 per cent of the population are extremely racist, 35 per cent are racist to some degree, 19 per cent are extremely tolerant, and 30 per cent are inclined towards tolerance. Racism is positively correlated with age, non-participation in the work force, little education, low socio-economic status, religious affiliation (especially with fundamentalist sects), and political conservatism. Richmond (1970) learned that Blacks and Asians were four times more likely than Whites to experience discrimination in employment and eight times more likely in housing. Ramcharan (1974) showed that 58 per cent of West Indians encountered discrimination in employment and 37 per cent in housing. In 1977 the Ontario Human Rights Commission reported that 58 per cent of their case load was race-related.

In a field study where actors posed as job applicants, Henry and Ginzberg (1985) learned that Whites have three times as many chances of being hired as Blacks, given similar qualifications. Another study, by Billingsley and Muszynski (1985), showed that a large majority of employers have no policies to prevent discrimination or to promote equity in employment. While evidence clearly shows that such measures are badly needed, most employers do not admit that there is a need and do not want such policies. These and other studies advocate that human rights at work need to be enforced by stronger sanctions than now exist. Governments should provide for training, education, and close monitoring of widespread practices among employers that deny basic rights to a large part of the population, rob society of a rich resource in human potential, and spread conditions that can lead to unrest and violence.

Robson and Breems (1985), in a study of Indo-Canadians in Vancouver, found that one-half of them experienced one or two ethnically hostile incidents over a two-year period. One-quarter were subjected to between four and twenty-four hostile experiences. Almost one in two was called names or threatened, one-quarter saw offensive graffiti, one in seven suffered property damage, one in nine was discriminated against at work, and one in fourteen was physically attacked. Ethnic abuse was most frequent in low-income areas and where there was a heavy concentration of Indo-Canadians. One-quarter of majority Canadians would prefer that Indo-Canadians not live in their neighbourhood, and almost one-half felt that immigration should be limited for people with yellow skin, compared with one-sixth who would keep out English-speaking Europeans. The researchers recommend that more resources be made available to prevent abuse, especially through the police, and to aid its victims.

Many social scientists are involved in policy research in education. Their major aim is to disclose blockages to equal opportunity, not only in access but also in participation in the rewards that attend higher education. Structured limitations in education which penalize certain groups are a violation of human rights. Abundant evidence of the need for change has been provided by such researchers as Breton (1972), Pavalko and Bishop (1966), Hall and McFarlane (1962), Pike (1970), Porter (1965) and Porter, Porter, and Blishen (1973, 1982), and Anisef (1980, 1982). Breton, in a large-scale national survey, advocated polyvalent or single-track schools, improved counselling, and equalizing standards by sex, ethnicity, and social class. Porter, Porter, and Blishen found that, among those with high mental ability, twice as large a proportion of grade 12 students from high-status families expected to enter university as from low-status families. Girls from low-income backgrounds are particularly disadvantaged. Anisef, Paasche, and Turrittin (1980), in a longitudinal study of Ontario youth, produced further evidence of unequal opportunity by class, gender, and rural (as against urban) community. Anisef and associates recommended (1982) that provincial governments should provide compensatory programs for economically disadvantaged children at the pre-kindergarten, elementary, and secondary levels.

Crysdale and MacKay (1985), reporting on a longitudinal intervention program in a working-class area in Toronto, showed that grade 9 and 10 students with low-income backgrounds could be assisted in staying longer at school or returning for post-secondary education if assistance was provided in the form of tutoring, counselling, and work experience. Especially helpful was a program of work-for-pay one school day a week under supervision of teachers and employers. Crysdale and MacKay also recommended intervention at an early age, with grass-roots programs for upgrading.

Some universities provide a base for research into international relations and these may serve as advocates for foreign policy which fosters human rights. An example is York University's Centre for Research on Latin America and the Caribbean. It acts in collaboration with social science research centres in countries where authoritarian regimes have closed university research institutes. It often gains access through church auspices abroad. Under faculty direction, twenty-five research associates, some from Third World countries, are working on the Chile Project.

Policy research in Quebec is often related to advocacy in human rights but is too extensive for inclusion here. It has played a foremost role in raising public consciousness as well as in informing policy makers concerning measures to advance human rights in that province.

Associations of social scientists, like those of doctors, lawyers, dentists, architects, engineers, and other professionals, engage in policy research in two ways. One is internal, to advance the interests of members. The other is external, to achieve the best interests of society as a whole. Within academic associations particularly, advocacy may be a source of disagreement, in substance and principle. One reason is that tradition favours abstraction rather than application, and although the classic notion of the separation between the general and particular has diminished, it is very much alive among influential academics. Tenure and the notion of academic freedom protect critics and innovators from the harshest types of repression, but academics who advocate changes in public policy risk effective, informal sanctions, often within the universities. The bolder among them persist in the belief that over the long run their findings will be vindicated by social experience.

Social scientists are protected against the worst abuses by the Canadian Association of University Teachers and by faculty unions. They often collaborate with related disciplines and universities through the Social Science Federation of Canada, which, although funded in part by the federal government, considers that advocacy is one of its main functions.

Research findings are not always good news for established interests. One way governments and powerful private groups may retard criticism is to reduce university funding and, in particular, social science research. Recently some highly placed business leaders have attacked universities intemperately, although others work with them to improve research of a technical nature. Under financial stringency, social research has a rocky road ahead. But excellence in policy, as well as basic research, in the long run will ensure advancement in the social disciplines and in the societies to which they are responsible.

In Canada we take for granted the expectation that good policy research will have long-term beneficial effects on social structure and practice. The advocacy embedded in this policy research is not suppressed with arbitrary arrest of researchers, torture, and possible death. In many parts of the world advocacy research is done at grave peril, as in Chile under ultra-conservative military dictatorship. Yet, as Landstreet and associates describe above, more than thirty advocacy research centres began operating, with the protection of the church and support of the international social science community. This surely is the most indisputable evidence of the extreme relevance of advocacy research, not only for the integrity of social science but for the recovery of justice and freedom. In a society where the denial of human rights is a fact of everyday life, advocacy research is one of the few means of recourse for powerless people and nourishes a tiny but bright spark of hope for future enlightenment and just development.

REFERENCES

Anisef, Paul, Gottfried Paasche, and Anton Turrittin. 1980. *Is the Die Cast?* Toronto: Ministry of Colleges and Universities.

Anisef, Paul, Norman Okihiro, and Carl James. 1982. *Losers and Winners: The Pursuit of Equality and Social Justice in Higher Education.* Toronto: Butterworths.

Armstrong, Pat, and Hugh Armstrong. 1978. *The Double Ghetto.* Toronto: McClelland and Stewart.

– 1983. *A Working Majority: What Women Must Do for Pay.* Ottawa: Advisory Council on the Status of Women.

Balikci, Asen. 1967. *At the Spring Sea Ice Camp, Part I.* Ottawa: National Film Board.

– 1971. *Yesterday-Today: The Netsilik Eskimos.* Montreal: National Film Board.

– 1972. *Netsilik Eskimos Today.* Montreal: National Film Board.

Billingsley, Brenda, and Leon Muszynski. 1985. *No Discrimination Here?* Toronto: Urban Alliance on Race Relations and Social Planning Council of Metropolitan Toronto.

Berger, Thomas. 1977. *Northern Frontier, Northern Homeland: The Report of the Mackenzie Valley Pipeline Inquiry.* Ottawa: Ministry of Supply and Services.

Bregha, François. 1981. *Bob Blair's Pipeline.* Toronto: James Lorimer.

Breton, Raymond. 1972. *Social and Academic Factors in the Career Decisions of Canadian Youth.* Ottawa: Information Canada.

Brody, Hugh. 1975. *The Peoples' Land.* Harmondsworth, England: Penguin.

– 1981. *Maps and Dreams.* Vancouver: Douglas and McIntyre.

Canadian Conference of Catholic Bishops. 1983. *Ethical Reflections on the Economic Crisis.* Ottawa.

Clement, Wallace. 1975. *The Canadian Corporate Elite.* Toronto: McClelland and Stewart.

Crysdale, Stewart. 1961. *The Industrial Struggle and Protestant Ethics in Canada.* Toronto: Ryerson Press.

– 1991. *Families under Stress.* Toronto: Thompson Educational Publishing.

Crysdale, Stewart, and Harry MacKay. 1985. *Youth's Passage through School to Work: Eastside and Northend Youth Compared over a Decade.* Downsview, Ontario: Department of Sociology, Atkinson College, York University.

Eichler, Margrit. 1983. *Families in Canada Today*. Toronto: Gage.

Falardeau, Jean-Charles. 1974. "Antécedents, Débuts, et Croissance de la Sociologie au Québec." *Recherches Sociographiques* 15:135–65.

Forcese, Dennis. 1975. *The Canadian Class Structure*. Toronto: McGraw-Hill Ryerson.

Hall, Oswald, and Bruce McFarlane. 1962. *Transition from School to Work*. Ottawa: Department of Labour.

Henry, Frances. 1978. *The Dynamics of Racism in Canada*. Downsview: Department of Anthropology, York University.

Henry, Frances, and Effie Ginzberg. 1985. *Who Gets the Work? A Test of Racial Discrimination in Employment*. Toronto: Urban Alliance on Race Relations and the Social Planning Council of Metropolitan Toronto.

Hiller, Harry. 1980. "Paradigmatic Shifts, Indigenization and the Development of Sociology in Canada" *Journal of the History of the Behavioural Sciences* 16:263–74.

Hutchinson, Roger. 1984. "The Dene and Project North: Partners in Mission." In W. Westfall, L. Rousseau, F. Harvey, and J. Simpson, eds., *Religion/Culture: Comparative Canadian Studies*. Toronto: Association for Canadian Studies.

Leyton, Elliott. 1975. *Dying Hard: The Ravages of Industrial Carnage*. Toronto: McClelland and Stewart.

Lockhart, Alexander. 1982. "The Insider-Outsider Dialectic in Native Socio-Economic Development: A Case Study in Process Understanding." *Canadian Journal of Native Studies*, no. 1: 159–68.

– 1985. "Northern Development Policy: Hinterland Communities and Metropolitan Academics." Plenary Address, Western Association of Sociology and Anthropology, February, Lakehead University, Thunder Bay, Ontario.

Luxton, Meg. 1980. *More than a Labour of Love: Three Generations of Women's Work in the Home*. Toronto: Women's Educational Press.

Mackie, Marlene. 1983. *Exploring Gender Relations: A Canadian Perspective*. Toronto: Butterworths.

Marchak, Patricia. 1976. "Women, Work and Unions in Canada." *International Journal of Sociology* 5, no. 4: 39–61.

Matthews, Ralph. 1976. *There's No Better Place Than Here: Social Change in Three Newfoundland Communities*. Toronto: Irwin Press.

McCormack, Thelma. 1981. "Good Theories or Just Theories? Toward a Feminist Philosophy of Social Science." *Women's Studies International Quarterly* 4, no. 1: 1–12.

Meissner, Martin. 1977. "The Sexual Division of Labour and Inequality." In M. Stephenson, ed., *Women in Canada*. Rev. ed. Don Mills, Ontario: General Publishing.

– 1980. "The Domestic Economy: Now You See It, Now You Don't." Unpublished. Vancouver: University of British Columbia.

O'Brien, Mary. 1981. *The Politics of Reproduction*. Boston: Routledge and Kegan Paul.

Pavalko, Ronald, and David Bishop. 1966. "Socio-economic Status and College Plans: A Study of Canadian High School Students." *Sociology of Education* 39, no. 3: 288–98.

Pike, Robert. 1970. *Who Doesn't Get to University – and Why*. Ottawa: Association of Universities and Colleges in Canada.

Pineo, Peter C., and E. Dianne Looker. 1983. "Class and Conformity in the Canadian Setting." *Canadian Journal of Sociology* 8, no. 3: 293–317.

Porter, John. 1965. *The Verticcal Mosaic: An Analysis of Social Class and Power in Canada*. Toronto: University of Toronto Press.

– 1979. *The Measure of Canadian Society: Education, Equality and Opportunity*. Toronto: Gage.

Porter, Marion, John Porter, and Bernard Blishen. 1973. *Does Money Matter?* Revised and republished 1982. *Stations and Callings*. Toronto: Methuen.

Ramcharan, S. 1974. "Adaptation of West Indians in Canada." Unpublished Ph.D. dissertation, York University.

Richmond, A.E. 1976. "Black and Asian Immigrants in Britain and Canada: Some Comparisons." *Journal Community Relations* 4, no. 4.

Robson, R.A.H., and Brad Breems. 1985. *Ethnic Conflict in Vancouver: An Empirical Study*. Vancouver: B.C. Civil Liberties Association.

Rocher, Guy. 1970. "L'Avenir de la Sociologie au Canada." In Jan J. Loubser, ed., *The Future of Sociology in Canada*. Montreal: Canadian Sociology and Anthropology Association.

Salisbury, Richard F. 1976. *Development of Attitudes to Development among the Native Peoples of the MacKenzie District*. Montreal: McGill University.

Salisbury, Richard F., et. al. 1972. *Development and James Bay: Socio-economic Implications of the Hydro-electric Project*. Montreal: McGill University.

Smelser, Neil J. 1984. "Research and Theory Have Altered Ogburn Vision." ASA Footnotes. Washington: American Sociological Association.

Smith, Dorothy. 1977. *Feminism and Marxism*. Vancouver: New Star Books.

– 1985. *Women, Class, Family and the State*. Toronto: Garamond.

Smith, Dorothy, and Naomi Hersom. 1982. *Women and the Canadian Labour Force*. Ottawa: Social Science and Humanities Research Council of Canada.

Tepperman, Lorne. 1975. *Social Mobility in Canada*. Toronto: McGraw-Hill Ryerson.

Wilson, S.J. 1982. *Women, the Family and the Economy*. Toronto: McGraw-Hill Ryerson.

Index

Contributors

HOWARD ADELMAN, Refugee Documentation Centre, and Department of Philosophy, Atkinson College, York University.

JOHN CLEVELAND, Department of Sociology, University of Toronto.

STEWART CRYSDALE, Department of Sociology, Atkinson College, York University.

DON DIPPO, Faculty of Education, York University.

PETER HARRIES-JONES, (editor), Department of Anthropology, York University.

ELSPETH HEYWORTH, Executive Director, Dixon Hall, Toronto.

PETER LANDSTREET, JINNY ARANCIBIA, MARCELO CHARLIN, HARRY DÍAZ, and JACQUES DOYER, Centre for Latin American and Carribean Studies, York University.

RONNIE LEAH, Department of Sociology, University of Lethbridge.

STAN MARSHALL, Instructor of Industrial Sociology, The Labour College of Canada, Ottawa, and Research Officer, Canadian Union of Public Employees.

GARETH MORGAN, Faculty of Administrative Studies, York University.

TIM REES and CAROL TATOR, Urban Alliance on Race Relations, Toronto.

METTA SPENCER, Department of Sociology, Erindale Campus, University of Toronto and Editor of *Peace Magazine*.